THE DRAGON'S QUANTUM LEAP

Transforming from a Mechanized to an Informatized Force

Timothy L. Thomas

D1009055

Foreign Military Studies Office (FMSO)
Fort Leavenworth, KS
2009

The author works for the Foreign Military Studies Office (FMSO), Fort Leavenworth, Kansas. FMSO is a component of the US Army's Training and Doctrine Command (TRADOC). The office is charged with preparing studies and assessments based on the reading of foreign and domestic publications and through contacts with a network of foreign and US military and civilian security specialists. FMSO researches, writes, and publishes from unclassified sources about the military establishments, doctrines, and practices of selected foreign armed forces. It also studies a variety of civil-military and transnational security issues affecting the US and its military forces. FMSO products are prepared for the US Army and other services, the Department of Defense, as well as nonDoD organizations to include the Treasury and Justice Departments.

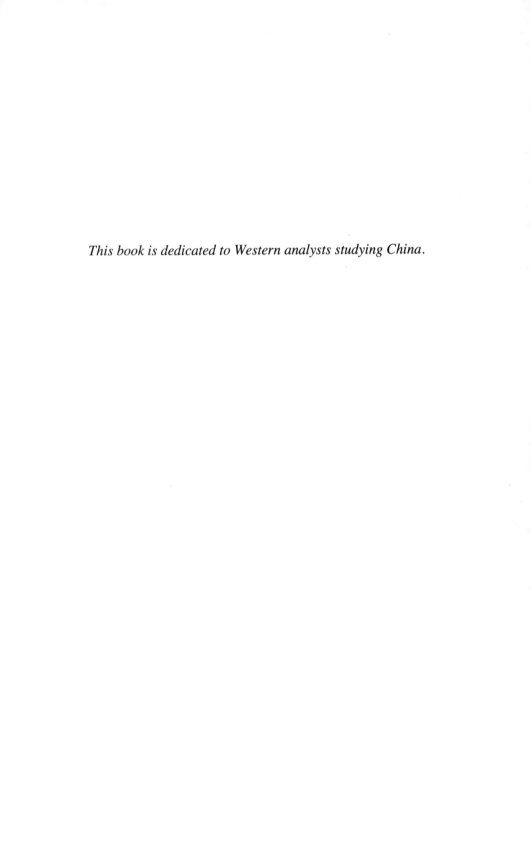

This book is dedicated to Western analysts studying China.

ACKNOWLEDGEMENT

The author used only open-source translations for the construction of this document. Since the author does not speak Chinese, he fully utilized the translation talents of the Open Source Center (formerly the Foreign Broadcast Information Service or FBIS) and other government contracted Chinese translators in order to write this book. The author is solely responsible for the selection and analysis of the material others translated.

In particular, the author would like to acknowledge the support of Mr. Charles A. Martinson III of Fort Leavenworth who designed the cover artwork. Mr. Martinson's visualization of the contents of this book is unique. His creativity is truly his trademark. The author would like to thank Mr. Robert Love of the Foreign Military Studies Office. Mr. Love monitored commercial translations of some material used in this work and ensured their timely delivery. Mr. Karl Prinslow, former Deputy Director of FMSO, ensured that funding for the translation of Chinese material was available. Finally, the author would like to express his thanks to FMSO director Mr. Tom Wilhelm for providing his support and encouragement for the project.

It is the intent of this book to provide US analysts with the details of changes in China's mode of thinking as it transitions from a mechanized to an informatized force. The author would like to thank the Training and Doctrine Command (TRADOC) G-2 for funding the second printing of this book in 2011.

FOREWORD

Chinese observations of warfare in the information age have resulted in a widespread transformation and metamorphosis of the People's Liberation Army (PLA) from a mechanized to an informatized force. This transformation has affected nearly every aspect of China's military from strategy to logistics to educational development.

The Dragon's Quantum Leap intends to peel back the transformation process and uncover the impact of new modes of thought on several key segments of military development (culture, stratagems, crisis management, deception, and reconnaissance among other elements) that digital-age thought is affecting. It expands the scope but not the basic theoretical theme of the author's two previous works on Chinese information warfare concepts. They were Dragon Bytes, which covered Chinese IW activities from 1999-2003; and Decoding the Virtual Dragon, which covered Chinese IW activities from 2003-2006. The Dragon's Quantum Leap updates these concepts and activities to mid-2009 and completes the author's trilogy on the topic. As with the author's previous works, this book primarily uses original Chinese source material.

New military thinking in the PLA, in conjunction with digital advancements in other areas (economic, diplomatic, and so on), has resulted in the closer integration of military and civilian planning and actions. As a result of these improvements, Chinese military theory and systems will be more flexible and competitive, enabling the PLA to become an aspiring superpower in the twenty-first century. The Dragon's Quantum Leap examines this transformation in detail. The book will cause the general military reader and the Chinese security specialist to think in different terms about Chinese military activities and to consider things yet unconsidered.

Tom Wilhelm
Director
Foreign Military Studies
Office
2009

TABLE OF CONTENTS

INTRODUCTION

Accelerating the informatization buildup of the Chinese military and constructing the informatized armed forces as quickly as possible form the core thinking of Comrade Jiang Zemin regarding the strengthening of the buildup of the modernization of national defense and the armed forces. This is what is primarily entailed in the revolution in military affairs with Chinese characteristics...[1]

The People's Liberation Army (PLA) of China has watched and studied western wartime experiences over the past twenty years. The PLA has accumulated "lessons learned" from these experiences and applied them to China's training exercises and included them in their educational curriculums. This has enabled China to better prepare for potential conflicts and to predict with some degree of certainty the nature of future war in an information age context.

The study of information-age conflicts has had a profound effect on China's military leaders and organizational structure. This is expressed in the PLA's integrated approach to military affairs, combining its ingrained historical proclivities (use of the dialectic and a comprehensive approach, focus on deception and strategy, seeking out strategic advantage or *shi,* etc.) with new technological concepts. This integration is manifested in the PLA's new mode of thinking, the focus of this book. The PLA's new mode of thinking encourages innovation and creativity. It takes the best ideas from China's military history and combines them with new concepts and visions resulting from the current discussion of information age developments.

The principal motivators for these changes were the use of information technologies by the United States (US) and its coalition partners in the recent wars in Iraq and Afghanistan; the US-led North Atlantic Treaty Organization's (NATO) conflict with Serbia over Kosovo in 1999; and the 1996 confrontation between China and the US over Taiwan. PLA theorists studied these high-tech applications and came away impressed (bordering on awe) with the enhancements that information technologies offered.

The Chinese response was to begin building a theoretical and tactical

---

[1] Wang Baocun, "A View of the Informatization Buildup of the Chinese Military," Information Warfare in China, Xinhua Publishing, 2005, New Military Affairs Reference (Special Edition), p. 116.

1

framework to support a military transformation with Chinese characteristics that would keep them competitive in the coming years. PLA leaders believe these changes are required for China to remain competitive in the current world environment. The focus of the transformation was on two levels: transforming from a mechanized to an informatized force[2] and updating the PLA's mode of thinking. China's military culture, theoretical developments, and planning and preparations for war have all been affected.

Incoming Pacific Command commander Admiral Robert Willard has noted that "China has EXCEEDED most of our intelligence estimates of their capability and capacity every year. They've grown at an unprecedented rate in those capabilities."[3] The Dragon's Quantum Leap discusses several of the developments in China's mode of thought that have enabled this transformation. The focus is on the integration of the old and new, which has injected digital devices and new life into campaign stratagems and deception; and on the desire to think creatively or "outside the box" and produce new concepts such as "beyond means warfare," war engineering, system attack warfare, and non-war military operations. Other issues have also been affected, such as China's concept of crisis management, military culture, and information warfare.

The Chinese military has enhanced its "informatized warfare" capabilities across the board. This transformation is often referred to as a "leap frog" development from a mechanized to an informatized force. However, as retired Chinese information warfare specialist General Wang Baocun notes, as the power of weapons and equipment grows qualitatively the combat capabilities of China's forces grow exponentially. Therefore the all-inclusive nature of the transformation could also be termed a "quantum leap" in military thinking and modernization in synchronization with modern developments worldwide—not just a leap frog endeavor.

To fully understand this quantum leap, one needs to consider a wide array of activities in the PLA and think as comprehensively as the Chinese do. Focusing on a single area does not provide the proper scope and depth of the transformation. Chinese military documents selected for this work highlight

---

[2] Several terms (cyber, digital, network) that are information-related in English are translated from Chinese into English in a number of ways (informationization, informationalization, etc.). In this work, informatization will be used as a noun and informatized as an adjective in place of these variants. When quotes or books/articles are referenced, the translator's version of the term will be employed.

[3] James A. Lyons, "Countering Beijing's New Weapon," Washington Times, 6 December 2009, p. B3.

several of these dramatic technical and theoretical shifts in the PLA. The end result is the realization that the PLA is on a fast track in its transformation from a mechanized to an informatized force and in the introduction of a new mode of thinking. This book shines particular light on the latter aspect of this transformation. However, the reader should be reminded that no book's material on the PLA is truly "up to date." That is, even though the material herein covers Chinese writings through 2009, who really knows to what level the PLA has advanced at the present time? This survey only scratches the surface of all the available texts on the PLA and its new mode of thinking.

The book is divided into three parts. Part One examines the ideas behind new modes of thinking (the book Unrestricted War, an article that a Chinese general wrote on new modes of thought, and a case study of new modes of thought in the PLA's military culture). Part Two examines some of the changes to ancient Chinese concepts in the information age (deception and stratagems). Also discussed are changes in the PLA's crisis management concept. Part Three focuses more closely on digital thought (the PLA's digital reconnaissance, an examination of a book dedicated to the idea of information war in China, and a look at how Taiwan views the Chinese concept of information war). Part Four comprises the conclusions one draws from this work.

Chapter One examines the 1999 book Unrestricted War and the responses of the international community to this highly controversial work. It is this author's opinion that the Chinese may have done the US a favor by publishing this work since it opened the eyes of many US planners and tacticians to the potential attack options of a host of nation-states and insurgents. The book may have played a small role in the development of China's informatized concept due to the variety of warfare options it offers. It played a much larger role, it appears, as a catalyst for the introduction of a new mode of thinking for the PLA.

Chapter Two discusses the impact of systems and informatized processes on military thought, describing the transition to new modes of thinking based on innovation. The chapter examines one author's method of integrating information technology into a Sun Tzu stratagem; and another author's twelve recommendations for new modes of thought in the PLA. The Chinese stress innovation and creative thinking. They believe that even though China wasn't the first to develop information warfare concepts, it still has a chance to be the most effective in using new information technologies. New concepts such as "war engineering" and "system attack warfare" are examined along with some subtle changes in military culture.

Chapter Three examines sixty-six articles on military culture written primarily by PLA authors in the journal <u>China Military Science</u>. The discussion covers Chinese traditional culture and what the PLA refers to as "advanced military culture," the latter being a product of the information age. The analysis describes how military culture has progressed in the PLA through the years and offers the reader insights into China's prejudices about the West. This is one of the few discussions available on PLA culture from a Chinese military academy source.

Chapter Four describes Chinese deception theory. The chapter starts by looking back at China's historical record and fascination with deception. The chapter then analyzes how China has applied modern day technologies to its deception theory especially with regard to camouflage techniques and efforts to fool reconnaissance assets. These applications encourage continued study of deception techniques both on the battlefield and in the virtual world since they are so realistic and applicable to the contemporary digital world.

Chapter Five takes a look at campaign stratagems from a high-tech vantage point. The chapter examines how to create and apply campaign stratagems in accordance with high-tech equipment and what technological forte is required of twenty-first century commanders. One interesting focal point is the list of issues that Chinese commanders must master to become proficient in the digital-age: dialectical thought, logical thinking, thinking in images, three-dimensional thought, unconventional thought, and associative thought. This chapter, based on the book <u>Campaign Stratagems</u>, is of great interest since its detailed discussion of various campaign stratagems is applicable to any armed force.

Chapter Six discusses the PLA's focus on high-technology crisis management responses. The chapter highlights the Chinese response to the May 2008 Sichuan Province earthquake in which upwards of 90,000 people perished. Of interest to military specialists is that the PLA's high-tech response is viewed by Chinese theorists as a non-military, high-tech response that helps prepare the PLA for informatized warfare. Non-military actions are described as well. They are becoming an important ingredient of the PLA's new mode of thinking. Perhaps this is the most important chapter in the book with regard to potential cooperation with the Chinese, since crisis management offers China and any potential opponent a method through which to avert a potential crisis. The Chinese are working to improve their current crisis management system and western analysts should follow these developments closely.

4

Chapter Seven is a look at the PLA's long-range electronic-reconnaissance concept. It discusses, in a temporal manner, the development of the PLA's active-offensive thinking in regard to information warfare. This focus represents a change from China's traditional active-defense concept. How and when China might use its active-offensive concepts for purposes other than reconnaissance is unclear, but, as general concepts, they are worrisome. It does not bode well for future cooperation and stability if Chinese theorists really do believe (as they openly state) that China can offset an opponent's information superiority only if China strikes first.

Chapter Eight is a summary of the Chinese book Information Warfare in China. Published in 2005, the work compiles the writings of some of the best retired PLA theoreticians and strategists: Wang Baocun, Shen Weiguang, Wang Pufeng, and Li Bingyan, to name but a few. The book includes discussions of both the theory and technological underpinnings of IW. While there is not as much information in the book as one would desire on the development of a new mode of thinking, the discussion does uncover some Chinese interests of value to analysts.

Chapter Nine discusses the thoughts of Taiwanese IW specialists who regularly examine the PLA's information warfare concepts. The chapter focuses on Taiwan's perception of the PLA's revolution in military affairs, political work, information warfare concepts, electronic warfare, and the PLA's plethora of information warfare institutes. The examination reveals that Taiwan, perhaps due to its intimacy with the Chinese language and culture, picks up on aspects of China's information warfare developments that Westerners neglect. These aspects include acupuncture warfare, highly-controlled warfare, and political work Web sites, all items of interest to people studying a new mode of thinking.

Chapter Ten lists the conclusions this analysis has generated, focusing on the main issue of this text: the impact of the transformation from a mechanized to an informatized force on modes of thought in the PLA. The list of conclusions is indicative of the challenges facing western armies as they confront the opportunities for cooperation or potential conflict with the PLA.

There are also four appendixes. Appendix One covers information-related articles in the PLA journal China Military Science over the past few years. Appendix Two analyzes two Chinese concepts and their adaptation to the information age, the concept of *shi* and the thirty-six stratagems of war. Appendix Three offers definitions of additional deception-related terms not discussed in Chapter Four. Appendix Four lists the table of contents of five books of relevance for the topic of new modes of thought based on a transformation from a mechanized to an informatized force.

This work completes a trilogy on Chinese information warfare issues. The work <u>Dragon Bytes</u> covers Chinese IW activities from 1999-2003; <u>Decoding the Virtual Dragon</u> covers Chinese IW activities from 2003-2006; and <u>The Dragon's Quantum Leap</u> covers the period from 2006-2009, with some additional material included from earlier years. Hopefully these three works can serve as a guide to a western understanding of the PLA's transformation efforts in the information age. It is the purpose of these works to help western analysts draw a more realistic picture of the challenge the PLA presents in the IW arena—and a picture for areas of potential collaboration.

PART ONE:

The Book <u>Unrestricted Warfare</u>, New Modes of Thought, and Military Culture

CHAPTER ONE: <u>UNRESTRICTED WARFARE</u>: INSTIGATOR OF A NEW MODE OF THINKING?

This chapter analyzes the controversial aspects of this book and examines several novel Chinese concepts that have received scant attention in the West.

...proposing a new concept of weapons does not require relying on the springboard of new technology, it just demands lucid and incisive thinking. However, this is not a strong point of the Americans, who are slaves to technology in their thinking.[4]

Introduction

In 1999 the Chinese released a book titled <u>Unrestricted Warfare</u>.[5] The book caused an uproar among Western analysts for its anti-American overtones and recommended employment of an unrestricted set of warfighting measures that appeared to go beyond the laws of armed conflict. In hindsight, the book also may have served as one of the primary catalysts for a new mode of thinking in the People's Liberation Army (PLA).

At the time of the book's release, the PLA was still in a state of awe over the military prowess that the United States (US) and its alliance partners had demonstrated in the 1991 war with Iraq and in the mid-1990s internecine conflict in Yugoslavia. A key component to the West's success in each case was its reliance on a new set of military options focused on information technologies (IT). In Iraq IT included the expanded use of simulations and precision weaponry for the first time. With regard to Yugoslavia, the Chinese witnessed how the Dayton Accords Peace Process (involving the Presidents of Serbia, Bosnia, and Croatia) utilized IT simulations and map-making abilities to "end the war without fighting," an often-stated Chinese military aspiration.

The PLA felt quite helpless in the face of such a prominent IT-based military force. The concepts of <u>Unrestricted Warfare</u> provided the PLA with a plausible method for confronting and perhaps winning a war against such a superior opponent. According to the book's authors, this could be accomplished with combinations of means employed in an unrestricted fashion and with the use of new theories and techniques.

---

[4] Qiao Liang and Wang Xiangsui, <u>Unrestricted Warfare</u>, Pan American Publishing Company, Panama City, Panama, 2002, p. 15.

[5] According to several Chinese linguists, a closer translation of the title is "Beyond Limits Warfare." However, due to its more common usage and translation, the title <u>Unrestricted Warfare</u> will be used in this chapter.

10

For the West, the book represents the first collection of thoughts from Chinese officers that seriously interpreted the evolving nature of war. The 1999 book was prescient in several regards, such as its discussions of hybrid wars, non-war military actions, and "combinations of actions" designed to win or thwart war. All three of these issues eventually rose to be the focus of theorists world-wide.

Two PLA colonels, Qiao Liang and Wang Xiangsui, co-authored the book. Many US authorities assumed outright that this controversial work was sanctioned by the Chinese Communist Party due to its military roots. Such works don't normally find their way to the public without official sanction. However, senior civilian leaders in China reportedly were forced to read the book after its publication to see what all the international fuss was about. While not dispelling all doubts, this fact does make it seem more unlikely that the work had the sanction of the highest authorities when first released.

Wang stated later that the 1996 Chinese maneuvers in the Taiwan Straits (designed by China to prevent Taiwan from taking steps toward independence) used a combination of factors to deter Taiwan. This success, and the recognition that other countries were using combinations of issues (military, economic, diplomatic, etc.) in their conflicts (Iraq, Kosovo, etc.), was the final push needed for him and Qiao to write Unrestricted Warfare.[6]

This chapter begins with an examination of the background of the authors and some initial comments from the Chinese about Unrestricted Warfare. The focus then switches to key aspects of the book seldom highlighted by Western pundits, aspects from which the US can learn much about the Chinese way of war and about Chinese views of the US military. The chapter concludes with 1999-2001 post-publication interviews with authors Qiao Liang and Wang Xiangsui about their book. The authors' views of their book in hindsight are of interest as they reinterpret some controversial aspects of their work.

---

[6] "Ingenious Remarks by the Author of 'Transfinite Warfare' on Using Force against Taiwan," Hong Kong Tai Yang Pao, 24 November 1999, p. D4, as translated and downloaded from the Open Source Center website, document number FTS 19991220001805. The term "Transfinite Warfare" is actually a variation of the translation of "Unrestricted Warfare."

Who are These Officer Authors?

Qiao Liang was born in 1954 to a military family. A member of the Committee of the Chinese Writers' Association, he was a Deputy Director of the Writing Office of the Political Department of the Air Force in 2005. He was designated a special researcher for the Strategic Research Center of the Air Force and served as a Professor at the Shanghai Defense Strategy Research Institute. At the Eighth International Sun Tzu Art of War Symposium in November 2009 he was identified as a Major General in the air force serving as a professor at the Air Force Command College. He is a "grade one writer." His novels include Gateway to Doomsday, Spiritual Banner, and The Great Glacial River. He has cooperated with other authors to write On Military Officer Quality, A Review of the World's Big Military Powers, A Listing of the Rankings of Global Military Powers, and The New Warring States Period. He has studied military theory for many years and read most of the great works of Chinese military history. [7]

Wang Xiangsui was also born in 1954, in Guangzhou, and joined the armed forces in 1970. He has been a political instructor, a political commissar of a wing, a regimental political commissar, a deputy political commissar for a division, and a researcher. In 2005 he was the Director and Professor of the Center for Strategic Studies at the Beijing University of Aeronautics and Astronautics. He was also Director of the Academic Department of the National Security Policy Research Committee of the China Research Society of Policy Science. In cooperation with other authors he has written On Military Officer Quality, A Review of the World's Big Military Powers, and A Record of the World's Past Major Wars. [8] He has retired from military service and is a civilian academic at the present time, and reportedly is still serving as the Director of the Center for Strategic Studies.

Qiao and Wang have worked together on several book projects in addition to the ones cited above. For example, they co-authored two chapters in the Chinese military book On the Chinese Revolution in Military Affairs. This book features some of the best Chinese strategists and to be included in this work demonstrates not only their abilities to write on many topics but also their highly regarded reputations. One of their chapters in the book, written with Liu Yazhou, was titled "Taking War to the Air and China's Air Force." Liu, Qiao,

---

[7] Qiao Liang and Wang Xiangsui, "Do We Advocate Terrorism?," Shanghai Guoji Zhanwang, 1 November 2005, pp. 86-89, published in the March 2000 issue of Juanchuan Zhishi, as translated and downloaded from the OSC website, document number CPP20051227318001.

[8] Ibid.

and Wang's chapter discusses the primary place of the offensive in modern combat and the important role of the Chinese Air Force in fulfilling that requirement. The air war is where China feels it can win limited war under informatized conditions.[9]

The other chapter in the book was co-authored by just Qiao and Wang. It is titled "Fully Calculating the Costs and Profits of War." Wang and Qiao discuss the US-led war with Iraq. They state that the "beyond limits" concept of bribing Iraqi generals maximized results and was much less expensive than using only the air force. The war also resulted in the acquisition of political profit. Wang and Qiao state that US President George Bush wanted to lay a foundation for his reelection; Secretary of Defense Donald Rumsfeld wanted to use the war to promote lightening reforms in the US military; and General Tommy Franks wanted to prove that the Army still maintained an irreplaceable role even in modern warfare. These are all understandable opinions from someone writing from abroad.[10]

The Book Causes a Stir in the US and China

Unrestricted Warfare has been the focus of many heated discussions and close analyses in the US and abroad. It is easy to understand why the book has attracted so many readers in the US. It offers a completely new theoretical form of warfare that has no boundaries; it offers a critical analysis of the US; and it is the product of a country billed as a rising superpower in the twenty-first century. Further, the book bypasses traditional modes of war, integrates all forces and means, and recommends fighting against the enemy from all angles.[11] For these reasons and others, the Chinese authors used the term "unrestricted" in the title.

A subtitle stating "China's Master Plan to Destroy America" was added to a 2002 English translation of the book. The translation is the work of the Pan American Publishing Company, Panama City, Panama. The subtitle and a 9/11 photo of the burning Twin Towers were portrayed on the cover of the Pan American work. To the uninformed reader it appears that China had something

---

[9] Liu Yazhou, Qiao Liang, Wang Xiangsui, "Taking War to the Air and China's Air Force," The Chinese Revolution in Military Affairs, ed. Shen Weiguang, New China Press, 2003, pp. 48-62.
[10] Qiao Liang and Wang Xiangsui, "Fully Calculating the Costs and Profits of War," The Chinese Revolution in Military Affairs, ed. Shen Weiguang, New China Press, 2003, pp. 174-186.
[11] Tung Yi, no title, Hong Kong Sing Tao Jih Pao, 12 February 2001, p. A18, as translated and downloaded from the OSC website, document number CPP20010212000047.

to do with the 9/11 tragedy. Such sensationalism has added to the hyperbole and hysteria surrounding the book since most Americans can only read the English version. The cover of the Chinese version of the book appears to have two laser beams coming from China that are focused on a satellite stationed over China while a jet fighter circles nearby.

In addition to the furor over Unrestricted Warfare in the US, the book was subjected to harsh criticism in China that was not well documented and discussed overseas. Chinese lawyers and military officials alike discounted the book's importance due to legal issues. Critics asked whether the advocacy of unlimited war was at odds with just war theory. Other Chinese analysts criticized the book's content for its distance from the Marxist point of war and for its support for questionable actions (terrorism, etc.) that were damaging China's international image. The authors reportedly were called before the Academy of Military Sciences and Ministry of Foreign Affairs in 2000 and subjected to official criticism.

In addition to the inquiries of lawyers and official military and foreign affairs figures, there were several pointed domestic criticisms of Unrestricted Warfare. A daily newspaper owned by the People's Republic of China (PRC), the Hong Kong Ta Kung Pao, presented a strongly worded criticism of the book. The author of the article, Kao Chieh-chien, used a question and answer technique to present his views.

First, Kao questions whether unrestricted warfare techniques will be effective. Authors Qiao and Wang had recommended using a combination of unrestricted means, to include command, finance, hackers, and so on. Kao notes that this might put state security and military strategies above state development strategies which could weaken national strength and economic development. There are also political restrictions that the authors appear to ignore. Qiao and Wang recommended that the basic rule of unrestricted war should be "the best way to achieve a goal. Any means compatible with this principle can be considered the best means." They add that this method is considered "to be an out-and-out Machiavelli." Kao notes that this is a break with traditional Chinese ethics and encourages one to act like terrorists, two paths Kao does not support.[12]

---

[12] Kao Chieh-chien, "What Limits Has 'Unrestricted Warfare' Exceeded—Also Discussing the Phenomenon Where 'Readers and Experts Stick to Their Own Views,'" Hong Kong Ta Kung Pao, 21 June 2000, as translated and downloaded from the OSC website, document number CPP20000621000055.

Second, Kao questions whether <u>Unrestricted Warfare</u> has been misread. Kao writes that in some places, Qiao and Wang "are humming [sic] and hawing in an effort to have their bread buttered on both sides, not that the readers misread the book." In this case, Kao is referring to incidents where Qiao, for example, said he does not support terrorism, then later adds that if the British and US can use terrorist methods, why can't the Chinese? Qiao later states that "saying without doing it [terrorism]" is using "theoretical deterrence." Kao writes that such thought is purely a fool's paradise and that "military thinking without the restriction of ethics is the ruthless thinking of heartless and mindless tyrannies." Instead of dreaming up combinations of methods, one's first thoughts should be whether a war should be fought or can be fought. Without these considerations, one is simply an armchair strategist.[13]

Third, Kao questions whether there are limits for military thinking. Kao feels that Qiao and Wang believe war is unavoidable and that the enemy has been determined. This has confined their research to a small area. Kao adds

> It has taken the travails of three generations of statesmen to turn the United States from the number one enemy in battlefields into a potential constructive and strategic partner, but to regress Sino-US relations into antagonistic relations, it takes only a slight error in thought; one has only to say no or to go beyond the limits, and Sino-US relations will slide down easily to an unmanageable extent.[14]

Finally, Kao questions the conscience of military experts and the silence of civilian specialists. He notes that it is never a good omen for the country when "the voice of specialists and scholars of the humanities and social sciences is buried by the same story in the media and that military experts are in high and vigorous spirits and receive the spotlight." He asks how in China "soldiers can have more freedom of speech than the common people in politically sensitive issues?" Kao ends his article by calling for more control of "civil officers" over the military and continuing the focus on economic development as the crucial task.[15]

Kao's criticism was buttressed by international critics who blasted the book. Some of the methods that Qiao and Wang advanced were deemed extreme and cause for worry regarding China's commitment to ban chemical

---

[13] Ibid.
[14] Ibid.
[15] Ibid.

and biological weapons.[16] However, in spite of the domestic and international uproar over the book, a September 1999 Chinese news article indicated that the book had gained traction and a high level of interest in China. <u>Unrestricted Warfare</u> was reprinted five times with 40,000 copies in circulation. Central Military Commission Chairman Jiang Zemin and Defense Minister Chi Haotian reportedly ordered the book.[17] By February 2001 the book was in its seventh printing, totaling 70,000 books. Qiao stated that 120 generals had contacted him and requested the book.[18]

Thus <u>Unrestricted Warfare</u> appears to have generated much discussion among members of the Chinese military and civilian elite. The book's popularity at home and abroad cannot be denied albeit for different reasons. It appears that when the initial furor over the book subsided, many people in China realized that this was an interesting book with lots of innovative thought as to how to confront the US. The book implied that unrestricted warfare could serve as a cognitive countermeasure to US technological advantages in 1999 and that unrestricted warfare could intimidate or scare US decision-makers with China's potential use of asymmetric warfare capabilities. However, the book could also have been using an old Chinese stratagem, to appear strong when weak, through these threats. For Chinese readers, the book's anti-American overtone supports PLA resolve against US military actions. It offers PLA servicemen confidence in the thinking ability of their leaders to find new ways for the "inferior to defeat the superior."

For the US, <u>Unrestricted Warfare</u> has provided a potential template of how terrorists, insurgents, or nation-states might attack the US from a non US-based doctrinal perspective. The book has made the US military pay attention to other methods of potential conflict and future war scenarios. It has not paralyzed US strategists as some suggest but, on the contrary, has mobilized and prepared them for a potential onslaught of creative activities. Qiao and Wang's book initially, at least, placed China squarely in US crosshairs as a result of their manuscript.

---

[16] Ming Zhang, "War without Rules," <u>Bulletin of the Atomic Scientists,</u> December 1999, at http://rempost.bolgspot.com/2006/01/war-without-rules.html.
[17] Chiang Hsun and Liu Ning-jung, "Completely New Method of Unrestricted Warfare," Hong Kong <u>Yazhou Zhoukan</u>, 20 September 1999, pp. 38-40, as translated and downloaded from the OSC website, document number FTS19991016000039.
[18] Tung Yi.

A Discussion of <u>Unrestricted Warfare</u>: Looking for Nuggets

<u>Unrestricted Warfare</u> has gained some notoriety in the West. It has a place in both Wikipedia and in ConflictWiki. These are mainly short summaries of book reviews on the text, although ConflictWiki goes into more detail.

Dr. James D. Perry, an analyst for Science Applications International Corporation (SAIC), wrote a review of <u>Unrestricted Warfare</u> for <u>Aerospace Power Journal</u> in the summer of 2000. He notes that the book was not a blueprint for a "dirty war" against the West as many suggested but a call for innovative thinking on future warfare. Thus Perry does not look at the book as a master plan to destroy America. Authors Qiao and Wang discuss technological and political changes that may shape future battlefields and these battlefields, Perry adds, could be everywhere and include many different topics (for example, trade warfare, financial warfare, terrorism, ecological warfare, computer-network attack, media warfare, drug warfare, and psychological warfare among other methods).

Perry wrote that Qiao, interviewed in 1999, criticized Slobodan Milosevic for "playing by the rules" against the US in Kosovo. This battlefield offered a fertile ground for unrestricted thinking that Milosevic did not exploit. He should have used the rules of <u>Unrestricted Warfare</u> and sent surface-to-air missile teams into Western Europe to attack NATO planes as they took off from air bases, Qiao noted. Qiao stated that the US was smarter in that it didn't restrict itself to purely military means in Kosovo, since "media war, news restrictions, trade sanctions, and financial attacks (such as freezing the other party's assets)" were employed against the Federal Republic of Yugoslavia.[19] These are measures the US has been using for years, however, and indicate that Qiao and Wang's work on combinations in warfare is not something new in every respect. Rather many of their ideas were actions that they hadn't considered in the past.

This author is in agreement with Perry that <u>Unrestricted Warfare</u> was a special book for its time (1999) for several reasons. First, it introduced some ideas that are only now being further developed in both China and the US. In the case of China it was the introduction in <u>Unrestricted Warfare</u> in 1999 of the concept of non-military operations. This concept has been a current focus of the Chinese military press (for example, a special section on non-military operations was developed in a 2008 issue of <u>China Military Science</u>). For the US, the concept introduced in <u>Unrestricted Warfare</u> and a topic of current

---

[19] James D. Perry, "Operation Allied Force: the View from Beijing," <u>Aerospace Power Journal</u>, Summer 2000, pp. 78-90.

discussion in the US is hybrid wars. Frank Hoffman, for example, wrote about hybrid war in a 2009 issue of <u>Joint Force Quarterly</u>. <u>Unrestricted Warfare</u> discussed both of these issues ten years ago.

Second, the book offered a good description of US strengths and weaknesses from Qiao and Wang's perspective. Surprisingly, a US weakness was identified as the concept of full spectrum war. To the authors, the concept is too conventionally focused and does not comprehensively engage all of the aspects of warfare as does <u>Unrestricted Warfare</u>. Finally, the book discussed in detail some Chinese concepts that were new to the non-Chinese specialist, such as the golden section, the side rule, the empty basket, and the extended domain (each concept is explained in detail below). In short, Qiao and Wang appear to have been poised at the leading edge of new thinking in 1999. <u>Unrestricted War</u> introduced a new mode of thinking into the PLA. For the US, the book offered a glimpse into some creative yet threatening Chinese thought.

<u>The Dragon's Quantum Leap</u> focuses on new modes of thinking which are now central to several contemporary PLA developments. Some of the new modes of thought found in <u>Unrestricted War</u> are listed below in the form of selected quotes that fall into one of two categories, either Chinese views of US warfare strengths and weaknesses; or Chinese views of the contemporary operational environment. Following the selected quotes is a general discussion of Qiao and Wang's views of new concept weapons and other specific Chinese topics.

Chinese Views of Strong and Weak Points of the American Way of War
Strong Points:
On the US Use of Lessons Learned: "It truly seems as if the Americans are always able to find the key to open the door of the next military action among the lessons of each military action."[20]

On Goldwater-Nichols: "The emergence of the 'Reorganization Act' in the United States and the effects it produced in the US military are food for thought, and any country which hopes to win a war in the twenty-first century must inevitably face the option of either 'reorganizing' or being defeated. There is no other way."[21]

---

[20] Qiao and Wang, <u>Unrestricted Warfare</u>, p. 51.
[21] Ibid., p. 53.

On the Results of the Gulf War: "It is already destined to become the starting point for the theory of 'omni-dimensional combat' proposed by the elite of the US Army when they suddenly woke up."[22]

On Helicopters, America's "Flying Cowboys:" "…very few people recall that it was the helicopters, not some of the other favorite new weapons, that performed first-rate service in 'Desert Storm'…This was definitely the most deeply significant tactical operation of the ground war during the war. It proclaimed that, from this point, helicopters were perfectly capable of conducting large-scale operations independently…there is no doubt that it is just a question of time before it [helicopter] drives the tank from the battlefield…Furthermore, the new concepts of a 'flying army' and 'flying ground warfare' in which the helicopter is the main battle weapon may become standard military jargon and appear in every military dictionary." [23]

On the US Air Force: "…General McPeak…was able to achieve his dream of breaking down the barriers between the strategic and tactical air forces and establish mixed air force wings, as well as his use of the 'subtract seven and add four' approach following the war to bring about the most richly original reform of the Air Force command structure in its history."[24]

On Costly Weapons: "What you must know is that this is a nationality that has never been willing to pay the price of life and, moreover, has always vied for victory at all costs. The appearance of high-technology weaponry can now satisfy these extravagant hopes of the American people."[25]

Weak points:
On Technology Dependence: "Moreover, who now dares state with certainty that in future wars this heavy spending will not result in an electronic Maginot line that is weak because of its excessive dependence on a single technology?"[26]

On the Diminished Role of the Navy in Desert Storm: "If the Gulf War is really seen as a big elephant, then it can be said that the US Navy's front fin is hardly touching the fur of the elephant, which is just the same as saying it is not touching the elephant at all."[27]

---

[22] Ibid., p. 54.

[23] Ibid., pp. 56-58.

[24] Ibid., p. 62.

[25] Ibid., p. 75.

[26] Ibid., p. 70.

[27] Ibid., p. 72.

On a Lack of Thinking: "Having thought lag behind reality (much less to speak of surpassing it) is not only a shortcoming of American soldiers, but it is very typical of them."[28] "They [Americans] believe that as long as the Edisons of today do not sink into sleep, the gate to victory will always be open to Americans. Self-confidence such as this has made them forget one simple fact—it is not so much that war follows the fixed race course of the rivalry of technology and weaponry as it is a game field with continually changing direction and many irregular factors. Whether you wear Adidas or Nike cannot guarantee you will become the winner."[29] "...proposing a new concept of weapons does not require relying on the springboard of new technology, it just demands lucid and incisive thinking. However, this is not a strong point of the Americans, who are slaves to technology in their thinking."[30]

On Overreliance on Weaponry: "Warfare'[s]...high-technology, high-investment, high-expenditure, and high-payback features make its requirements for military strategy and combat skill far lower than its requirements for the technological performance of weaponry."[31]

On Institutional Reforms' Impact on National Strategy: "The institutional reforms that began after the Gulf War...even had a far-reaching effect on America's national strategy...in handling international affairs the US government has become increasingly fond of using force, makes moves more quickly, and seeks revenge for the smallest grievances."[32]

On Lacking an Opponent like the Soviet Union: "... what is surprising is that such a large nation unexpectedly does not have a unified strategy and command structure to deal with the threat [of non-military war, such as terrorists]. What makes one even more so wonder whether to laugh or cry is that unexpectedly they have forty-nine departments and offices responsible for anti-terrorist activities, but there is very little coordination and cooperation among them."[33]

---

[28] Ibid., p. 121.

[29] Ibid., p. 77.

[30] Ibid., p. 15.

[31] Ibid., p. 76.

[32] Ibid., p. 81.

[33] Ibid., p. 107.

Chinese Views on Changes in the Contemporary Strategic Environment

On Thinking about the "Empty Basket" and the 24 Methods of War:[34]
"The combination of which we speak is just this type of empty basket, an empty basket of military thinking. It is not the same as any of the very strongly directed methods of operation of the past, for only when the basket is filled with specific targets and contents does it begin to have directionality and aim. The key to whether or not victory is won in a war is nowhere else but in what things you are able to pack into this basket."[35]

On Hidden Agendas: "Only a handful of soldiers are likely to grasp a principle that every statesman already knows: that the biggest difference between contemporary wars and the wars of the past is that, in contemporary wars, the overt goal and the covert goal are often two different matters."[36]

On New Technological Spaces and Battlefields: "We can anticipate that every major alteration or extension of the battlespace of the future will depend on whether a certain kind of technological invention, or a number of technologies in combination, can create a brand new technological space."[37] "Thus, warfare will simultaneously evolve in the macroscopic, 'mesoscopic', and microscopic spheres…"[38]

On the Term "Unrestricted War:" "When we suddenly realize that all these non-war actions may be the new factors constituting future warfare, we have to come up with a new name for this new form of war: warfare which transcends all boundaries and limits, in short: unrestricted warfare."[39]

On the Economic Factor Replacing the Military Factor: "…military threats are already often no longer the major factors affecting national security…these traditional factors are increasingly becoming more intertwined with grabbing resources, contending for markets, controlling capital, trade sanctions, and

---

[34] Ibid., p. 123. The 24 methods of warfare proposed in the book are atomic, diplomatic, financial, conventional, network, trade, bio-chemical, intelligence, resource, ecological, psychological, economic aid, space, tactical, regulatory, electronic, smuggling, sanction, guerrilla, drug, media, terrorist, virtual (deterrence), and ideological.

[35] Ibid., pp. 124-125.

[36] Ibid., p. 28.

[37] Ibid., p. 31.

[38] Ibid., p. 31. Mesoscopic, according to Qiao and Wang, is the area between macroscopic and microscopic.

[39] Ibid., p. 5.

21

other economic factors, to the extent that they [traditional factors] are even becoming secondary to these factors."[40]

On the Extended Domain View: "Actually, it is not only the US but all nations which worship the view of modern sovereignty that have already unconsciously expanded the borders of security to a multiplicity of domains, including politics, economics, material resources, nationalities, religion, culture, networks, geography, environment, and other space, etc. This type of 'extended domain view' is a premise for the survival and development of modern sovereign nations as well as for their striving to have influence in the world."[41]

On an Extended Domain Strategy: "Such a strategy takes all things into consideration that are involved in each aspect of the security index of the interests of the entire nations, as well as superimposes political (national will, values, and cohesion) and military factors on the economy, culture, foreign relations, technology, environment, natural resources, nationalities, and other parameters before one can draw out a complete 'extended domain' which superposes both national interests and national security—a large strategic situation map."[42]

On Combining Different Types of War: "With combination there is abundance, with combination there are a myriad of changes, and with combination there is diversity. Combination has nearly increased the means of modern warfare to the infinite..."[43]

On Desert Storm: "We have no intention of helping the Americans create a myth but when 'Desert Storm' unfolded and concluded for all to see...who could say that a classic war heralding the arrival of warfare in the age of technical integration-globalization had not opened wide the main front door to the mysterious and strange history of warfare..."[44] "...it does represent the first and most concentrated use of a large number of new and advanced weapons since their appearance, as well as a testing ground for the revolution in military affairs triggered by this, and this point is sufficient to earn it the position of a classic in the history of warfare..."[45]

---

[40] Ibid., p. 95.
[41] Ibid., p. 96.
[42] Ibid., p. 97.
[43] Ibid., p. 98.
[44] Ibid., p. 48.
[45] Ibid., p. 63.

On the Importance of Information Technology: "We can say with certainty that this is the most important revolution in the history of technology, its revolutionary significance is not merely in that it is a brand new technology itself, but more in that it is a kind of bonding agent which can lightly penetrate the layers of barriers between technologies and link various technologies which appear to be totally unrelated."[46]

On Future War and Information War: "Even if in future wars all the weapons have information components embedded in them and are fully computerized, we can still not term such war information warfare, and at most we can just call it computerized warfare. This is because, regardless of how important information technology is, it cannot completely supplant the functions and roles of each technology per se."[47]

On the Difference in Computerized War and Information War: "Computerized warfare in the broad sense and information warfare in the narrow sense are two completely different things. The former refers to the various forms of warfare which are enhanced and accompanied by information technology, while the latter primarily refers to war in which information technology is used to obtain or suppress information."[48]

On Tactics Leading, Weapons Following: "...when the Americans proposed the concept of 'building the weapons to fit the fight,' it triggered the greatest single change in the relationship between weapons and tactics since the advent of war. First determine the modes of combat, then develop the weapons, and in this regard, the first stab that the Americans took at this was 'air-land battle.' The currently popular 'digitized battlefield' and 'digitized units' which have given rise to much discussion represent their most recent attempt."[49]

On National Interests: "...Iraq had seized the entire West by the throat. Lifelines are naturally more important than face, and the United States had no choice but to take it seriously..."[50]

On the New Form of Alliances: "In the new age, going it alone is not only unwise, it is also not a realistic option."[51] "More profoundly, the appearance of

---

[46] Ibid., p. 3.
[47] Ibid., p. 9.
[48] Ibid.
[49] Ibid., p. 12.
[50] Ibid., p. 48.
[51] Ibid., p. 49.

the 'overnight' alliance brought an era to a close. That is, the era of fixed-form alliances..."[52]

On the Media: "Unlike battlefield propaganda, which has an excessively subjective tinge and is easily rejected by an opponent or neutral individuals, because it is cleverly cloaked as objective reporting, the media has a quiet impact that is hard to gauge."[53]

On the Difficulty of Being a Soldier Today: "It is very obvious that none of the soldiers in any one nation possesses sufficient mental preparation against this type of new war which completely goes beyond military space. However, this is actually a severe reality which all soldiers must face."[54]

On International Rules of War: "Small nations hope to use the rules to protect their own interests, while large nations attempt to utilize the rules to control other nations."[55]

This ends the section on selected quotes from Unrestricted Warfare. The next section highlights some of the important general concepts of the book.

General Discussion of Key Points in Unrestricted Warfare

Qiao and Wang offer some specific innovations and developments (especially in the book's final three chapters) that require more explanation. Each topic is covered below from the perspective of these two officers. They include the following concepts: combined war that goes beyond limits; new concept weapons versus a new concept of weapons; the side-principal rule; the golden section rule; the "civilianization" of war (the degree of participation of the entire population in war, such as the use of hackers); breaking ideological boundaries; and the new "essential principles" of warfare.

Combined War that Goes Beyond Limits: Qiao and Wang write that the concept of warfare has been expanded due to the diversity of means available today. Any future war will be a "cocktail mixture" or combination of means beyond the traditional battlefield.[56] Combinations introduce diversity and abundance into the conduct of warfare. Qiao and Wang believe "what is truly important is whether or not one understands what goes with what to implement

---

[52] Ibid., p. 50.
[53] Ibid., p. 60.
[54] Ibid., p. 108.
[55] Ibid., p. 109.
[56] Ibid., p. 43.

combinations."[57] Combinations of non-traditional means will challenge the logic, laws, and traditional models of warfare.[58] In defining combined war that goes beyond limits, Qiao and Wang write:

> But in fact, unlimited surpassing of limits is impossible to achieve. Any surpassing of limits can only be done within certain restrictions. That is, 'going beyond limits' certainly does not equate to 'no limits,' only to the expansion of 'limited.' That is, to go beyond the intrinsic boundaries of a certain area or a certain direction, and to combine opportunities and means in more areas or in more directions, so as to achieve a set objective.[59]

The authors thus imply most clearly that the term "unrestricted" doesn't really work as a translation of the title of their book. Rather, "exceeding limits" seems to better express the title of their book. The authors stress that the concept of combined war is first of all a way of thinking, and only afterwards is it a method.[60] Qiao and Wang believe the ability to transcend ideology is the first requirement of exceeding limits. Only then can the second meaning, to transcend limits and boundaries, take effect. The latter involves selecting the most appropriate means but not necessarily the most extreme means.[61]

New Concept Weapons versus a New Concept of Weapons: Man-made earthquakes, tsunamis, weather disasters, subsonic waves, and new biological and chemical weapons all constitute new concept weapons (NCW).[62] Kinetic-energy weapons, directed-energy weapons, sub-sonic weapons, geophysical weapons, solar-energy weapons, meteorological weapons, and gene weapons are also NCW.[63] These new concept weapons differ from a new concept of weapons. The latter include stock market crashes, computer viruses, and rumors or scandals as new weapons. A hacker in general and a non-state actor in some instances can help create trade war; financial war; new types of terror warfare; ecological, psychological, and smuggling war; media, drug, network, and technological war; and fabricated, resource, culture, and international law warfare.[64] Technology is no longer the main factor. A new concept of weapons implies using things that initially benefit mankind to harm mankind. China's

---

[57] Ibid., p. 119.
[58] Ibid., p. 120.
[59] Ibid., p. 155.
[60] Ibid., p. 171.
[61] Ibid., p. 154.
[62] Ibid., p. 16.
[63] Ibid., p. 24.
[64] Ibid., pp. 38-43.

awareness of things must expand since anything can become a weapon, Qiao and Wang note.[65] These "kinder weapons" may try to paralyze or undermine but they do not intend to produce casualties. They may be the watershed between the old and new weapons of war.[66]

The Side-Principal Rule: The side-principal [spelling per the document] rule is apparently another way to consider a concept being "asymmetric" since it implies striking an object from any direction other than head-on. Qiao and Wang write that "the side-principal rule is opposed to all forms of parallel placement, balance, symmetry, being all-encompassing, and smoothness, but, instead, advocates using the sword to cut the side."[67] Frontal collisions must be avoided. This "is the most basic grammar of victory for the ancient article of war."[68] However, the concept doesn't always exclude a frontal collision if such a move imposes surprise on an adversary. A side element is a deviation in "terms of lines of thought and essence, instead of deviation in form." Thus if one is not expecting a frontal assault, it can be applied as a surprise move that utilizes the side-principal rule (a deviation in thought) to achieve success.[69]

Golden Section Warfare: The number .618 is known as the rule of the golden section. It refers to a mathematical ratio and was originally considered by artists as the golden rule of aesthetics. The number became a basic design scale which, in the case of the Parthenon, for example, was found to be the ratio of vertical lines to horizontal lines. American J. Kieffer in 1953 and the Chinese mathematician Hua Luogeng turned this number into the "optimum seeking method." This optimization can refer to number of soldiers and force. It often appears in attack or defend ratios of forces such as 2:3, 3:5, 5:8, and 8:13.[70] These ratios usually ensure success if one is on the right side of the .618 rule. Qiao and Wang state that .618 can be found in the arc of a cavalry sword, the apex of the flying trajectory of a bullet shell or ballistic missile, and in the optimum bomb-release altitude and distance for an aircraft in dive bombing mode. In these cases (no further explanation was provided, which makes it difficult to prove) the .618 principle also applies.[71]

The Civilianization of War: Qiao and Wang believe that future war will be conducted in non-war spheres. Winning wars with non-war means has become

---

[65] Ibid., p. 16.
[66] Ibid., p. 20.
[67] Ibid., p. 141.
[68] Ibid.
[69] Ibid., p. 147.
[70] Ibid., p. 148.
[71] Ibid., pp. 130-136.

a reality, even though the outline of the "civilianization" of such a concept isn't yet clear. The civilianization of war (People's War in the information age?) has been a theme of several writers since the publication of <u>Unrestricted Warfare</u>.[72]

Breaking Ideological Boundaries (supra-domains, supra-means, supra-tiers): Transcending ideology is the first requirement of exceeding limits in Qiao and Wang's opinion, as mentioned above. To do so requires supra-domain, supra-means, and supra-tier combinations. Those involved in warfare must break free from the confines of domains and the boundaries of ideology in order to enter a state of freedom of thought. There is now no domain that cannot be used. The Chinese are good at understanding and using this fact while Americans are not, according to Qiao and Wang.[73] It is necessary to select which domain will be the main battlefield to achieve the objectives of war, domains that may not be military.[74] Domains must become playing cards deftly shuffled in Chinese hands.[75] Non-state organizations may, for example, combine kidnapping, assassinations, hackers, and currency speculation as an example of supra-means.[76]

Means are methods or tools through which one can obtain an objective. Supra-means could include "buying or gaining control of stocks to turn another country's newspapers and television stations into tools of media warfare." Or it could include using assassination against financial speculators in Wang and Qiao's opinion.[77]

With regard to supra-tier levels, Qiao and Wang state that war no longer needs to progress from one level to another until a "moment of destiny" is reached.[78] Rather, that moment of destiny is now something that can be created through combinations. To be able to continuously create such moments is something to be achieved, a winning strategy that should be used often. Warfare could thus be "changed into a dragon with interchangeable limbs, torsos, and heads which we could put together as we like, and which could swing freely in any direction."[79] At the national level the PLA's actions could also include non-military actions that correspond to strategy.[80]

---

[72] Ibid., pp. 144-145.
[73] Ibid., p. 161.
[74] Ibid., p. 163.
[75] Ibid., p. 164.
[76] Ibid., p. 166.
[77] Ibid., p. 164.
[78] Ibid., p. 168.
[79] Ibid., pp. 168-169.
[80] Ibid., p. 170.

Essential Principles: Qiao and Wang believe the Gulf War changed the nature of war as it was once understood. The authors define warfare in the following manner:

> Warfare can be military, or it can be quasi-military, or it can be non-military. It can use violence, or it can be nonviolent. It can be a confrontation between professional soldiers, or one between newly emerging forces consisting primarily of ordinary people or experts. These characteristics of beyond-limits war are the watershed between it and traditional warfare, as well as the starting line for new types of warfare.[81]

This new nature of war results in new principles of war with which no one is familiar, the authors add. These principles include omni-directionality, synchrony, limited objectives, unlimited measures, asymmetry, minimal consumption, multi-dimensional coordination, and the adjustment and control of the entire process.

Omni-directionality means considering all factors associated with unrestricted war. The idea is to use all war resources, prevent blind spots, move in an unrestricted manner, and orient at will. Through the use of this 360 degree method the situation can be properly ascertained as well.[82]

Synchrony has replaced phasing as an important planning principle according to Qiao and Wang. It implies doing something within the same time period but does not imply "simultaneity." The authors note that unrestricted war could also be dubbed "designated time warfare." They believe that the US has not expanded this battlefield concept beyond the military.[83]

Limited objectives imply not pursuing objectives beyond one's reach. If objectives are outside the reach of available measures then defeat is certain. Qiao and Wang use a speech by President Clinton to emphasize this point. They note that Clinton sought on one occasion to promise action when America's national interests and sense of values were in danger. Actions can be achieved through the use of power but changing values is outside the reach of power as an objective in Wang and Qiao's opinion.[84]

---

[81] Ibid., p. 177.
[82] Ibid.
[83] Ibid., p. 179.
[84] Ibid., p. 180.

28

Unlimited measures refer to employing measures beyond boundaries or restrictions to achieve limited objectives. The implication is to disobey the law when implementing such measures.[85]

Asymmetry means hitting an opponent where he least expects it or following a train of thought that opposes a line of symmetry. Asymmetrical factors should be examined when considering a main axis of attack, a center of gravity, or force disposition and deployment. It is necessary to work on developing a line of action that creates power for oneself and allows the situation to develop as intended.[86]

The *minimal consumption* principle refers to making rational use of combat resources. It has three components: rationality is more important than thrift; the size of combat consumption is decided by the form of combat; and the consumption of combat means can be lowered by using more measures. Here again the authors advise a force to "combine the superiorities of several kinds of combat resources in several kinds of areas to form up a completely new form of combat" and thereby minimize consumption.[87]

Multidimensional coordination means coordinating different spheres and forces to accomplish an objective. These different spheres include geography, history, culture, ethnic identity, and the influence of international organizations. This is especially important today since any sphere can become a battlefield.[88]

Finally, there is the essential principle of the *adjustment and control of the entire process*. This refers to obtaining feedback during an operation and making the proper revisions. Control over this process is very important.[89]

The future battlefield's military sphere will be but one of several domains to which these essential principles apply. With the increased stature of non-military activities and their impact on future military and non-military battlefields, control over these domains will become particularly important. According to the authors, control is a point that China focuses on constantly while the US tends to focus more on dominance and superiority than control.

---

[85] Ibid., p. 181.
[86] Ibid., pp. 181-182.
[87] Ibid., pp. 182-183.
[88] Ibid., pp. 183-184.
[89] Ibid., p. 185.

Qiao's Newspaper Interviews on <u>Unrestricted Warfare</u>, 1999-2001

The publication of <u>Unrestricted Warfare</u> generated a series of author interviews with the Chinese and Taiwanese press. One of the first interviews was with Qiao and it took place in June 1999 with the newspaper <u>Zhongguo Qingnian Bao</u>, which the China Youth League sponsors. Qiao stated that no other country in the world can match US superiority in military technology. Therefore other nations must depend on non-military actions as much as military actions to defeat a nation so equipped. It is a way for a weak country to cope with a larger evil.[90] Beyond-limits or unrestricted warfare is required to defeat or at least injure such a superior opponent. This type of warfare is more humane than conventional war and may require the overlapping of several methods, Qiao notes, such as "Schwarzkopf (commander) plus Soros (finance) plus bin Laden (terrorist) type tactics."[91] The most ominous part of the interview was Qiao's belief that war with the US is "inevitable." This is because China will grow strong only at the cost of consuming much of the world's resources which will put it in direct competition and eventually conflict with the US.[92]

In a September 1999 interview Qiao said he realized that war was not the only way to force ones' will on another party and that the purpose of the book was to develop a "new war theory" similar to that formed earlier by Clausewitz. This can be accomplished by the "dislocation" method in which one upsets the "order of the cards in one's own hand and reorganizes them in accordance with the needs of war and interests of that time."[93]

In the September interview Qiao listed "military war methods" as atomic, conventional, biological, chemical, ecological, space, electronic, guerrilla, and terrorist warfare; "above-military war methods" as diplomatic, network, intelligence, psychological, technological, smuggling, drug, and fictitious warfare; and applicable "non-military war methods" as financial, trade, resources, economic aid, legal, sanction, media, and ideological warfare. He noted that he was not proposing that China follow non-military war actions but that if all else failed and the country's existence was at stake, it must consider such issues. Thus his strident tone seems to have diminished

---

[90] Sha Lin, "Two Senior Colonels and 'No-Limit Warfare,'" <u>Zhongguo Qingnian Bao</u>, 28 June 1999, p. 5, as translated and downloaded from https://www.opensource.gov, document number FTS19990728000697.

[91] Ibid.

[92] Ibid.

[93] Ma Ling, "Special Topic on Important News," <u>Ta Kung Pao</u>, 19 September 1999, p. B3, as translated and downloaded from www.opensource.gov, document number FTS19991005000805.

somewhat between June and September. Qiao states that the US has already used the principles of unrestricted warfare without knowing it. He notes, for example, that the US in Iraq used conventional plus diplomatic plus sanctions plus legal plus media plus psychological plus intelligence warfare all at the same time.[94]

In March 2000 in <u>Liaowang</u>, the weekly journal of China's official news agency Xinhua, Qiao stated that, with regard to non-military actions, "our study, analysis, and pointing out the possibility of such actions does not at all equate to approval of it..."[95] Qiao added that the US makes rules for their interests and puts domestic laws above international laws, breaking the latter as they see fit. The intervention by the North Atlantic Treaty Organization (NATO) into the Federal Republic of Yugoslavia (FRY) over human rights issues at the expense of the FRY's national sovereignty is a good example in his opinion. He then notes that "the concept of unrestricted warfare that we proposed does not at all mean breaking all the rules," a statement quite at odds with Qiao's statements in other articles.[96] He added that the intent of <u>Unrestricted Warfare</u> was to provide an approach, an option, and a new kind of military thinking for strategic military studies.[97]

In a June 2000 interview, this time with Taiwan's press, Qiao stated that the book is popular because of its innovative content. He was quick to add that the book does not represent an official PLA viewpoint. Qiao said the book has allowed for more guesswork by people concerned with cross-strait issues but that a certain geographical reality cannot be avoided. Taiwan is a "geo-prisoner" of the mainland. He said a reason for writing the book was to stress the absurdity that the US can lay down the existing international norms on the one hand and, on the other, change them at will. He added that this does not mean that China will break international norms arbitrarily as the US has done.[98]

Of course, the events of 9/11 gave the Chinese press a reason to reenergize their interest in Qiao and Wang, just as their popularity was

---

[94] Ibid.
[95] Staff reporter, "Unrestricted War—New Concept of War Presented by Non-Military Experts," Beijing <u>Liaowang</u>, 13 March 2000, No. 11, pp. 55-56, as translated and downloaded from the OSC website, document number CPP20000322000070.
[96] Ibid.
[97] Ibid.
[98] Yuan Leyi, "War Does Not Have a Law; A Strong Enemy Can be Outwitted with 'Unrestricted Warfare'...," Taipei <u>Chung-Kuo Shih-Pao</u>, 30 June 2000, p. 14, as translated and downloaded from the OSC website, document number CPP20000712000045.

beginning to wane. For example, a PRC-owned newspaper praised the authors for their foresight in predicting that high-tech means outside of military means would be used by terrorists. The effect was strategic and the US, too self-willed and conceited, finally paid for the enemies it had made over the years, according to Qiao and Wang. They added that perhaps the US will reflect on these events and make some changes to its foreign policy.[99] Qiao paid equal attention to the new insurgent capability, however, stating

> One of the byproducts of globalization resulting from technological integration is global terrorist activities. Non-professional soldiers and non-government organizations constitute a growing threat to the sovereign state. Increasingly they are the opponents of all professional armies. Next to non-professional fighters, the professional army looks powerful beyond compare. In the new era, however, the professional army is the dinosaur that cannot adapt. Non-professional fighters, on the other hand, are like raptors, full of life. They could use their sharp teeth to bite off half the world.[100]

A few years later, in November 2005, an article on Unrestricted Warfare was published in the Shanghai Guoji Zhanwang. In this article authors Qiao and Wang answered questions from interested readers. First, readers wanted to know if the book would fuel the West's China threat theory. The authors answered that this had already happened and that the Russian example (the disintegration of the USSR) should make China wary of US theories of this type. The authors state that their book, on the other hand, raises the issue of the state terrorism of big Western countries that threatens the world. Their book opposes terrorism, Qiao and Wang note, especially state terrorism.[101]

Qiao and Wang expressed their opinion again that 'going beyond limits' does not equate to 'no limits,' only to an expansion of 'limited.' Further, the word unrestricted refers to "non-military war actions and to going beyond the military sphere to open up new battlefields and find new combat

---

[99] Ma Ling, no title, Hong Kong Ta Kung Pao, 13 September 2001, as translated and downloaded from the OSC website, document number CPP20010913000078.
[100] Jiang Xun, "Terrorism As New Form of War in the 21st Century," Hong Kong Yazhou Zhoukan, 17 September 2001, No. 38, pp. 41- 42, as translated and downloaded from the OSC website, document number CPP20010920000063.
[101] Qiao Liang and Wang Xiangsui, "Do We Advocate Terrorism?" Shanghai Guoji Zhanwang, 1 November 2005, pp. 86-89, originally published in the March 2000 issue of Jianchuan Zhishi, as translated and downloaded from the OSC website, document number CPP20051227318001.

measures."[102] Combined war that goes beyond limits is "to go beyond the intrinsic boundaries of a certain area or a certain direction, and to combine opportunities and means in more areas or in more directions so as to achieve a set objective."[103] Their book appears to be aimed at the US when in fact the US was used as the threat only because it is the world leader in terms of equipment, mobility, and military theory. Rather, the authors conclude, their work is aimed at any nation that would harm China's national interests.[104] Obviously, Qiao and Wang's logic is highly debatable from a US viewpoint.

Conclusions

Qiao and Wang believe that an underdeveloped country like China that has never sought hegemony cannot follow blindly behind developed countries like the US and try to develop high-tech weaponry. Rather it must establish new ways of thinking and readjust its strategies, theories, and concepts to ensure national security. Unrestricted Warfare tells the PLA how to do this.[105] In this sense it is the first step among many in adopting a new mode of thinking as the force transforms from a mechanized to an informatized presence.

Zheng Liming, writing for China's official news service Zhongguo Xinwen She, noted that Unrestricted Warfare constitutes

A sagacious grasping of the current lag in military thought that people were still unaware of, points out the fatal weaknesses existing in US military thought and its unavoidable fragility in modern warfare, and reminds people that today, with economic globalization and constant social changes, there is an increasingly wide range of factors that have a bearing on national security and that there is a really great possibility that nonmilitary means and nonmilitary actions will win victory and the initiative in a future war.[106]

Qiao and Wang's discussion in Unrestricted Warfare is well represented by this summary. The authors state that the diversity of means available for contemporary warfare (the twenty-four methods listed earlier) has enlarged the concept of war. The battlefield is everywhere and war may be

---

[102] Ibid.

[103] Ibid.

[104] Ibid.

[105] Zeng Liming, "Theoretical Breakthrough and Strategic Readjustment—A New Change in China's Idea of National Defense," Zhongguo Xinwen She, 28 December 1999, as translated and downloaded from the OSC website, document number FTS20000126000997.

[106] Ibid.

conducted in areas where military actions do not dominate. When combinations of these methods are put together, the result is termed a "cocktail warfare mixture." This mixture represents a gradual accumulation of links and competencies that are replacing a form of warfare that used to proceed from one level to the next. The authors stress that

> With combination there is abundance, with combination there are a myriad of changes, and with combination there is diversity. Combination has nearly increased the means of modern warfare to the infinite, and it has basically changed the definition of modern warfare bestowed by those in the past: warfare carried out using modern weapons and means of operation.[107]

The twenty-four methods they propose are not entirely new "means to compel the enemy to accept one's interests" but rather means that have been used continuously by nation-states over the past three decades. That is, the two colonels are not nearly as original in their thinking as many analysts world-wide give them credit. Their originality comes in adding the word "war" behind each of the methods, and in advancing a theory to really combine methods which US analysts and doctrine writers have not done to the same degree.

From a Western viewpoint, there are several lessons that one can learn from this discussion of <u>Unrestricted Warfare</u>. First of all is the danger of writing a provocative book if you are a representative of a nation-state! This book has generated all types of international concern and raised China's threat posture higher on the radar of other countries than it previously was. While the authors were responsible for this international scrutiny, they were not responsible for the manner in which some people tended to exploit the book and manipulate its content. For example, the English version of the book incorrectly associated the unrestricted warfare concept with 9/11 (and indicted China as a co-conspirator).

A second point of interest is the warning shot the book fires across the bow of US military thinking and operational concepts. US operations are currently focused on Iraq and Afghanistan. The authors note that a country placing an excessive focus on one type of enemy can be attacked by another outside of their field of vision.[108] US strategists as a result must pay close attention to the entire spectrum of threats, to foreign perspectives of the contemporary operational environment, and to ways that other nations plan to

---

[107] Qiao and Wang, p. 98.
[108] Ibid., p. 121.

manipulate it. Qiao and Wang note that the information age may not be all it is cracked up to be. The authors write that "it is difficult for high-tech troops to deal with unconventional warfare" and add that "perhaps there is a rule here, or at least it is an interesting phenomenon which is worth studying."[109] It is not known whether such a rule (how unconventional forces defeat high-technology forces) is under consideration or not in China.

A third point of interest to Western analysts is that the book underscores what apparently is a rising theory in China, non-war military actions. Such actions are now discussed in detail in Chinese military journals. For example the authoritative Chinese journal China Military Science, in Issue 3, 2008, dedicated its lead section on "Subject Discussion" to non-war military operations theory and practice. Six articles discussed: the study of non-war military operations; non-military operations during the Sichuan earthquake; the terrorist threat and new armed forces missions; legal issues surrounding non-war military operations; characteristics of naval non-war military operations; and the growth and termination of the US theory of non-war military operations.[110]

Fourth, Western analysts should pay attention to Unrestricted Warfare for a better understanding of how the Chinese view our militaries. There is clearly frustration with the US and its coalition partners that are expressed in the book. These frustrations also illuminate Chinese prejudices in their consideration of America's national security policies. One prejudice is that the authors only see negatives in US ventures abroad and rarely give the US credit for the humanitarian work it does all the time. This could involve things like Tsunami relief efforts or passing out food to those in need after earthquakes or other natural disasters. Another prejudice, perhaps more in line with reality, is the authors' perception that a real shortcoming of the US military is its tendency to allow thought to lag behind reality. Perhaps this latter statement is truer now than it was fifteen years ago simply due to the crush of deployments that the US military has faced. There has been precious little time to think.

According to several bloggers writing from a Western point of view, the PLA authors ignored US diplomatic efforts such as attempts to bring peace to the Middle East, US economic sanctions to force nations to abide by international and humanitarian law, US efforts to control the drug trade in Colombia and other countries, and other non-military US measures over the

---

[109] Ibid., p. 13.
[110] China Military Science, Issue 3, 2008, table of contents.

years. It is as if the authors read no newspapers in the 1990s that offered any insight on US international efforts in any of these fields.

Thus, while some of the negative points from a Chinese point of view should be taken into consideration by our military leaders, other points should just be ignored as they demonstrate a misunderstanding of Western military thought and actions. Qiao and Wang ignore much of the good that Western armies perform. The absence of this contextual aspect certainly leads the authors to the dire predictions and prejudices they expose on the pages of Unrestricted Warfare. A well-rounded critique of what America and other nations do in relief operations of all types worldwide would help alleviate some of their mistaken perspectives.

So, is Unrestricted Warfare China's master plan to destroy America as the books English translation contends? Is it a wild concept by irresponsible writers that deserves strong condemnation world-wide? Or is it a book that offers insights into Chinese thinking and indicates where the Chinese military is heading? This author sides with the latter proposition. Unrestricted Warfare is an interesting thought piece not previously advanced by military theorists at home or abroad, especially by a uniformed member of another nation-state. For this reason alone, it is worth reading. The text offers many new ways to consider the operational environment and ways to control it. As Qiao and Wang write

> For a long time both military people and politicians have become accustomed to employing a certain mode of thinking, that is, the major factor posing a threat to national security is the military power of an enemy state or potential enemy state. However, the wars and major incidents which have occurred during the last ten years of the twentieth century have provided to us in a calm and composed fashion proof that the opposite is true: military threats are already often no longer the major factors affecting national security.[111]

If America's military desires to break free from the Chinese label of "lacking lucid and incisive thinking," then theorists in the US should be considering NOW new combinations and cocktail mixtures since we are ten years removed from the publication of Unrestricted Warfare. Most assuredly the Chinese are doing so as this work goes to press.

---

[111] Qiao and Wang, p. 95.

CHAPTER TWO: THE "ART OF WAR" IN THE 21ST CENTURY

This chapter highlights how ancient military thinking and information age concepts are being integrated to produce new modes of thought. [112]

The theoretical thinking of each era, including the theoretical thinking of our times, is a historical product. It has completely different forms in different times and has completely different content. [113] Engels

Introduction

The history of warfare demonstrates that nations taking the lead in transforming their militaries during periods of revolutionary change have the best chance of seizing the initiative in future war. It is apparent that the book Unrestricted Warfare gives the PLA a new mode of thinking that encourages transformations of this type in the Chinese military.

The Chinese concept of "informatized warfare" represents a focused transformation of the nation's mode of thinking. Traditional and mechanized methods of thought work less well in an integrated and systems-oriented environment characterized by rapidly changing time-space relationships. The strategic focus of the transformation requires "changing the thinking style, introducing innovation in operational theory" according to one source. [114] Engel's prediction was correct. Modern times encourage change and the development of entirely different forms of military thought and content.

This chapter examines the PLA's new modes of thought. Included in the discussion are the integration of technology with ancient stratagems, the use of new concepts such as war engineering and system attack warfare, and the impact of culture on new modes of thought.

---

[112] A variant of this article appeared in the Summer, 2009 edition of India's military journal CLAWS, pp. 164-182.

[113] Selected Works of Marx and Engels, Beijing, The People's Press, 1995, Second Chinese Edition, Vol. 4, p. 248, as quoted in Deng Yifei, "A Revolution in Military Thinking in the Information Age," Beijing Zhongguo Junshi Kexue (China Military Science), No. 6, 2007, as translated and downloaded from the Open Source Center website, document number CPP20080527563002.

[114] Zhan Yu, "Strategic Considerations for Army Transformation," Beijing Zhongguo Junshi Kexue (China Military Science), 25 August 2008, pp. 86-97, as translated and downloaded from the OSC website, document number CPP20080825563003.

China's <u>White Paper</u>: Formalizing the Transformation Process

Evidence of change in PLA thought is found in the Chinese <u>White Paper on National Defense</u> released in January 2009. China's military <u>White Papers</u> have traditionally explained the general azimuth of the PLA's development. The terms "mechanized" and "mechanization" were used only seven times in the 2009 version while the terms "informatized" and "informationization"[115] were used nearly fifty times, clearly showing where the emphasis is now placed. Only the terms "nuclear" and "defense" exceeded these information-oriented terms in word count.[116]

The catalyst for a new thinking style emanates primarily from Chinese observations of and lessons learned from US and coalition actions in the Desert Storm and Kosovo operations, and then from US/coalition actions in Afghanistan and Iraq. These conflicts demonstrated the power and accuracy of a new type of thinking, one based on information age concepts.

The informatization of the armed forces, the PLA realizes, demands new modes of thinking that "possess more pronounced comprehensive, dynamic, flexible, effective, creative, and forward-looking thought functions"[117] than conventional military thought. Such demands result in completely new warfare concepts[118] that affect every branch of the military. In the PLA's opinion, these changes are transforming the military from a closed force into a modern information age power focusing on new missions and roles to include peacekeeping, military diplomacy, and joint antiterrorism maneuvers with other nations. These are some of the nonwar military actions addressed in <u>Unrestricted Warfare</u> and elsewhere in PLA publications. Most recently, the PLA's navy has accepted the mission of combating Somali pirates. Such changes not only indicate that China's military reform process is underway, but they also demonstrate that China is increasing its military potential and willingness to accept more missions. The end goal of change is to have the

---

[115] "Informationization" is equivalent to the English term "informatization."
[116] "Full Text: China's National Defense in 2008," <u>Xinhua</u> in English 0208 GMT 20 January 2009, as downloaded from the OSC website, document number CPP20090120968111.
[117] Li Deyi, "A Study of the Basic Characteristics of the Modes of Thinking in Informatized Warfare," Beijing <u>Zhongguo Junshi Kexue</u> (<u>China Military Science</u>), 20 August 2007, pp. 101-105, as translated and downloaded from the OSC website, document number CPP20081028682007.
[118] Ibid.

capability "to win local wars in the era of information,"[119] another focus of the 2009 White Paper.

The PLA's "informatized thought" transformation is the outer formal reflection of a much deeper reform of the entire Chinese military establishment, a transformation that will affect both doctrine and equipment. At the same time the fundamentals upon which the PLA's thought processes rest (use of the dialectic, comprehensive assessments, Sun Tzu's principles, stratagems, etc.) remains as the thought platform to which integrated and system-oriented applications will be attached. Perhaps in this sense not as much has changed as Chinese theorists like to posit. Mixing the old and the new is akin to having "Sun Tzu at the computer."

Informatized Thought: Can the Inferior Still Defeat the Superior?

The work of PLA Major Peng Hongqi demonstrates the application of informatized warfare concepts to age-old Chinese military principles that result in a new mode of thinking. His article, "A Brief Discussion of Using the Weak to Defeat the Strong under Informatized Conditions," was written for the authoritative journal China Military Science. The article offers nine ways that an information-based inferior force could attack an information-based superior force.[120] Thus Peng still believes that the inferior can defeat the superior, especially after reading of some insurgent successes against coalition forces.

Peng offers a number of methods to help an inferior informatized force (China) overcome a superior informatized force such as the US. First, Peng states that it is imperative that the weaker side in an information confrontation find a way to limit a superior opponent's control over information. The weaker side must adhere to the active offense, he notes, especially in peacetime. This latter assertion contradicts the active defense emphasis of China's White Paper. The offense in peacetime provides the inferior side with a moment of relative equality that changes the traditional law of the weak always being on the defensive. Active offense is an asymmetric operation that requires properly determining key targets such as those that control data and make decisions. An inferior force must strike first or lose its opportunity to subdue the enemy. Attacks must be continuous once initiated, Peng notes, and both the military and the people must be mobilized. Society's informatized elite must be

---

[119] "Military Support to Peaceful Development," China Daily, 6 January 2009, at http://www.china-wire.org/2009/01/military-support-to-peaceful-development.
[120] Peng Hongqi, "A Brief Discussion of Using the Weak to Defeat the Strong under Informatized Conditions," Beijing Zhongguo Junshi Kexue (China Military Science), No. 1, 2008, pp. 142-148, as translated and downloaded from the OSC website, document number CPP20080624563002.

absorbed into the military's plans since everyone with a notebook computer can become a combatant.[121]

In a surprise interpretation of United Nations (UN) regulations, Peng states that, according to the self-defense charter of the UN,

> the inferior side carrying out a preemptive strike to subdue the enemy stems from the need to seize freedom of military actions, which is fundamentally different than a powerful enemy interfering in the internal affairs of another country and carrying out aggressive "first strike" actions.

Thus Peng seems to imply that it is the RIGHT of an inferior force to attack a superior force first.[122]

A second way for an inferior informatized force to defeat a superior informatized force is through the manipulation of the latter's "price disparity," the point where psychological weakness occurs, and through the use of allies. Causing massive war losses and casualties may affect the will of the superior force to continue fighting before it affects the inferior force since the former fears paying the price for victory more than the inferior force. Winning the support of allies and destroying an opponent's coalition through persuasion and the use of the "righteousness of a war effort" are other ways the inferior can defeat the superior.[123]

Third, Peng states that one must grasp the laws and circumstances of informatized conditions that guide information-based societies and militaries. One such issue to exploit is that only 20 percent of systems actually play key roles in the sustenance of a society or military force. The other 80 percent are only of secondary importance. The most vulnerable and most important of the 20 percent are space systems, networked systems, and logistic systems in that order. These are the systems that should be targeted. Another key measure, Peng notes, is developing countermeasures in conjunction with strategy.[124]

Fourth, the enemy must not be allowed to control information superiority, especially "the control of perception." Control of perceptions allows an inferior force to induce information confusion in a superior force via information excess, information inflation, or information inundation.

---

[121] Ibid.
[122] Ibid.
[123] Ibid.
[124] Ibid.

"Technological blind spots" (those areas not covered by satellites) can also aide an inferior force's plans. Studying the operating principles, systems, and conditions of an adversary's technical and theoretical conditioning allows Chinese forces to nullify some components of an adversary's overall perception system.[125]

Fifth, Peng writes that an inferior force must conduct information reconnaissance and prepare confrontational responses as asymmetric checks and balances on an opponent's strategy. An inferior force must control an adversary's combat preparations. Protracted control over an enemy is a means by which effective control is maintained over time and space. Protracted control also requires demonstrating countermeasure potential to a superior opponent. Without such a demonstration, the adversary would have no reason to go along with a protracted fight.[126]

Sixth, much of an inferior force's reconnaissance can now be done surreptitiously on computers through the use of hackers or other civilian means. This enhances the PLA's ability to claim plausible deniability when accused of being part of the attack. Forces begin engagements and reconnaissance well before a conflict emerges. Peacetime collection of key information on another force's data collection and processing systems is vital to success and offers an opportunity to act before a war breaks out.[127] Peng states that one should

> ...treat the peacetime struggle for information supremacy as a 'genuine, perpetual, and never-ending battle' in preparation and implementation. It must practice strict information secrecy. The essence of information confrontation is to gain as much enemy information as possible and keep the enemy from gaining information on one's own side.[128]

China appears to have performed Peng's vision well if the number of accusations leveled against the mainland is any indicator. India, South Korea, Germany, Australia, the US, and others have all accused China of penetrating their computer systems. The Chinese government has denied all of these accusations against them. Peng also notes that "the only way the inferior side can compete with a powerful enemy is by taking full advantage of peacetime to energetically elevate its material and technological foundation."[129] Chapter Seven of this book focuses on just this issue.

---

[125] Ibid.
[126] Ibid.
[127] Ibid.
[128] Ibid.
[129] Ibid.

Seventh, Peng states that the process through which information is understood (and how it can be manipulated) is important for nations to understand. The struggles between reconnaissance and counter-reconnaissance and deception and counter-deception are indicative of why this requirement is so important. One side can collect huge amounts of information on the other side, but if 50 percent of that information is deceptive input, then the side collecting information can be placed at a significant disadvantage.[130] Verifying data reliability is a requirement that cannot be delayed.

Eighth, Peng writes that the initiative in battle can only be won when "external potential" is achieved. External potential means using clandestine special operations to disrupt enemy plans, using the media to advertise the crimes of an enemy force, and applying external pressure on the enemy from other countries. External operations are important because science and technology are shrinking the power of spirit, strategy, and other non-technical elements. Outside pressures must be increased on these elements as a result.[131]

Finally, Peng contradicts many of his colleagues who search for so-called "trump" weapons. He believes there is too much emphasis on trump weapons since weapons alone cannot decide a conflict. They can be countered by other trump weapons that also contain asymmetric superiorities or by creative thought processes. Inferior forces are required to find technological niches and occupy a small space in that field if they are to maintain some type of counterforce (and thus balance) when dealing with a superior opponent. Optimizing the use of existing technologies, using strengths to make up for weaknesses, putting together things that are weak to make something strong, and using structural changes to enhance combat strength are other effective measures.[132]

Peng's article indicates that informatized war is a confrontation of not only technologies but also knowledge and the information age talents of people. The slant of Peng's article is very important since it offers thoughts foreign to many US analysts who don't (can't) think as Peng does due to our own prisms and limitations (legal, ethical, cultural, etc.). Peng's thinking approaches several of the thought processes in Unrestricted Warfare.

---

[130] Ibid.
[131] Ibid.
[132] Ibid.

Peng's use of a simple thought from the era of Sun Tzu, how "the inferior can defeat the superior," demonstrates that even in the information age the PLA can use ancient thought. Peng is not the only author who has written about integrating strategies into the informatized warfare paradigm. For example, a Jiefangjun Bao article in January 2008 examined warfare strategies for network attack and defense. These strategies included "preserving and breaking," "attacking and defending," "peculiarity and straightness," "showing the shape," "form and force," and "using space" to influence the struggle over network space.[133] All of these are variations of ancient stratagems.

Changing a "Mode of Thinking"

The information age offers Chinese leaders a unique chance to make a "quantum leap" in military affairs and bypass many long years of research and production of mechanized equipment. However, the transformation from a mechanized to an informatized force requires changes to the military's mode of thought. The PLA has to learn how to apply new technologies and to develop new thinking styles quickly or risk falling further behind. Military leaders are confronted with digital, high speed versions of command information, control information, early warning information, survey information, intelligence information, systems information, and evaluation information that change the way operations are conceived and executed, according to several prominent Chinese authors.

Targets have also changed. The foci of Chinese information attacks are enemy command centers, information systems, and information capabilities rather than troop formations as in the past. Battles will be fought over information resources at both the tactical and strategic levels. New modes of thinking are required to protect operations, logistics, and other associated areas.[134]

Li Deyi, Deputy Chair of the Department of Warfare Theory and Strategic Research at the PLA's Military Academy of Science, highlights what must change (and why) in the PLA's mode of thinking. He states:

1.   Changing the mode of thinking is a requirement for ensuring victory in future war. Conventional thinking needs to move

---

[133] Liu Wanxin, Dang Wanlong, and Zhang Dan, "Network Attack and Protection also Need Strategies," Beijing Jiefangjun Bao (Liberation Army Daily), 2 January 2008, p. 6, as translated and downloaded from the OSC website, document number CPP20080102436002.
[134] Li.

from individual system engagement toward systemized thought and system-to-system engagements. Group and organizational decision-making replace individual thought.

2. Strategy and technology are unified for planning purposes. The information superhighway can produce information misdirection, spread the fog of war, and interfere with and disrupt the enemy's strategic perceptions. Electronic deception, camouflage, and interference along with viral infiltration and interference with/deception of satellites can cause enemy errors in judgment.

3. Systems methodology has broken armies away from singular cause and effect determinism that is characteristic of conventional warfare. Systems use information, information technology, and information system modes of thought to reduce an enemy's combat effectiveness.

4. Information and information technology determine combat effectiveness, victory, and defeat in war. They stand alongside materials and power as one of the three major strategic resources.

5. Information deterrence (that is, information technology, weaponry, and resource deterrence as well as counter-information deterrence) are new modes of strategic thought and are important new deterrent forces just behind nuclear deterrence in achieving national strategic objectives.

6. New modes of thinking will enable breakthroughs in control theory.

7. New modes of thinking integrate information reasoning, analysis, strategic capabilities, and the experiences of warfare with information collection and storage, information processing, information transmission, and the logical reasoning capabilities of computers and artificial intelligence. C4ISR system decision-making is scientific, collective, real-time, and precise.

8. Systemized warfare is represented by activities that have organization, planning, objectives, measures, layers, and steps. It is networked thought built on a network foundation. Networks are systems so systemization thinking is also "networkization" thinking, another new mode of thought.

9. The design of military system architectures, defensive alignments, and attack countermeasures must utilize qualitative and quantitative analysis. Precise analysis, planning, design, guidance, and management are the

requirements of the man/machine process for new thinking.[135]

Li is not the only Chinese leader to emphasize the need for new thinking styles. Major General Zhan Yu, commandant of the Shijiazhunag Army Command Academy, believes new problems will emerge that transform solutions based on books toward solutions based on practical experience/facts. This transformation requires a change from conservative to creative thought. Personnel must discuss what has never been discussed and do what has never been done. This is not a transformation of thought that deals with emergencies but rather with long-term perspectives. Finally, Zhan agrees with Li on at least one point. He notes that new modes of thought can be viewed as a "systems engineering" project. Modes of thought must change from singular or individual areas to systemic thought that is integrated.[136]

Another leader emphasizing change was the Dean of the Department of Military Political Work of Shijiazhunag Army Command College, Senior Colonel Deng Yifei. He writes that change requires foresight, flexibility, effectiveness, and awareness of how information resources are expanding infinitely and being transmitted in an unobstructed way. Information technical tools enable more complex and precise planning, release the energy of thinking, and inspire creative thought. Information resources have turned into a multiplier of thinking effectiveness.[137] In the information age, Deng believes that creative thinking is the pivot point for innovative thought and the "golden key" to the door to success and victory in war.[138]

War Engineering: An Example of a New Mode of Thought

Major General Hu Xiaofeng, a professor in the Information Operations and Command Training-Teaching and Research Department at China's National Defense University, noted that the age of informatization requires new approaches to the study and management of information age wars. War engineering is one of these new approaches.[139] It appears to be an updated version of the Chinese concept of war control.

---

[135] Li.

[136] Zhan Yu.

[137] Deng Yifei, "A Revolution in Military Thinking in the Information Age," Beijing Zhongguo Junshi Kexue (China Military Science), No. 6, 2007, as translated and downloaded from the OSC website, document number CPP20080527563002.

[138] Ibid.

[139] Hu Xiaofeng, "The Basics of War Engineering," Beijing Zhongguo Junshi Kexue (China Military Science), No. 3, 2007, as translated and downloaded from the OSC website, document number CPP20070927478001.

War engineering arose, Hu contends, from the requirement to find a method to study, manage, and control information age war systems. Chinese war engineering is "a method of systems engineering that studies, designs, tests, controls, and evaluates war systems and that is guided by systematic thinking, based on information technology."[140] The most important element of war engineering is to maintain control of war systems. Through war systems, control of the course of operations is possible.[141] The concept is centered on managing warfare and has total victory as its goal.

War engineering looks at combat as a nonlinear, complex adaptive system. War engineering studies, designs, and manages war requirements, theories, experiments, and processes. It has five parts: requirements, planning, testing, control, and evaluation engineering. Control engineering, the most important element, consists of strategic, campaign, and tactical command information systems which monitor situations, control decision-making, handle anomalies, and evaluate results.[142]

Hu concludes his thoughts on war engineering by quoting Engels, who noted that "it wasn't the inventors of new material measures; it was the first person who, in the correct manner, used a new measure that had already been invented." Hu believes China is searching for a way to be the first to use US inventions to their benefit and prove Engels correct. China hopes to be able to manage and control war instead of reacting to it and to make wartime changes in advance (through simulations) instead of making changes as war requires or demands. War engineering, according to Hu, will be one of several catalysts that promote the further development of information war studies as China transforms its military from a mechanized to an informatized force.[143]

System Attack Warfare: Another New Mode of Thought

New modes of thinking require, above all else, creativity and innovation. Dai Qingmin, the Director of the All-PLA Informatization Consultation Committee (and former head of the Electronic Warfare Department of the Chinese General Staff), wrote an important article regarding innovation and informatized thought in 2007 in China Military Science. He discussed information attack theories, not active defense theories, and he stressed the importance of innovative developments.

---

[140] Ibid.
[141] Ibid.
[142] Ibid.
[143] Ibid.

Innovation, Dai writes, is the precursor to the further development of military technology, weapon modernization, organizational restructuring, and changes in military practice.[144] The basic task of innovation in the information age is to "reveal the law of informatized warfare, put forward a corresponding strategy for informatized warfare, and formulate the principles for informatized operations."[145] Innovation creates new transformation theories, systems integration theories, and service and arms building theories.[146] Technical informatized innovation must take into account issues not considered in the past in China, Dai notes, such as fair competition, a sound investment mechanism, a legal system for protecting intellectual property rights, and an effective human resources cultivation mechanism.[147]

In another 2007 article, this time in the Liberation Army Daily, Dai wrote that one innovative change is to use "system attack warfare as a guide." Coming from a person of such renown, this is a very important statement and one that should concern the West. There is no mention of active defense in Dai's writing here, just attack options. He also stated that it is imperative to grasp the initiative in future war, take information dominance as a core principle, and develop informatization operations theories ahead of time.[148] According to Dai, these actions require an objective analysis of the contradictions that exist in the current stage of informatization,[149] and the focus should be on those that can be exploited. These points and concerns differ markedly from mechanized thought, where China stressed active defense and an interest in attacking only after first being attacked. Now, Dai states that

> System attack warfare is the basic thought of our armed forces for fighting operations in the environment of informatization. System attack warfare stresses the use of asymmetric offensive actions to seize battlefield control in all battle domains, using elite forces and

---

[144] Dai Qingmin, "Ensure Historical Orientation and Promote Comprehensive Innovation of Military Informationization," Beijing Zhongguo Junshi Kexue (China Military Science), No. 1, 2007, as translated and downloaded from the OSC website, document number CPP20070512563001.

[145] Ibid.

[146] Ibid.

[147] Ibid.

[148] Dai Qingmin, "Further Understanding on Laws of Military Informatization Building," Beijing Jiefangjun Bao (Liberation Army Daily), 13 February 2007, p. 6, as translated and downloaded from the OSC website, document number CPP20070213721038.

[149] Ibid.

composite operation means that mix hard and soft attacks to focus attacks on the core and weak links of the enemy operation system...[150]

Problems that the PLA will have to overcome, according to Dai, as a change is made from a traditional to an informatized mode of thought, include: structural problems such as breaking down section barriers and department interests; the current inability to independently innovate; and the clarification of unclear demands for the construction of an information network.[151] Military innovations must solve these problems.

Zhang Zhiping and Ye Haiyuan, in their work on the transformation of the military with Chinese characteristics, also discussed innovation. They state that innovation must include new viewpoints, concepts, and thoughts. Operations theory, for example, might include information warfare, spatial warfare, precision operations, and integrated joint operations. The development of strategies for operational issues will be particularly important for future informatized warfare concepts.[152] Once again, the focus is on combining technology with strategies as other military authors have repeatedly stressed.

Major General Zhan Yu, cited previously in this chapter, offers other thoughts on innovation in operations theory. He states that systemic destructive attack must be emphasized; information must take a leading role; and firepower will control the process of operations, with precision operations the highest state to be pursued. The PLA's operational style must change to be of the joint, non-linear, precision, and non-engagement (no direct contact) types. Finally, combat capability must undergo a transformation in command and control, information operations, precision-strike capability, strategic maneuver, fast assault, special operations capability, and comprehensive-defense capability for the conduct of informatized warfare. This will enable a qualitative leap in military organization and force structure.[153] Where Zhan sees a qualitative leap, this author believes the PLA's progress is more akin to a quantum leap.

Culture Affects Innovation Trends

According to Chinese analysts, China's new mode of thinking will develop differently than would a corresponding transformation of thought in the

---

[150] Ibid.

[151] Ibid.

[152] Zhang Zhiping, Ye Haiyuan, "Trends in World Military Development: Accelerating Military Transformation with Chinese Characteristics," Beijing Renmin Ribao (Internet Version), 9 April 2008, p. 7, as translated and downloaded from the OSC website, document number CPP20080409710003.

[153] Zhan Yu.

West. This is due to the impact of Chinese culture and history on innovation and due to the development of two types of thought processes, metaphysical and dialectical. No further explanation was offered.

Innovation affects culture and vice versa. Authors Xiao Dongsong, a doctoral student in military studies at China's National Defense University, and Li Qing, an associate professor in the Teaching and Research Section for Political Theory at National Defense University, wrote about the effects of culture on innovation. The authors state that knowledge is gained from cognitive reflections on the essence, patterns, properties, and features of the external world. Values are reflected in the way things and processes are used, resulting in a series of "value reflections, value assessments, value principles, and value concepts to form a value system for society."[154] Informatized thought (such as that produced over the Internet) has greatly changed "how we know" and has created new modes of thought. Wikipedia is perhaps the best example of putting a new spin on "what we know." "What we know" is determined by the hundreds of individuals who contribute to Wikipedia, and their personal agendas are unknown.

Xiao and Li define culture as "the organic unity of knowledge systems, value systems, and methodological systems of thought."[155] Knowledge system innovation includes new phenomena that must be recognized, analyzed, and summarized. This will require that existing knowledge categories for military actions, truth, philosophy, and information war be processed and refitted. Existing categories of knowledge (ethics, etiquette, benevolence, justice, gain and harm, material substances, actions, systems, control, information, etc.) must adopt new measures as well.[156]

Value system innovation is the result of different assessments in attitudes, interests, enthusiasms, and mental dynamics. Value assessment systems of different societies are reflected in conditions such as geography, demography, customs, and means of production. It is also reflected in how religion and people, individuals and groups, mind and strength, and morality and gain are related (and which are the most important to a culture).[157] A

---

[154] Xiao Dongsong and Li Qing, "Analysis of the Impact of Culture on the Innovation of Military Theories," Beijing Zhongguo Junshi Kexue (China Military Science), 2002, No. 3, pp. 31-39. For more information on Chinese military culture in the information age, see Chapter Three.
[155] Ibid.
[156] Ibid.
[157] Ibid.

methodological system of thought is then created out of "how we know and by what means we know the external world."[158]

As a methodological system of thought, culture provides military theory with innovative tools for thought and with the logical means and patterns for processing information. As an example, Xiao and Li contrast Greek and Chinese thought:

> The early Greek method of thought was a simple and substantial way of thinking, in that the essence of things was within the things themselves. As such it held that one should understand the substance, that is, the thing in and of itself in order to grasp the essential nature and pattern of said thing. By contrast, the method of thought in Chinese antiquity was a simple and relational way of thinking, in that the essence of things was reflected in the relationship between a given thing and other things. As such, understanding a thing meant understanding various types of relationships. These two different methods of thinking provide two different anchor points for thinking; one is substantial, and the other relational.[159]

Xiao and Li also contrast views in the West and in China on the concept of war. They noted:

> The West placed emphasis upon seeing war as an entity, in that new viewpoints, ideas, and theories were extracted during the process of bringing war in and of itself to light. China, however, placed war within a larger relational world, and extracted new viewpoints, ideas, and theories by means of revealing the relationships between war and politics, war and economics, war and the natural environment, and war and leadership.[160]

In terms of logical thought patterns, the West uses metaphysics which is based on analysis and decomposition according to Xiao and Li. A subject is understood as a static and isolated presence that is broken down into a series of mutually independent elements and these elements are analyzed as a means of gaining a precise understanding of the subject. China uses dialectical thought. Here the logical patterns of thought are represented by a high degree of analysis with a high degree of integration. Understanding a subject is seen as a presence

---

[158] Ibid.
[159] Ibid.
[160] Ibid.

51

with common links and actions. A comprehensive examination of the relationships between the possible and actual, history and the future, and the whole and the part is performed in order to gain an understanding of the essential nature and pattern of things.[161]

New modes of thought are affected by this cultural thought process. A person brought up in the Chinese system will analyze information age developments and apply them differently than someone brought up in a Western society who performs the same analysis, according to this way of thinking.

One's level of expertise in military practice, according to Xiao and Li, also affects one's attempts at innovation. In the area of military practice the PLA is weak since it has not fought a high-tech war yet. But the PLA's work on war theory appears strong and focused on inculcating information age technologies into the force. The PLA is attaching particular significance to an examination of philosophical, historical, and scientific culture. Philosophy considers the connections and development of various aspects of nature and society; military history helps summarize the lessons of military culture; and science, in particular the impact of technology (with information technology at its core), has caused fundamental changes in both societal and military activities. Theories of information war and associated theories (Third Wave, etc.) have evolved from these developments.[162]

Xiao and Li believe the use of technology (such as the development of simulations) has led to a closer understanding of military practice and a corresponding move away from Confucianist practice. Technology has encouraged China to move away from traditional military thought and toward an advanced culture, one that takes into consideration new developments and results in innovation in military theory.[163]

The authors conclude that the development of an advanced military culture will increase the knowledge level of officers and troops, their scientific knowledge and culture levels, and Chinese combat power. At the same time, the Marxist value system must be updated and enriched in areas such as patriotic devotion. In a reversal of traditional values and modes of thought, now the qualitative must be emphasized over the quantitative and effectiveness emphasized over fairness.[164]

---

[161] Ibid.
[162] Ibid.
[163] Ibid.
[164] Ibid.

Final recommendations by Xiao and Li included the following:

Continue to create, learn, and understand new methods of thinking. Pay attention to the latest changes and results of research and understand the content and essential characteristics of modern methodology.

Strengthen the systematic buildup of methods of thinking to include philosophical, sociological, physiological, and psychological methods; and combine and integrate them. Study the structure, logic, and means by which this new organic system can be employed.[165]

The next chapter will discuss in more detail the changes that have occurred in Chinese military culture as a result of information age developments.

Conclusions

Innovations and creative thinking, in the view of the PLA, are the keys to victory in future war. This requires escaping from the grasp of mechanized thought and finding new and innovative ways to implement informatized thinking. Innovations involve finding new ways to apply ancient stratagems to information age developments. In a certain sense, a new mode of thinking is an asymmetric answer to a competitor with technological prowess but who has failed to apply these advances to their fullest. Engels belief that "it wasn't the inventors of new material measures; it was the first person who, in the correct manner, used a new measure that had already been invented" could find new applicability in the information age. Sun Tzu's principles integrated with systems thinking may provide such a cognitive advantage.

The PLA is moving from a mechanized to an informatized force as fast as possible. For example, the PLA's University of Science and Technology (UST) reports it is cultivating junior commanders for joint operations under informatized conditions. Five training systems have been formed, to include a command information engineering system. Courses have increased their content on complex electromagnetic environments, information security, and psychological operations.[166]

---

[165] Ibid.

[166] Liu Geng'an and Ma Shengwei, "PLA UST Cultivates New-Type Military Talents," Beijing Jiefangjun Bao (Liberation Army Daily), 5 January 2009, as translated and downloaded from the OSC website, document number CPP20090105702014.

Peng's analysis and recommendations on how the inferior could defeat the superior were the closest examples of an actual way to apply Sun Tzu-type methods to the information age. Li Deyi listed twelve changes in the PLA's mode of thinking that must be integrated into informatized thought. Systems methodology, information deterrence, control theory, and other factors were highlighted. Some of his recommendations share a common reference point with Western information age theory while others do not. Those in the latter category should be closely examined by Western analysts for their potential implications or use.

General Dai's new mode of thinking focused more on systems and innovation than on applying old principles of war. He stated that to grasp the initiative in future war China must take system attack warfare as its guide and develop informatization operations theories ahead of time.[167] The Chinese, like other nations, believe it is better to worry about things before they happen instead of after the fact when it is too late. War engineering, innovation, and creativity are required ahead of time in order to affect efficiency, management, strategy, organization, and theory with information means.[168]

Cultural proclivities provide military theory with some of the tools for innovative thought. Xiao and Li's contrast of Greek and Chinese thought was noteworthy. While Greek thought emphasizes understanding the substance of something, Chinese thought stresses thinking of things in relation to one another. As the authors noted, these two different methods of thinking provide two different anchor points for thought: one is substantial and the other relational.[169] It is thus to be expected that Chinese theoreticians will be looking for all types of relational aspects associated with informatized thought.

While the West uses metaphysics China uses dialectical thought. The dialectic enhances the development of countermeasures merely by its thought process of thesis, anti-thesis, synthesis. This requires that Western analysts conduct a close analysis of the links, actions, and counteractions that the PLA stresses and how they are being integrated into the force. A comprehensive examination of the relationships between the possible and actual, history and the future, and the whole and the part is performed in the PLA in order to gain an understanding of the essential nature and pattern of things.[170]

---

[167] Dai Qingmin, "Further Understanding on Laws of Military Informatization Building."
[168] Ibid.
[169] Xiao and Li.
[170] Ibid.

In summary, it is quite apparent that the PLA's approach to informatized war will vary from Western modes of information age thought. This is not unexpected. Perhaps, however, too few Westerners appreciate the specific aspects of these differences and ignore such developments at their risk. To better understand the Chinese and find ways to work together with them or to develop counters to their creative thinking (as they develop counters to our way of thinking) it is strongly recommended that Western analysts study the Chinese as they study us—in detail. We must learn from them as they have learned from us. We can start by better understanding their new modes of thought—and warning them of some of the perils they are contemplating and introducing.

CHAPTER THREE: CHINESE INFORMATION AGE MILITARY CULTURE

This chapter examines the development of military culture in China as presented in China Military Science over the past several years.

> In confrontations on the future battlefield, what is scarier than inferior technology is inferior thinking.[171]

Introduction

With over 5000 years of history, officers and academicians of the People's Liberation Army (PLA) have much information on which to base their books and articles about China's rich tradition of military culture. For a Western audience, there is much to learn about (and from) the Chinese. For example, while most Western audiences like to think of Sun Tzu's maxim of "winning without fighting" as representative of Chinese military culture, Chinese Colonel Jin Lixin disagrees. He wrote that being able to break the enemy's resistance without fighting "is the rarest of rarities." What Chinese history demonstrates, according to Jin, is an offensive philosophy of "attacking the enemy's army in the field."[172]

A few test questions on Chinese military thinking further demonstrate the West's unfamiliarity with PLA culture. To answer the following four questions, select from Karl Marx, Sun Tzu, Mao Zedong, or Deng Xiaoping: Whose philosophy and military thought serves as the advanced culture of military thought in China?[173] Whose philosophy serves as the PLAs guiding principle?[174] Who developed People's War?[175] Who said that the biggest mistake is to miss an opportunity to send superior military forces against the

---

[171] Deng Yifei, "Realizing a Historic Leapfrog in Military Thinking Mode," Guangming Daily, 17 January 2008 as translated and downloaded from the Open Source Center website, document number CPP20080219563001.

[172] Jin Lixin, "Ye Jianying and Traditional Chinese Military Culture," China Military Science, 2002, No. 1, pp. 65-72.

[173] Fang Yonggang, "Defining Advanced Chinese Military Culture," China Military Science, 2005, No. 6, pp. 73-83.

[174] Peng Guangqian and Yao Youzhi, editors, The Science of Military Strategy, Military Science Publishing House, Academy of Military Science of the Chinese People's Liberation Army, English version, 2005, p. 150.

[175] Ibid., pp. 121, 126.

enemy?[176] The answers to these questions can be found in the footnote to this sentence.[177]

The Chinese believe that the cyber/information age has helped them transform their rich traditional military culture into what they term as an "advanced military culture." The primary factors behind this change are the PLA's recognition of the influence of technology on strategy, the penetration of China's traditional culture by modern media, and the creation of high-technology strategic psychological warfare concepts. In the words of one author, China must construct socialist culture with Chinese characteristics; must create cultural diffusion hardware and software over which China has autonomous intellectual property rights; and, most important for Western audiences, China must take action to "propel China's culture industry and media industry beyond China's borders in an effort to take over the international culture market."[178] Western media outlets and militaries should be made aware of this Chinese effort.

This chapter will focus on Chinese military culture based on selected articles that express the thoughts of PLA officers and academicians over the past eight years. The discussion does not include a typical PLA soldier's military cultural focus (the oath, flag, colors, and other military representations) but rather military thought and philosophy. The lessons learned from this examination are extensive and at times surprising in both context and substance. The examination exposes potential Chinese predispositions and thus intentions for further scrutiny and interpretation, and exposes Chinese thinking and prejudices about US military culture. The examination begins, however, with a short overview of the manner in which this analysis was conducted.

The Journal China Military Science

China Military Science is a core PLA military periodical. It serves as the sole source of information for this chapter. The journal is published bimonthly and is sponsored by the PLA's Academy of Military Science and by the Chinese Military Science Association. Therefore the chapter reflects the thoughts of the Academy's officers and academicians and its content is controlled by the editors. China Military Science addresses issues of strategy,

---

[176] Ibid., p. 288.

[177] The answer to all of these questions is Karl Marx. If you correctly selected the Prussian-born philosopher as the answer to all of these questions, consider yourself among the very few to do so.

[178] Wang Shudao, "Modern Cultural Diffusion and National Security," China Military Science, 2005, No. 3, pp. 64-69.

history, defense, troop building, combat theory, and international military studies in addition to culture. The journal has won numerous awards in China.

The material examined covered the eight years (1999-2007) of the journal, where no less than 66 articles had the word "culture" in an article's title. Of the 66 articles[179] examined, fourteen were history related, twelve were foreign military related, three were Communist Party related, seven were strategy related, six were society related, and twenty-four were purely military related. The latter category included law, camp culture, spiritual construction, combat power, military theories, advanced and future culture, systems, science and technology, modernization, worship, the environment, frontier defense, duty, national defense, and harmony and balance. Twenty-eight articles on culture were published in 2002 alone, the apparent height of interest and discussion on the subject. From 2000 to the last issue of 2002, the journal published six "groups" devoted to military culture under the title "Theoretical Study of Chinese Military Culture." In each set there were approximately five or six culture-related articles.[180]

Definitions

To understand Chinese military culture a few important terms must be defined upfront. These terms are important for the remainder of the discussion that follows. The terms that are defined are culture, military culture, traditional military culture, Marxist culture, and advanced military culture, the latter being the focus of this chapter.

Culture

Fang Yonggang, a doctoral student at the Dalian Naval Academy, notes that culture is the object of the strength of people. It is the sum of the material and mental results created during a historical process that transforms nature, society, and people. It is a conceptual system of social ideology (philosophy, politics, law, ethics, and art). Fang states that culture is described in three ways. First, he uses scholar Liang Shubins's definition of culture, which states that "culture is everything that our life depends upon…the meaning of culture is surely in economics and politics, but it encompasses everything." Second, Fang states that culture refers to mental culture, to include philosophy, art, religion, language, logic, natural science, and other forms of knowledge such as the

---

[179] Five issues between 1999-2007 were not available for examination in the library of the author's place of employment, the Foreign Military Studies Office at Fort Leavenworth, Kansas.

[180] The discussion is understandably far from conclusive but rather attempts to offer an introductory point of view for discussing Chinese military culture.

humanities and social sciences, human thought and consciousness, ways of thinking and acting, customs and habits, education, cultural institutions, and social organizational forms. Third, Fang notes that culture refers to the mental activities and products established upon a definite economic foundation and adapted to definite political institutions. [181]

Zhang Xiaojun and Xu Jia define culture differently. They cited China's 1982 Concise Social Sciences Dictionary to define culture as "the sum of the material wealth and the spiritual wealth created by mankind in the course of social development." Zhang and Xu add that culture is "the social messages carried by the system of consensual symbols and its products and developments." [182]

Military Culture

Wu Mengchao, a Major General in 2002 and Vice President of the Nanjing Political Academy, defines military culture as a pattern of ideas attached to the potential military strength of an armed force (equipment, personnel, institutions, and training), to warfare (combat strength and its application), and to society (transformation from national strength to military strength). Military culture occurs when societal culture is shifted to military activities. Historical observations and logic (based on the past, present, and future of an object) determine military culture as well. The more developed a society is, the stronger is its cultural accumulation and the stronger the mental power of its people. Military cultural content is a qualitative indicator of military building. [183]

Fang Yonggang discusses Chinese military culture in a 2005 article. He states that military culture is a conceptual, complex entity formed from military knowledge systems, military value systems, and systems of military cognitive methods. It is the cultural basis formed from the combat strength of the armed forces. [184]

Wang Zhaohai, in 2007, defines military culture as "the sum and substance of the ideology gradually formed among members of the military through military practice, consisting of the knowledge system, concepts of values, and methods of thought and conduct. It is the historical precipitate of

---

[181] Fang Yonggang.
[182] Zhang Xiaojun and Xu Jia, "A Comparison of the Features of the Traditions of Chinese and US Strategic Culture," China Military Science, 2004, No. 2, pp. 112-115.
[183] Wu Mengchao, "Where is Our Military Culture? On the Present-Day Forms of Our Military Culture," China Military Science, 2002, No. 3, pp. 20-23.
[184] Fang Yonggang.

the spiritual production and spiritual life of members of the military. It is the carrier of symbols of values for the military and members of the military."[185]

Traditional Military Culture

Jin Lixin's 2002 work on Marshall Ye Jianying's view of military culture listed key points for understanding traditional Chinese military culture. They are:

- Clarity of Goal. Ye's goal was to emphasize the past to benefit the present. He advocated using China's precious historical inheritance to apply success and avoid defeats in these changing times.
- Take a Firm Stand. China must use Marxist and Mao Zedong thoughts as weapons to dissect, sort out, and critique ancient military heritage using a scientific and dialectic attitude.
- Deal Strictly with Concrete Matters. Open up research into military science, and seek truth from facts. Remain down to earth and don't make something out of nothing. General rules are more universal.
- Weed through the Old to Bring Forth the New. One must "assume an impressive posture" by bringing the bow back but not shooting, demonstrating that one is ready to do battle. This is active defense.[186]

This latter point is much like present day deterrence thought and the Chinese concept of *shi* (see Appendix Two for a detailed description of *shi*).

Marxist Military Culture

Liu Dingchang and Wang Yi, in 2002, write that Marxist military culture includes both software (thought, scholarship, science, etc.) and hardware (infrastructure, equipment, and training) and has five levels. They are:

- The culture of military thought which includes military dialectics and basic theory about war and strategy
- The culture of military scholarship which includes the sciences of strategy, campaigns, tactics, and war mobilization, among others

---

[185] Wang Zhaohai, "Tentative Analysis of the Development of Harmonious Culture and Military Cultural Development," China Military Science, 2007, No. 1, pp. 47-56.
[186] Jin Lixin.

- The culture of military technology which includes military science and technology and military training
- The culture of military systems which includes the systems of leadership and political work
- The culture of military infrastructure which includes military organization and equipment.[187]

Advanced Military Culture

Fang Yonggang defined advanced military culture as merely an extension of advanced culture but with specific differences between soldiers and civilians in ideas, aesthetic values, and means of continuity. Drawing upon its superior military cultural heritage and forward orientation, advanced military culture must change in accordance with temporal and spatial conditions (such as cultural qualities, psychological features, and individual characteristics of officers and troops). Change includes examining the rational components of foreign military cultures.[188]

Wang Zhen, a professor in the Political Department of the Chinese Navy's Dalian Ship Academy and the chief editor of the work <u>Theory for Building the Communist Party of China</u>, noted in 2005 that while China's modern military culture is guided by Marxism, Mao Zedong military thought is an important component of China's modern advanced military culture. Wang states that modern advanced military culture is differentiated from China's ancient and modern military culture by profound changes in military concepts. In particular, the emergence of Mao Zedong military thought shattered traditional thought and reformed important traditional concepts. This revolutionary change was manifested in the following ways:

- It used the purpose of the new People's Army to explain the instrumental value of the army. No longer were armies tools of the ruling class to make war but now the PLA works for the people to spread propaganda, organize the masses, arm the masses, help the masses establish a revolutionary political power, organize the establishment of the Communist Party, and make war if necessary.
- It used a cultural perspective of the party commanding the guns to thoroughly transform the cultural perspective of the gun alone being supreme. That is, the gun was not the only element of respect. Rather, the Party commands the guns and not vice versa.

---

[187] Liu Dingchang and Wang Yi, "The Fundamental Features of Marxist Military Culture," <u>China Military Science</u>, 2002, No. 4, pp. 19-25.
[188] Fang Yonggang.

- It used materialist dialectics to make innovations and develop theories and strategies in Chinese and foreign military cultures. Mao, being knowledgeable in ancient, foreign, and Marxist writings, attached importance to deriving the best from both local and foreign military thought, especially theory and strategy. Revolutionary wars are just, and counterrevolutionary wars unjust. [189]

Wang defined advanced military culture as "the military culture concepts and military culture system that are established under the guidance of correct military values." Mao's military thought clarified scientific military values and allowed military concept culture, military system culture, and military action culture to take shape as a scientific system. [190]

The Move from Traditional to Advanced Culture

Military culture is transitioning in accordance with the Chinese military's move from a mechanized to an informatized force and with the world's transition from a Cold War environment to a digital age marked by global economic and social integration. The move to advanced military culture does not mean, of course, that traditional cultural thought is being tossed out. Rather, it is being updated in correspondence with today's digital context. For example, traditional concepts such as the preservation of unity, the pursuit of peace, and emphasis on rational thought all remain part of advanced military culture. [191] Updating military culture simply ensures that the culture of military thought does not suffer from inferior thinking but keeps up with the times.

One main concern serves as a motivating factor for the PLA to transform from traditional military culture to advanced military culture. This concern is that some PLA members believe Western culture is penetrating China via digitized public opinion means. Wang Shudao, an Assistant Professor in the Military Personnel Management Department of the Xian Political Institute, is one who believes that Western penetration of the media has forced a cultural transformation. [192] The digital age has introduced more cultural diffusion in China due to access to other cultures ideologies and philosophies.

Cultural diffusion, according to Wang, is a means to pass on, promote, and develop cultural content. It can act positively (supporting the PLA) or

---

[189] Wang Zhen, "Mao Zedong Military Thought and China's Advanced Military Culture," China Military Science, 2005, No. 1, pp. 53-62.
[190] Ibid.
[191] Wang Zhaohai.
[192] Wang Shudao.

negatively (enabling the disintegration of the PLA) and has two layers of meaning. The first is the diffusion of culture itself, its semiotic characteristics and system of meaning. The second is diffusion activities through definitive media both internal (within a community) and external (among different communities, known as intercultural diffusion or cross-cultural diffusion).[193] These activities use modern information technology and specialized media. There are five elements: the diffuser of culture; a specific system of meanings; a definitive semiotic system; specialized media; and the target of cultural diffusion. Modern cultural diffusion is based on high-technology, is global in scope, and can be used as a combat power additive.[194]

Cultural diffusion in the information age has new forms. These are:

- With respect to cultural symbols—artificial language and logic symbols are in the process of replacing traditional material and written symbols as the carriers of cultural information and the transmission of systems of meanings
- With respect to communication technology—digital information technology and virtual reality technology are replacing traditional printing and electronic technologies
- With respect to diffuse media—satellite radio, television media, and computer network media are increasingly replacing traditional paper publication media.[195]

Wang sees three challenges to China. First is the challenge to China's national spirit, the latter touted as the essence of China's military culture. This challenge is caused by exposure to other lifestyles and to Western "libertarianism." This has introduced feelings of cultural inferiority among some Chinese. A second challenge is that presented to socialist ideals. The penetration of China by digitized systems has offered the West a chance to highlight their capitalist system and values. A third challenge is that presented to socialist information and the public opinion environment in general in China. Wang believes there is an "information supermarket" that has resulted in a loss of control and management over information in China. Citizens are not able to distinguish between good information and "information detrimental to the stability of Chinese society, interfering with the direction of public opinion and social psychology."[196] The diffusion of Western values has caused, according to

---

[193] Wang Shudao.
[194] Ibid.
[195] Ibid.
[196] Ibid.

Wang, a crisis in beliefs and an upheaval in convictions, hedonism, and extreme egoism.[197]

Wang believes that cultural diffusion is a new form of soft power that can affect national security. In response, China must adapt a preventative cultural diffusion strategy in order to regain the strategic initiative in what Wang describes as the "cultural psychological warfare of the new period."[198] The West's cultural diffusion has not only intervened into China, it has established a "strategic containment of the cultural layer" that has allowed the West to gain the initiative in cultural psychological warfare. Three recommendations were made by Wang:

- Proactive defense must be China's strategy to control the diffusion of Chinese culture since the West is in a position of relative strength. The hypocrisy of the West's anti-Chinese forces must be exposed.
- The Party must exert control over cultural diffusion. It must vigorously develop advanced culture, integrating traditional and modern diffusion media and national and private sector media to propagate national spirit and basic national values.
- Socialist culture with Chinese characteristics must serve as an essential condition for the implementation of cultural counterattacks and what Wang describes as "cultural attack psychological warfare."[199]

Advanced military cultural thought should continue to innovate and change, to take the best from the West, and to elevate quality on a level above quantity in terms of importance. These requirements are mandated by the changes accompanying the digital age. For example, with regard to the quality over quantity concept, Liu Dingchang, then a Senior Colonel and President of the Nanjing Institute of Politics at Shanghai, and Wang Yi, a Senior Colonel and the Political Commissar of the same institute, noted in 2002 that

China's quantitative fighting strength is determined by the socialist political system, the population, economic factors, and natural geography. These factors are in constant flux based on modifications to military strategy. Qualitative aspects of fighting strength refer to the quality of military affairs, politics, technology, culture, health, and the

---

[197] Ibid.
[198] Ibid.
[199] Ibid.

psychological caliber and disciplinary style of the officers and troops as well as the caliber of military thought, strategy, and tactics. Marxist military culture has always placed great emphasis on the quality of the army.[200]

Wu Mengchao states that strong values and knowledge are two areas of measurement to help determine the development of an advanced military culture. Values emphasize the character of people. Chinese internal values include a peaceful disposition based on an active defense concept, an emphasis on strategic thinking, the use of deterrence whenever possible, and a benevolent approach. China's military values are handed down from a historical study of Confucianism and Mohist, Daoist, and Legalist thought. Knowledge, the other area of measurement, emphasizes the scientific nature of culture. It includes learning from Marxist ideology, focusing on science and technology, and studying lessons learned from actual practice. [201]

Revelations for a Non-Chinese Expert

For the average Western analyst who is not a Chinese expert, there are several points of interest embedded in Chinese discussions of culture. Among the most important issues are:

- How technology must be embedded into strategy, the latter serving as the strongest military cultural element of China
- The importance of Marxism to contemporary Chinese military culture and philosophy
- Contradictions to some commonly accepted Sun Tzu and Mao Zedong phraseology
- The role of intellectuals in the development of Chinese military culture and thought
- The importance of strategic psychological warfare and persuasive media to the enhancement or degradation of military culture, to include persuasive simulations
- The impact of informatization on military culture.

Strategy and Information Technology

It should come as no surprise that the focus of many Chinese cultural writings is the issue of strategy. The Chinese have studied strategy closely for thousands of years. The revelation for a Western reader is not the PLA's continued study of strategy but the manner in which they intend to improve it.

---

[200] Liu Dingchang and Wang Yi.
[201] Wu Mengchao.

Major General (retired) Li Bingyan, a Senior Editor of the <u>Liberation Army Daily</u>, the PLA's major newspaper, offered some of the best suggestions in this regard. He is well-known in China and abroad for his writings on military strategy. He has authored, among many works, a new edition of <u>The Thirty-Six Stratagems</u> and <u>Strategies of the Ancients</u>.

Li points out three differences in Western and Eastern thought. First, Westerners focus on technology while Easterners focus on strategy. Li believes this is because Westerners created a socio-cultural environment where science and technology were esteemed while Easterners incorporated nature into human affairs and believed that changes in society were linked to changes in nature.[202] This is an important point for western analysts to consider.

Second, when Westerners look at a problem, Li thinks they focus on a single point. Easterners, on the other hand, develop a comprehensive way of looking at a problem, what Li terms a "twin-lens" approach (or a comprehensive approach). Third, when examining relationships, Li believes that Westerners view coordination and struggle as incompatible. Easterners, on the other hand, seek a point of equilibrium between coordination and struggle advocating a battle of wits and eventual harmony and not a reliance on force.

Li states that China must not rely on strategy alone in its battle of wits any longer. Rather, China should learn from the West and integrate strategy with technology.[203] In this sense he aims to improve the quality of strategy in China.

Li notes that there is a reason beside "incorporating nature into human affairs" for China's slow acceptance of technology. During the Western Han era (206 BC—25 AD), China was governed by the concepts of "reject a hundred schools of thought, esteem only Confucianism" and "emphasize officials, not technology." Officials, viewed as saviors of the people, blocked anyone venturing toward science, as the latter was deemed work for men who were clever with their hands. Li terms this a negative element of Chinese culture. As a result, Chinese strategy was forced down the narrow road of deceit and trickery, where stratagems play a major role.[204] In Li's opinion, China studies the use of strategy to win victory while the West studies the use of force to achieve victory. Since the Chinese believe that war is not only a contest of

---

[202] Li Bingyan, "Emphasis on Strategy: Demonstrating the Culture of Eastern Military Studies," <u>China Military Science</u>, 2002, No. 5, pp. 80-85.
[203] Ibid.
[204] Ibid.

material forces but also a battle of wits, they stress subjective (flexible, creative thinking) factors in war.

Lin Ronglin, a Colonel and professor at the Naval Command Institute, and Cui Tao, an MA candidate at the same institute, agree with Li. They write that the integration of stratagems and technology is important.[205] The authors conclude that "not only must we continue traditional Chinese military thought on strategy, we must also emphasize the borrowing of Western information technology advantages in order to adapt to information wars of the future."[206]

Lin and Cui list four reasons for China's emphasis on strategy:

- War has rules and by recognizing the rules, one could use other strategies to trounce the enemy.
- The full utilization of the subjective mobility of those involved in a conflict is required. Based on objective factors, subjective efforts are used to obtain victory.
- Both sides in a war are flexible. Both hide the truth and show falsehoods, and both compete in intelligence and bravery. The use of deception is necessary.
- War must be in the service of a particular political end and serve as a means to that end.[207]

Marxism

Fang Yonggang wrote in 2005 that it was Mao who began the integration of Marxist thought into the Chinese revolution. This began an innovation in military culture that allowed China to show that it is adaptive and able to integrate traditional military strategy and philosophy with science and technology from the West.[208]

Marxist writings have had a much greater impact on Chinese military philosophy than many non-Chinese experts (such as this author) could ever expect. The Chinese give Marx and Engels credit for strongly influencing many of the key aspects of their military thought. This influence should never be underestimated. Wang Zhaohai notes as late as 2007 that Marxism is the

---

[205] Lin Ronglin and Cui Tao, "Innovation in Chinese Military Thinking through Comparison with the West," China Military Science, 2006, No. 5, pp. 117-124.
[206] Ibid.
[207] Ibid.
[208] Fang Yonggang.

guiding ideology and correct direction of development for Chinese thought. He adds that the core element of military culture is the socialist value system.[209]

Marxism is considered an essential aspect of traditional Chinese military culture, even though it is a nineteenth century concept. Jin Lixin, a Colonel and assistant researcher at the Academy of Military Science's Encyclopedic Research Department, wrote in 2002 about Marshall Ye Jianying's view of traditional Chinese military culture's Marxist and dialectical connections.[210] He notes that Ye read the Marxist/Leninist classics and Chinese and foreign history of all kinds. Further, Jin notes with regard to Marxism and the dialectic, "study and draw on dialectical thinking in ancient military strategies and tactics, especially Sun Tzu's Art of War. Solving the contradiction of the unity of opposites—the enemy and oneself—was the premise for conducting all military activities." The one "without or hollow" is vacuous and the one "with or solid" is substantial (attack what is weak, avoid what is strong).[211]

Liu and Wang write that this ideological aspect of military culture is supported by Marxism's cornerstones, dialectical materialism and historical materialism.[212] Marxist dialectical materialism, they write, reveals objective facts and inherent relationships that outmoded metaphysical precepts cannot. Relationships include, for example, those between war and culture, the buildup of the national economy and the armed forces, the people and weapons and equipment, and a series of dialectical relationships within the military (attacking and defending, weakness and strength, superiority and inferiority, and so on).[213]

Historical materialism provides a theoretical basis for patterns of social development, for the form of a socialist economy, and for methods of production. Mao Zedong, Deng Xiaoping, and Jiang Zemin, the authors note, have developed Marxist military culture with Chinese characteristics although they didn't specify just what these characteristics were.[214]

Authors Liu and Wang discount the contributions of Clausewitz and Jomini to military culture by stating that "military cultures prior to the advent of Marxism are limited by historical conditions, in particular because they are

---

[209] Wang Zhaohai.
[210] Jin Lixin.
[211] Ibid.
[212] Liu and Wang.
[213] Ibid.
[214] Ibid.

not guided by scientific concepts of the world or methodologies. As such, they have many drawbacks in terms of their content and function which fundamentally hold back any further progress for them."[215]

Jin offers some historical offensive-oriented Chinese military doctrine for Western readers to ponder.[216] On the one hand, Confucian, Daoist, and other Chinese doctrines have repudiated war for thousands of years in books. On the other hand, Marshall Ye Jianying's military theories, according to Jin, include seeing value in war and value in fighting (instead of "winning without fighting"). Ye saw progress for China in the conduct of war and used the War of Resistance against Japan as an example. This war formed a unified people's war front, unified the government, unified the military, formed resistance leaders, and founded the Political Department. "This overall view of Ye Jianying's concerning the value of war is clearly of an epochal and scientific nature."[217] Jin added that "Looking back through the volumes of China's 5,000 year history, what we see more of is 'attacking the enemy's army in the field' with shining spears, armored horses, and fierce combat, and 'besieging walled cities' by beheading generals, capturing banners, and blood baths; truly being able to 'break the enemy's resistance without fighting' is the rarest of rarities."[218] Thus Westerners should keep a wary eye on China's military buildup for good reason.

These two thoughts, war helps China progress and "the rarest of rarities" is breaking the enemy's resistance without fighting, are truly different thoughts than Westerners are accustomed to hearing. Finally, Jin stresses time and again that Ye's focus is on applying lessons learned from the past to present day situations. One must learn and adapt.

The Role of Intellectuals
Wang Xingsheng was a senior Colonel in 2002. He was the Director of the Fifth Research Office of the Chinese Academy of Military Science's Military Systems Research Department. Wang wrote that ancient Chinese intellectuals paid attention to military matters and that they greatly enriched the story and tradition behind China's military culture. Scholars focused on war prevention, opposed wars of annexation, but advocated war for moral principles. What arose was a scholarly group of military strategists that

---

[215] Ibid.
[216] Jin.
[217] Ibid.
[218] Ibid.

remained active even during the period of Confucianism. Several were later designated as officers due to their extensive knowledge of strategic affairs.[219]

Ancient Chinese intellectuals focused on military matters in the following ways:

- They directly threw themselves into military struggles of the times. There were two groups—intellectuals that the emperor appointed as generals (some like Sun Tzu and Sun Bin became outstanding commanders and strategists) and intellectuals who served as officials or military aids and took part in the planning and decision-making in army tents (such as Zhang Liang and Xiao He).
- They wrote books on the art of war and war policy complete with notes and commentaries on them. They described how to enhance war preparations, inspire morale, study strategy, amass forces, and restore the country.
- They summarized military successes, failures, gains, and losses while researching and constructing history.
- They wrote prose that reflected war and military life. A considerable portion of Chinese poems are about military matters.
- They created novels with war as the main object of discussion which spread military culture and helped in the accumulation of the military cultural psychology of the nation.[220]

Ancient intellectual writings thus have significantly shaped the style of Chinese military culture. Wang believes both ancient and modern intellectuals have enhanced the concept of national unity, imbued Chinese military culture with a distinctively patriotic and heroic hue, and caused Chinese military culture to assume an even more pacifistic and compassionate spirit for the state of the world and its people.[221] Further, intellectuals provide Chinese military culture with incisive language and an aesthetic characteristic that blend philosophy and poetic appeal in a concise, comprehensive, innovative, and universal manner. Perhaps most important, intellectuals promote a military style of thinking that is good at strategy and adept at the use of indirect methods.[222] Why did strategy develop earlier in China than in other

---

[219] Wang Xingsheng, "Chinese Intellectuals Paying Close Attention to Military Issues: Tradition and Its Impact on Military Culture," China Military Science, 2002, No. 6, pp. 23-27.

[220] Ibid.

[221] Ibid.

[222] Ibid.

nationalities? Wang believes that the answer may be grounded in the fact that intellectuals did not come from families with military backgrounds in most cases. They were thus unfamiliar with issues on an operational level and only dealt with strategic issues. Further, the battle of wits between two sides interested and excited Chinese scholars. The novels and plays they wrote further popularized strategy.[223]

Psychological and Cognitive Issues, Persuasion, and National Character
Yan Xiaofeng, Deputy Director of the Philosophy Teaching and Research Office of the Marxism Teaching and Research Department at National Defense University, writes that the strength of strategic psychological warfare (SPW) comes from national culture.

Yan states that national culture is defined from a series of issues. They are:

- National culture is the combination of factors, including a country's national spirit, ideologies, traditions, customs, ways of thinking, and the quality of sciences.
- National culture is the development of a nation's economy and politics. They are interdependent.
- National culture is a combination of a nation's various concrete cultures such as various forms of social ideology and social psychology. The former includes political and legal thinking, morals, art, religions, sciences, philosophy, and so on. The latter includes feelings, will, habits, and interests.
- In the national culture system, national spirit is the essence and ideology is the symbol. National spirit is the national faith, belief, character, and quality that a nation develops under certain national, historic, and production conditions.
- National culture is a system that has complex structure and abundant content.
- Finally, national culture is a country's image. Advanced national culture is a powerful strategic weapon in strategic psychological warfare. It shows to the world a civilized image that "our country loves peace, insists on justice, and pursues advancement."[224]

---

[223] Ibid.
[224] Yan Xiaofeng, "Competition and the Contest of National Culture," <u>China Military Science</u>, 2004, No. 4, pp. 57-63.

In the case of China, Yan believes that there are two reasons why China's national culture is so strong: a sense of national dignity developed over thousands of years which enable a sense of identification and belonging; and the influence of the Chinese Communist Party. The latter has created a culture of democracy that enables justice, advancement, and enlightenment according to Yan.[225]

Another country's culture often becomes the target of SPW. The party that launches SPW is trying to make another country's people, especially the elites, accept, become interested in, or long for the values, thoughts, ideas, life styles, and even social systems of another country. With this understanding, and the Chinese focus on preventing the spread of foreign information within its culture, China probably considers US policy makers as experts in creating SPW.

Yan continues that it is also important to eliminate hostility in the target country and to create favorable opinions of the party launching SPW. If war does erupt, opposing counties will then have more difficulty developing hatred and a fight-to-the-death mentality if a favorable opinion of the country has preceded war's outbreak. The measure of effectiveness for SPW's success is whether China is able to conquer and replace another country's culture[226] and to resist SPW efforts of other countries.

In the information age, boundaries are more porous which allows for the dissemination of national culture with fewer logistical and technical restrictions. SPW can be conducted at a level of competition and contest over national culture where one really can win without fighting. The information era has created new ways to consider time, space, progress, and the tools of war. Entire war strategies can now be based strictly on the competition between the national cultures of two countries. Information is used to destroy an opposing forces identification with and dependence on its national culture. Such abstract war can work as well as actual war in Yan's opinion. The changing nature of access and influence in the information age has made China more protective of its culture which is an important element of China's comprehensive national power.[227]

Chen Bingyan and Wang Yanzheng, graduate students at Shijiazhuang Army Command College; and Wang Zhenxing, a professor and master's

[225] Ibid.
[226] Ibid.
[227] Ibid.

candidate advisor at the College, wrote a very good article on psychological warfare. Titled "Enhancing China's Excellent Culture and Erecting a National Psychological Great Wall," the article underscored the importance of "warding off the cultural expansion and psychological attacks of the West" and "promoting the transformation of advanced culture into an excellent national psychology."[228] The authors define national culture as the product of spiritual and material civilization created by a nation in the historical course of its existence and development.[229]

The authors note how information technology is influencing China's advanced military culture. In the authors' opinion

> Life in society has entered an unprecedented information environment. The explosive development in high technology centered around information technology has been accompanied by the increased informatization of society. This type of information environment is the result of advances in society, and is an objective fact from which there is no turning back for any country or nation. However, the information environment is an artificial environment, and the content it transmits reflects the social cognitive values of different countries and interest groups.[230]

Building and promoting China's national culture requires that China erect a national psychological Great Wall between itself and the West. China must "oppose those who separate the culture of Marxist thought from traditional Chinese culture and the world's national cultures, or put them in opposition to each other, which risks restricting the methods of the culture of Marxist thought."[231] To that end, a correct orientation toward public opinion must be secured.

China must do four things to maintain its culture according to Chen, Wang, and Wang. First it must establish dedicated institutions responsible for planning, modifying, and managing the work of SPW; second, research into issues of national psychology must be increased; third, specific cultural

---

[228] Cheng Bingyan, Wang Yanzheng, and Wang Zhenxing, "Enhancing China's Excellent Culture and Erecting a National Psychological Great Wall," China Military Science, 2002, No. 5, pp. 59-67.
[229] Ibid.
[230] Ibid.
[231] Ibid.

education and propaganda work must be carried out; and finally, a professional information and guidance team (s) must be established.[232]

Other authors focused on the development of cultural awareness and techniques to persuade the media. Wang Lin, a Senior Colonel and Professor of Military Journalism and Communication at the PLA's Nanjing Institute of Politics; Wang Yitao, a Captain and Xinhua PLA Branch Journalist; and Wang Guibin (no title provided) wrote a 2005 article that discusses media strategies to use in cultural wars with the West and other nations.[233] Media warfare is defined as an information battle where adversaries fight for dominance of message output and maximum effect on communication. These messages can disguise hostility and aggressiveness and increase public opinion and support. Cultural characteristics to be studied include customs, religion, moral values, behaviors, literature, the arts, and so on that can achieve a desired cultural effect. Information selection criteria include cultural flaws of other nations.[234]

The authors write that China needs to create professional institutes that conduct cultural effects research and in-depth preparatory work to keep research up-to-date and ensure speedy propaganda responses if needed. Spiritual and material cultural effects should be studied. In particular, there is a need to understand and use information platforms such as the Internet. Finally, appropriate cultural battle simulations must be developed to accumulate the necessary information and experience to improve one's own defensive abilities in media warfare.[235]

Media strategies include directing the public's attention to a focal point of common interest; using contrast, such as revealing and disclosing the illegitimacy of an adversary action and then explaining why friendly actions are both legitimate and inevitable; using the persuasive effect of strong cultural leaders, those active and influential in dispersing objective facts and subjective judgments (artists, scientists, teachers, and athletes, among others); and using the strategy of repetition of cultural effects specific to the given culture and its background.[236]

The Impact of Informatization on Military Culture

---

[232] Ibid.
[233] Wang Lin, Wang Yitao, and Wang Guibin, "A Study on the Strategy of Cultural Effects in Media Warfare," China Military Science, 2005, No. 6, pp. 120-128.
[234] Ibid.
[235] Ibid.
[236] Ibid.

The digital age has squarely impacted military culture in China as the preceding paragraphs indicate. Yao Gaohong, a professor and doctoral candidate advisor (and editor of the Journal of Nanjing's Institute of Politics) and Du Yongji, a doctoral candidate at the Nanjing Institute of Politics, write that "for the construction of conditions for military culture which are adapted to the conditions of the informatized military, it is necessary that the conditions of traditional military culture are systematically reformed involving every aspect of the conditions of military culture."[237]

If reform is to involve every aspect of military culture, then weaponry and equipment, military organizations, military thought, and other aspects will be affected by the digital age. The PLA must "establish military values, modes of thinking, and a cultural psychology which are adapted to the conditions of informatized war so that the transformation in cultural concepts is the premise upon which the new conditions of military culture are constructed."[238] This includes the ethics of informatized war, the rules of war, and the ways of using armed force. Yao and Du list the six elements of military culture as

- Military theory
- Military systems
- Military values
- Military ethics
- Military psychology
- Military thinking.[239]

Yao and Du focus the conclusion of their article on the development of several issues. First is the obvious need to integrate military and social cultures (since informatization has blurred the boundaries between what is and is not military). Second is the development and understanding of twenty-first century trends caused by information technology (knowledge-based forces, intelligent weapons, the digital battlefield, and informatized war and deterrence strategies). Third is the requirement to understand an opponent's military culture, particularly his military value pursuits and the direction of his strategic thinking. Finally, there is the need to develop new innovations in military theory since the first to do so will have the advantage in future military battles. This requires not only carrying on one's own military cultural traditions but also learning from other military cultures. Yao and Du note that "gaining an

---

[237] Yao Gaohong and Du Yongji, "Main Trends of Military Cultural Development in the Twenty-First Century," China Military Science, 2002, No. 4, pp. 41-48.
[238] Ibid.
[239] Ibid.

understanding of another country's strategic culture and thinking is helpful for eliminating strategic misunderstandings and avoiding mistakes in strategic judgment."[240]

Some PLA Views of US Culture

Zhang Xiaojun, senior colonel and professor at the People's Liberation Army Foreign Languages Academy, and Xu Jia, a professor at the same academy, write often on military topics and strategic thinking. Their article under consideration here is on the topic of strategic culture. They define strategic culture as

> ...the social messages carried by the system of strategic symbols. Strategic culture is made up of two parts. One part is the continually produced social messages carried by the system of antagonistic symbols related to a conflictive nature, a violent usage, a connotation of security, and the qualities of an enemy and of threat. The other part is the continually produced social messages carried by the system of antagonistic symbols related to priorities, reasonable choice, and the evaluation of results.[241]

The authors believe strategic culture falls under the topic of "grand culture." It is subject to influence by spiritual culture, scientific and technological culture, institutional culture, and the material culture of a country. Its main categories include warfare concepts, national defense and security concepts, theories for gaining the upper hand, and so on. Zhang and Xu further go on to compare US and Chinese strategic culture in their article. They interpret Chinese strategic culture as dominated by pacifism and moral principles. They view US strategic culture as driven by profit and national interests.[242]

First, they write that Chinese traditional strategic culture emphasizes morality in warfare and values peace. This tradition respects inaction. Confucianist thinking was manifested in ancient military affairs and advocated benevolence and righteousness. Mohists were pacifists who advocated caution and fighting only for moral principles. These philosophies valued what was righteous and unrighteous. Sun Tzu's words reflect this philosophy.[243]

---

[240] Ibid.
[241] Zhang and Xu.
[242] Ibid.
[243] Ibid.

Apparently they discard the views of Chinese authors noted above (especially Jin) who have a different view of Chinese military culture.

In contrast, Zhang and Xu believe that Western culture is driven by profit and not morality. National interests are the center piece of US government affairs and the standard pursued by strategic decision-makers. The authors believe economic interests are the starting point for US strategic culture since the US is a capitalist country ruled by pragmatists. This enhances an orientation toward material gain.[244]

Second, Zhang and Xu compare defensive and offensive thinking in China and the US. They believe that China's strategic culture is more defensive and that even offensive actions are for defense. The US is offensively motivated and expansionist oriented, the authors write, and "expansion could ensure the growth of US capitalism, resolve contradictions in domestic economic contradictions, avoid divisions, and bring about national security."[245]

Third, the authors discuss the topic of strong and weak forces, which they describe as an important category in Chinese culture. Strong forces stand for attack and masculinity, and weak forces refer to defense and femininity. Chinese strategic culture is ideologically weak and uses weakness to gain victory according to Zhang and Xu. China believes that victory is gained from knowledge and not strength. Thus a weak defense can both hide one's capacities and allow one to bide one's time yet still allow for gaining mastery after an enemy has struck first. It represents the crystallization of the fusion of pacifist thought and dialectical thinking in strategic culture since it "focuses on the wisdom of seeking the complimentary in the contradictory."[246] US strategic culture, the authors note, stresses the opposite. It is focused on the worship of strength, the praise of attacks, and emphasis on competition and subjugation. There is a self-veneration of ideology and value concepts backed up by strong material forces.[247]

Finally, the authors state that there is a difference in economic backgrounds and thus approaches in China and the US. China is more of an agricultural force and the US is a commercial force. The Chinese people are attached to their native land and are unwilling to leave it. Thus they do not engage in expansionism. They place emphasis on ground defense and have light regard for maritime defense. Agriculture is the reason the country became rich

---

[244] Ibid.
[245] Ibid.
[246] Ibid.
[247] Ibid.

and made the military strong. Authors Zhang and Xu look at the US as a capitalist country rich in mercantilism, a country of immigrants, and for this reason US territory is always expanding. Expansion has been greatly assisted by an offensive naval force. Finally the authors write that the US uses the military to keep the country strong while China uses the prosperity of the country to make the military strong.[248]

In summation, Zhang and Xu note that China has a well established history of strategic culture. They write that Confucianist doctrine has held a dominant position since the Han Dynasty (which directly contradicts Chinese writers' focus on the influence of Marxism) and that caution has ruled when force has been used. With regard to the US, the authors write that Americans think of themselves as pacifist but the figures show otherwise.[249]

Ren Xiangqun offered another view of strategic culture. He is an assistant researcher at the Department of War Theory and Strategic Studies at the Military Science College and is a Colonel with a PhD in Military Science. Ren quotes Li Jijun, a retired general and well-known Chinese strategist, to start his analysis. Li wrote that "strategic culture is strategic thinking and strategic theory formed on the foundation of a certain history and cultural tradition of a people. This kind of thought and theory, according to Ren, is what guides strategic actions and impacts social culture and trends."[250] US mainstream cultural tradition is based on the thought, values, and behaviors of white, middle-class people. These are the political leaders, CEOs, university presidents, scientists, reporters, and novelists that have successfully influenced society. This tradition, according to Ren, focuses on manifest destiny in foreign affairs, individualism, commercialism, pragmatic philosophy, and social Darwinism.[251]

Chen, Wang, and Wang apparently agree with this assessment. They wrote in 2002 that

The Catholic Puritans among the early European immigrants felt superior in that they felt they were 'chosen by God' and had a 'manifest destiny to save the world' all of which mixed in with their mercantilism, expansionism, practicality, and social Darwinism to

---

[248] Ibid.
[249] Ibid.
[250] Ren Xiangqun, "The Influence of Mainstream Cultural Traditions on US War Decisions," China Military Science, 2004, No. 4, pp. 127-136.
[251] Ibid.

become the basis of the ideological culture of the United States and cognitive roots of the country's hegemonic mindset.[252]

Ren and the Chen, Wang, and Wang collective mention social Darwinism. This is an adjunct to Darwin's theory of "survival of the fittest" and refers to the US predilection that their social system will enable the "survival of the fittest" among the human species. They appear to use this concept interchangeably with the concept of manifest destiny, in both cases implying that the US sees a "right" (whether from God or nature) for imposing their system on others. At a Sun Tzu Art of War symposium, a Chinese moderator even went so far as to state that "if we can't clear up social Darwinism, we can't get rid of war. China must use Sun Tzu theory to solve the social Darwinism problem."

These articles and others from <u>China Military Science</u> are revealing for their prejudicial/one-sided treatment and judgment of US actions and corresponding aggrandizement of Chinese generosity and benevolence. Chinese analysts ignore US acts of benevolence, such as US attempts to bring peace to Bosnia or stop genocide in other areas of the world. The Chinese authors ignore these actions and focus only on what they term as expansionist and material motives. Meanwhile China's quiet moves into Africa and Central Asia are ignored.

In similar fashion, China accuses the US of self-veneration. Clearly a country basing its ideology around the communist cult of personality (Mao, Deng, Jiang, etc.) is conducting self-veneration albeit of a different type. For a nation supposedly focused on the people, this is difficult to understand. US ideology venerates the achievements of the common man in science and other areas as well as presidents and statesmen. In fact, political leaders are often the focus of scorn in the US media. Thus the strategic culture of both nations leads to different debates and interpretations. This is hard to deny.

Another example of a prejudicial assessment comes from the work of Fang Yonggang. He notes that internally, officers and troops in the PLA are united and "democracy within the Party, people's democracy, and inter-party democracy" are being promoted. Externally, the positive, proactive, and innovative reverence for the masses drives the PLA forward so that the prominent goal of "being of the people" is attained. This is inherently different from foreign military culture, Fang writes, particularly that of the West, whose

---

[252] Chen, Wang, and Wang.

values are oriented toward "serving a minority of the people" and "serving the capitalist class."[253]

China and the US may not correctly assess each other perhaps out of ignorance, oversights, or the overriding influence of their national strategic culture on their perceptions. Yao and Du note that the different approaches that countries have to their security interests influence the formation of their military values and the selection of their ways of military thinking.[254] The implication is that the more we understand strategic culture and the selection of security interests, the better we will be able to understand one another.

Wang Lin, Wang Yitao, and Wang Guibin, mentioned earlier, write in 2005 about a method by which to better understand one another (even though they were discussing the conduct of cultural wars at the time!). They write that when examining the cultural roots and characteristics of the core spirit of an enemy, subjects must avoid cultural prejudice when dealing with targets. One must actively utilize empathy toward the cultural proclivities of the target. To be truly empathetic, seven steps must be followed. It is these same steps, however, that could be applied to understand one another better in peacetime. That is, the seven step recommendation would work in times of war to get at enemy mind sets; or in peacetime to better work with one another and eliminate potential points of misunderstanding (especially in times of crises!). These steps are:

- One must share the inner state of someone and recreate that person's inner image.
- One must recognize the types of cultural diversity in society.
- One must know oneself and individuals in a given culture.
- One must eliminate one's own isolation from the environment.
- One must take on the other person's perspective and thinking.
- One must acquire experience through empathy obtained from the five steps above.
- One must restore his or her inner state, and re-experience one's own cultural state again. [255]

These same steps are used to conduct media warfare, according to the authors.

---

[253] Fang Yonggang.
[254] Ibid.
[255] Wang Lin, Wang Yitao, and Wang Guibin.

Other Important Aspects of Advanced Military Culture

The articles of Liu Tinghua, Yang Yuling, Fang Yonggang, and Wang Zhaohai in China Military Science also included several other issues worthy of consideration regarding advanced military culture. Liu Tinghua, a Director of the Research Office of the Historical Research Department of the Academy of Military Sciences, emphasizes the connection between strategy and history. In 2002, he wrote on military ideological and cultural lessons learned from the Chinese classic work I Ching since many of the I Ching lessons (combat preparedness, unity of the people and army, and the "just" use of force) have become Chinese cultural traditions.

Liu writes about the I Ching concept that the "superior man, when resting in safety, does not forget that danger may come; when in a state of security, he does not forget the possibility of ruin; and when all is in a state of order, he does not forget that disorder may come."[256] To strengthen national defense, the superior man must educate the people and nourish them; think of what might come and prepare for it; and keep weapons in good repair in case of unforeseen contingencies. The goal is to be ever vigilant and mindful of adversities and prepare for the worst. Further, the army must insist upon participating only in just wars (i.e., the liberation of people) and using only competent generals who possess integrity; fostering harmonious relations with people to create a unified military front; instituting rigorous discipline; utilizing flexibility (subjective initiative) in commands; luring the enemy into terrain; staying positive in the face of momentary setbacks; gaining a firm understanding of the nature of war; and treating prisoners of war with respect.[257] Chinese culture eventually absorbed most of these issues that were written about long ago.

However, Liu warns that the I Ching contains mysticism and irrational thought as well that must be countered by taking a scientific view. For example, there is the belief that a dangerous campaign will result if someone witnesses the immersion of a young fox's tail in water as it crosses a stream. This type of thinking must be countered.[258] In fact

Winning or losing a war is the result of a contest between soldiers and weapons and is influenced by terrain and weather conditions, along with how well commanders exercise their subjective initiative. It has

---

[256] Liu Tinghua, "Study of Military Ideology and Culture in the Book of Changes," China Military Science, 2002, No. 6, pp. 35-40.
[257] Ibid.
[258] Ibid.

nothing to do with divination, which was the result of the low level of scientific advancement at the time which led to the search for psychological comfort by means of praying to gods for protection.[259]

The preservation of unity is a major traditional theme that the Chinese carried over into advanced military culture. It is a national cultural tradition of some importance that is most often reflected in Chinese discussions about Taiwan. Yang Yuling, a PhD and the Director of the Military History and Culture Teaching and Research Section of the Xi'an Political Institute, wrote that "Culture plays a role that cannot be replaced by other social elements, namely the functions of coalescence, integration, assimilation, and standardization of the conduct and psychology of the social groups within a nation."[260] Culture, Yang believes, molds an identification psychology in people or a country through assimilation and acclimation, a "cognitive schematic" often referred to as nationality.[261] Yang adds that "for thousands of years, national unity has always been viewed as the highest political objective and as being in the highest interests of the nation" and for this reason national reunification with Taiwan remains a priority.[262]

Yang adds that values represent the scale from which standards of social conduct are measured and tested. Upholding unity is one of these values. National spirit or unity is a key element of identification psychology, reflected as patriotism. National unity provides will and vitality for the nation, is embedded in China's national spirit, and is "Chinese culture's rational and systematic recognition of the state's political objectives."[263] The cultivation of a cognitive psychology of shared culture should serve as "a strategic duty and basic stratagem for national reunification."[264]

Finally, Yang writes that national identity involves political, economic, cultural, and military factors, which he terms a systematic construct. It is also a construct that must change with the times. While China must maintain and manage an enduring memory of its traditions, it must also respond to cultural challenges brought on by changing times.[265]

---

[259] Ibid.
[260] Yang Yuling, "On Cultural Identification and National Reunification," China Military Science, 2005, No. 3, pp. 57-63.
[261] Ibid.
[262] Ibid.
[263] Ibid.
[264] Ibid.
[265] Ibid.

Fang Yonggang wrote a comprehensive paper on advanced military culture and its aspects. He states that advanced military culture in the PLA has six subsystems: military thought, military ethics, military institutions, military science and technology, military strategy, and military mental life.[266] His list is somewhat similar to that of Yao and Du mentioned earlier.

The first subsystem, military thought, refers to military culture at the level of reason and is expressed in philosophical and theoretical form. It reveals the innate connection between issues of war and economics, war and politics, war and culture, humans and weapons, and the laws of war.[267]

The second subsystem is military ethics. This subsystem is an internal system of standards of conduct for the armed forces internally. Marxist military ethics guide the Chinese military while carrying forward China's cultural traditions. Advanced military ethics obey the command of the Party, love of the military, respect for cadres, strict adherence to discipline, patriotic devotion, perseverance, integrity, hard work, and enlightened etiquette, providing a strong structural pillar for the fighting spirit of a PLA soldier.[268]

The third subsystem is the creation and development of military institutions—their form, nature, function, and implementation. These institutes integrate and standardize military activities and never cease to innovate and adapt to new technology and equipment or theories of fighting.[269]

The fourth subsystem is military science and technology. It consists of theory, ideology, consciousness, knowledge, quality, the capacity for innovation, systems of cognition, and a scientific attitude. It is in this subsystem that the factor of quality plays its major role (due to the cyber age) and edges out quantity in importance. Science and technology will have a major impact on increasing combat power and will require new types of thinking, ideological concepts, ideas about work, and methods of leadership suited to the demands of informatized war.[270]

The fifth subsystem is military strategy which reveals the quality, traditions, and reality beneath military culture. The roots of strategy began long ago and form a unique cultural tradition in Chinese history. Mao first integrated Marxist strategy into the Chinese revolution and this began an innovation in

---

[266] Fang Yonggang.
[267] Ibid.
[268] Ibid.
[269] Ibid.
[270] Ibid.

culture that allowed China to absorb lessons from the West. Chinese culture is thus adaptive and able to integrate traditional strategic culture with modern science and technology championed in the West.[271]

Finally, there is the subsystem of mental life manifested mainly in military literature and art. This subsystem allows for the creation of personal qualities consisting of idealistic beliefs that motivate soldiers to make contributions. It elicits a consciousness of national defense in people and improves combat power.[272]

In addition to the six subsystems mentioned by Fang, he also listed five functions of advanced Chinese military culture. They are guiding ideology, uniting military morale, creating mental incentives, providing intellectual support, and guiding scientific methods.[273]

Major General Wang Zhaohai, Chairman of the Political Department at the Academy of Military Sciences, writes that military culture can be dissected into form, era, region, and class. Military culture can be divided by form into military spiritual culture, the culture of military systems, the culture of military conduct, and the culture of military equipment. By era it can be divided into traditional military culture and modern military culture. By region, it can be divided into Chinese military culture and Western military culture. By class attributes, it can be divided into landlord military culture, capitalist culture, and proletariat military culture.[274] Military culture thus is an important concept that includes different aspects of military activity.

Conclusions

This discussion of Chinese military culture is, admittedly, limited to one journal. It has used only a few articles from a vast treasure trove of works on the issue. However, it serves as an introductory viewpoint on the topic and a contemporary one at that, fostered by the official journal of the Chinese Academy of Military Science.

The discussion initially highlighted six so-called "points of interest" that focused on some specific items of Chinese military culture. These points of interest were (1.) a Chinese analyst's opinion that "winning without fighting" is the "rarest of rarities" for Chinese history, where the sword has ruled. This

---

[271] Ibid.
[272] Ibid.
[273] Ibid.
[274] Wang Zhaohai.

point of view is at odds with the most popular assessment of Chinese military cultural history, a history based on humanity and benevolence (2.) the important role that Marxism plays for both its impact on culture and on military thought processes. The latter point includes the concept of the dialectical thought process among other Marxist ideas (3.) the focus some Chinese analysts placed on combining technology with strategy. There is a realization that pure strategic thoughts are not enough in a world where technology is driving equipment and concepts (4.) the more traditional focus on the role that intellectuals played (Sun Tzu was an intellectual who became a strategist). The focus on thought may be the reason that strategy surfaced as the main element in Chinese traditional thinking. The study of ancient Chinese history also demonstrates the importance of innovation and creativity in Chinese thinking, to include borrowing the best elements from Western military culture. Hopefully, US theorists are learning from Chinese history as well. (5.) a focus on strategic psychological warfare and the use of persuasive techniques via the media to influence situations. This includes the use of persuasive technique simulations and (6.) the digital age's impact on Chinese military culture in all its aspects (theory, ethics, science and technology, strategy, etc.), causing several significant shifts.

One conclusion that becomes evident upon reading Chinese military cultural material is that, for China, "military theory with the characteristics of our armed forces is the outcome of the combination of Marxist military theory with the concrete practice of China's revolutionary war."[275] That is, not only ancient military theory but Western and some contemporary Chinese history have strongly influenced military tradition in China. Another conclusion is that the digital age has genuinely threatened traditional military culture in China forcing the PLA to develop what it terms as advanced military culture.

The general discussion also includes definitions of several terms focused on culture: military culture, strategic culture, traditional and advanced military culture, and cultural wars. These definitions offer a general understanding of the importance of knowledge and values to the Chinese military as well as the important role that society at large plays in the formation of military culture. In addition the components of advanced military culture were described. Cultural warfare, for example, emphasized how to demonstrate empathy and truly get "into" a culture, requiring that the last step of the process was to "re-experience one's own cultural state again."

---

[275] Zheng Shenxia, "Establish and Implement Scientific Development Outlook and Push Forward the Construction of Military Theory in an All-Round Way," China Military Science, 2005, No. 4, pp. 1-9.

The discussion makes it clear that China's analysts are attempting to distill years of military culture as they decide on the direction in which the PLA's military culture should head as it transitions from traditional to advanced military cultural thinking. This fact alone should be of great interest to other nations. China's focus on military culture comes at a time when the PLA is becoming an increasingly important player on the world stage.

It is important for the US to study Chinese military culture not only to learn where it is headed but to understand what is of value from their ancient history. There are many aspects of Chinese military culture and theory that offer the Western analyst another way of viewing or solving a problem. The US, of course, should be as selective in choosing items from Chinese thought for its use as the Chinese are when choosing military concepts from a Western system. Wang Zhaohai noted that China "must not blindly accept foreign military culture when we seek to draw lessons from it, nor must we simply exclude foreign military culture because it conflicts with our own, and thereby overlook the positive and beneficial aspects."[276] We must do the same.

China's military cultural transition is occurring while its armed forces are transitioning from a mechanized to an informationized force. The PLA is learning how to operate in complex electromagnetic environments and how to conduct information warfare tactics. This revolutionary change in the conduct of warfare has left its mark on military culture and the evolution of advanced military culture is proof positive. China is very concerned over the penetration of its military culture by Western media and hopes to do better at constructing socialist culture with Chinese characteristics, creating cultural diffusion hardware and software over which China has autonomous intellectual property rights, and, as author Wang Shudao noted, taking action to expose the hypocrisy of Western anti-Chinese forces. China's approach must be proactive if it is to "propel China's culture industry and media industry beyond China's borders in an effort to take over the international culture market."[277]

Finally, a look at China's military culture, if properly analyzed, can expose predispositions and intentions that the US can utilize to better understand China's military leaders and thus potentially avert conflict. The increasingly aggressive Chinese behavior and growing defense budget, and the reconnaissance activities by units such as PLA hackers, indicate that the

---

[276] Wang Zhaohai.
[277] Wang Shudao, "Modern Cultural Diffusion and National Security," China Military Science, 2005, No. 3, pp. 64-69.

Chinese will be well-prepared to fight a future war in a strategic manner, one that other nations may not consider. As was noted earlier, what is scarier than inferior technology to some Chinese theorists is inferior thinking. It appears that in the case of the PLA, they are working hard to ensure that their thinking is not inferior but takes the best from East and West.

It is evident, based on the occasional conflicts that arise between China and the West, that both sides need to learn how to understand one another's intentions better. A closer study of military culture and an open debate among the two sides on the topic may provide one avenue (among many) to do so. Hopefully this analysis has opened a few doors to understanding the current concerns and reactions of the PLA to the threats it perceives to its military culture as well as offering a reverse look at Wang Shudao's position. That is, it is possible to expose the hypocrisy of China's anti-Western forces just as he hoped to expose the hypocrisy of the US's anti-Chinese forces. The dialectic works for either Chinese or Western thought.

PART TWO:

High-Tech Deception, Campaign Stratagems, and Crisis Management in the PLA

CHAPTER FOUR: CHINA'S MILITARY AND HIGH-TECH DECEPTION

This chapter examines the Chinese concept of deception and its use today under conditions of informatization.

War is a game of deception.[278]

Introduction

Chinese military theorists are quick to point out that information age deception is a powerful weapon that has some old and many new uses. For one thing, high-tech systems have increased opportunities to deceive or to uncover deception at the political, diplomatic, economic, and military levels of war preparation. Deception, military planners note, can be used to fool an enemy in peacetime by increasing the fog of war or establishing a high-tech "smoke screen" behind which aggressive actions can begin to take shape.[279] This indicates that preparations for deception activities still begin well before conflict occurs whether it is the study of opposing armies' decision-making habits and equipment parameters or the development and employment of realistic decoys.

Deception is historically ingrained in Chinese military thought. However, deception is also used against Chinese society on occasion. For example, the Chinese government uses virtual devices to deceive the population as necessary. A recent BBC report has details of something known as the "50 cent party." Bloggers receive 50 cents (50 Chinese cents or $.07 cents) for writing an entry that supports government policy. In this way paid commentators on policy issues help control public opinion and offset unpopular decrees. Online bloggers write entries with a positive spin about a policy in dispute. Such virtual deception has worked well, the report states, citing evidence from the public security bureau of the city of Jiaozuo in Henan Province. Chinese authorities, realizing they could not block or monitor news in

---

[278] Wu Rusong and Wu Xianlin, chief editors, <u>Sun Zi: The Art of War, Sun Bin: The Art of War</u>, People's China Publishing House, 1995, p. 24.

[279] Zhang Xianfend and Bie Yixun, "Visible Battlefield: New Trend in Informatized Strategic Camouflage," <u>Jiefangjun Bao</u>, 11 May 2005, p. 11, as translated and downloaded from the Open Source Center website, document number CPP20051019502002.

some localities, proposed using their own commentators. Today estimates are that there are tens of thousands of these commentators, the report noted.[280]

A more well-known and recent Chinese public use of information deception occurred at the 2008 Beijing Olympic Games. During the dazzling opening ceremony, one of the most impressive opening ceremonies in the history of the Olympics, fireworks lit up the sky over the course of a mile leading to the National Stadium (also known as the Bird's Nest). These fireworks were to represent footsteps leading to the stadium. A Beijing newspaper later revealed that a brighter set of footprints had been created and filmed much earlier in a special effects lab and this was shown on television instead of the real fireworks.[281] Thus millions of viewers were deceived into believing what they saw on the TV screens was a live broadcast.

This chapter will define and discuss this all-important concept of deception. It will highlight some information age deception advances, camouflage techniques, high-technology reconnaissance deception, and the deception-stratagem link (Appendix Three defines four additional deception terms, "decoy," "infrared decoy," "deceptive electronic jamming," and "radio communication deception"). The discussion will not further cover Chinese deception issues against Chinese society.

How Does the Chinese Military Understand Deception?

The Chinese Military Encyclopedia defines the term deception in the following manner:

Deception: A technical term from ancient Chinese military science. First seen in *Sun Zi – Laying Plans*: 'All warfare is based on deception.' During the Spring and Autumn Period and the Warring States Period, people broke free from the ideological fetters of humane and righteous warfare and 'turned out surprises and lay in ambush, using both variations and deceptions in the use of force' (*Book of Han – Yiwenzhi*). Military strategists suggested the idea of deception in the use of force in keeping with the scientific summarization of social reality at that time. Deception theory quite profoundly reflected the essence and laws of military struggles. Its basic substance was the use of pretense: 'The military stands on deception' (*Sun Zi – Military*

---

[280] Michael Bristow, "China's Internet 'Spin Doctors'," BBC News, Beijing, 16 December 2008.

[281] Aaron Barnhart, "Not-So-Special Effects," The Kansas City Star, 16 August 2008, p. F1.

Combat); 'There is no lack of deception and fakery between warring positions' (*Hanfeizi – Nanyi*). This is so because one simply cannot talk of virtue and morality in desperate battles of life and death – one can only confuse the enemy through deceit and feints and by exposing what is false and hiding what is real in order to conceal one's own plans. Only then can suddenness be achieved in military operations; only then can the enemy be attacked where he is unprepared; only then can one appear where the enemy is not anticipating; and only then can the initiative be grasped in military operations. Deception applies only to fighting an enemy: 'Use deception to strive for victory over an enemy; there must be trust when ruling the masses' (*Notes of the Eleven Scholars on Sun Zi – Laying Plans, Wang Xi's Notes*). Deception is an important substance in the military science of ancient China, and it has had a profound and lasting influence. (Qiu Xintian)[282]

According to Ma Jinsheng, Chinese author of the 1991 book <u>Military Deception</u>, military deception started 4,000 to 5,000 years ago in China. The concept has evolved over time and now constitutes a standard practice that involves covering up the truth, using ruses, and creating false impressions. It was not always this way. Initially, during China's Western Zhou Period (around 1100 B.C.), Ma notes that etiquette was extremely important and the idea was to be virtuous and not to start a war without a proper warning to the other side. Eventually the concept that "all is fair in war" took hold and deception became a major component in the planning and conduct of conflict. Survival won out over virtue and morals.[283]

One can safely assume, then, that Sun Tzu was a survivalist and not a moralist since he states most emphatically that "all warfare is based on deception." The <u>Art of War</u> includes sections on attack by stratagem, use of spies, and so on in addition to sections on deception. This implies that an active instead of a passive position must be taken. A successful deception operation will utilize surprise and spies, the discipline of troops, and knowledge of enemy culture and its decision-making criteria.[284] It must also be guided by strategy and research of the following issues before implementation:

- Study of one's own position and the position of the enemy

---

[282] <u>Chinese Military Encyclopedia</u>, Academy of Military Science Press, Volume 3, July 1997, p. 699.
[283] Ma Jinsheng, <u>Military Deception</u>, Military Science Press, 1991. Since only a translation was available to the author and not the original text, exact pages cannot be listed.
[284] Ibid.

- Study of available resources
- Research of friendly military strength
- Study of how an enemy force would react to friendly military strength
- Study of how an enemy force might change its battle formation or plan
- Determination of whether the use of threats is justified in lieu of deception.[285]

Deception's goal is to confuse the enemy force and mislead it. The three components of deception are the side originating the deception, the target of deception, and the medium through which the deceptive action is delivered (the latter may be based on direct [rumors] input, indirect [leaflets] input, or false impressions [troop deployments, fortifications]). Deception can be visible (leaflets) or invisible (rumors), although Sun Tzu appears to favor visible methods according to Ma.[286]

With regard to strategic deception, Ma writes that it has five characteristics and three ways to carry it out. The five characteristics of strategic deception are:

- Its scale is large.
- It may last for a long time.
- It can affect the overall progress and outcome of a war.
- It envisions that military deception will be carried out side by side with political and diplomatic deception.
- It is directed by a country's high command.[287]

Strategic deception is carried out by spreading peace rumors, assuming a friendly gesture, and concealing war preparations; misleading an enemy as to the time and place of a war's start; and misleading an enemy as to the place and type of aggression. Allies, friendly forces, and neutrals can also be made, unbeknownst to them, part of the deception plan.[288]

Basing strategy and tactics on deception is described by the editors of the book Campaign Stratagems as a law, one that allows planners to confuse the enemy, cause the enemy to make mistakes, and conceal their own intentions.

---

[285] Ibid.
[286] Ibid.
[287] Ibid.
[288] Ibid.

The editors (or translators) interchangeably use the terms deception and scheme. In this book, deception is defined as actions such as cheating and swindling, while the term scheme is defined as unexpected tactics.[289]

The list of deceptive methods from Sun Tzu's Art of War[290] is familiar:

- When attacking, one must appear unable to attack.
- When using force, one must appear passive.
- When near, one should appear far.
- When far, the enemy should think one is near.
- Hold out bait to entice the enemy.
- Feign disorder and crush him.
- If he is secure at all points, be prepared for him.
- If he has superior strength, evade him.
- If the enemy has a choleric temper, seek to irritate him.
- Pretend to be weak so that he may grow arrogant.
- If he is at ease, give him no rest.
- If his forces are united, separate them.
- Attack him where he is unprepared and appear where you are not expected.[291]

The website East-Asia-Intel reported in November 2006 that, according to the Chinese paper Zhanqi Bao, China must prepare a good plan, learn to show what is false and hide what is true, and remain flexible in order to deceive an enemy force. The intelligence an enemy gathers must be consistent with its subjective assessment. An enemy's media reporting must be controlled as well with no contradictions existing between military and civilian points of view on the situation at hand. If deception is to succeed, subjective reasoning also comes into play when a situation changes rapidly. If the enemy force cannot see the real objective of the information's initiator but only the false objectives laid out by friendly forces, then actions will be successful. In particular, China's approach must be comprehensive for deception to succeed:

We must collect and analyze the characteristics of enemy commanders, enemy units, and the battlefield. We must gain a clear understanding of the main reconnaissance measures and methods the enemy uses. We must take the intelligence collected and carefully analyze and study it,

---

[289] Zhang Xing Ye and Zhang Zhan Li, Campaign Stratagems, National Defense University, 2002, p. 75.
[290] Ibid.
[291] Ibid.

think hard about the situations our forces could encounter on the move, tie in with our actual situation and formulate countermeasures, and take truly practical measures of deception, to include the object of the deception, its content, method, security measures, and the timetable for its implementation.[292]

The Information Age and Deception

Another work of importance on military deception is the 1998 book Military Deception Methods by Liu Bing Chen and Wang Gang. These authors make it clear that eleven years ago the integration of technology and deception was on the mind of the PLA. An unnamed person at the PLA's Army Military Planning Institute's "Military Deception Methodology Research Center" wrote the book's introduction. Noting that the "new devil called 'information warfare' will be among us," the introduction underscores the necessity of combining deception with technology. With concepts introduced such as "let technology install wings on military deception methodology," the man-machine union in the author's opinion will become the "fourth tidal wave of Eastern intelligence."[293]

Western researchers of the People's Liberation Army (PLA) have been acutely aware of the importance of deception to Chinese theorists for centuries. Chinese classics such as The Secret Art of War: The Thirty-Six Stratagems emphasize often that deception is a military art form that can achieve military objectives. Further, military deception remains one of the key elements of Chinese information warfare theory and practice. In the information age, deception can play a huge role in perpetrating a catastrophic result for an enemy force. For example, encouraging someone to push the wrong button in an infrastructure complex via deceptive means could yield catastrophic results. It could initiate a cascade of events leading to the shutdown of vital systems.

Wars fought under high-tech conditions almost ensure, due to reconnaissance assets and precision-guided munitions, that once a force is discovered it will be annihilated. To deceive satellite reconnaissance requires technical advancements in camouflaging a force on various types of terrain, at sea, and in the air as well as a host of deceptive electronic methods to cause interpreters of satellite imagery to believe that what is true is false and what is false is true.

---

[292] East-Asia-Intel.com website, accessed 6 October 2008.
[293] Liu Bing Chen and Wang Gang, Military Deception Methods, Kun Lun Publishing Press, 1998. Since only a translation was available to the author and not the original text, exact pages cannot be listed.

China's military is studying how to deceive and manipulate the decision-making capability of foreign commanders in the field through the use of a series of high-tech developments. These include self-adapting biological materials that change texture and color like a chameleon and the creation of equipment that simulates military activity. There is also a focus on integrating high-technology equipment with stratagems (stratagems are designed to mislead enemy processes of perception, thinking, emotion, and will. They use objective realities together with subjective creativity to deceive or persuade). The deception chore has been made easier in some respects by the information age. Systems acquire, forward, and process information. Therefore, any measure designed to alter, control, or block information can conceivably deceive an enemy, especially a high-tech one.

In addition to high-tech means and stratagems, camouflage has traditionally been one of the main methods to deceive an enemy force on the battlefield. Today a large role is played by what the Chinese term "engineering camouflage." Camouflage conceals one's own side, deceives the enemy, improves battlefield survivability, and protects the integrity of one's combat operations. Simultaneously, camouflage interferes with enemy information systems, causes confusion among enemy decision-makers, degrades enemy high-tech weapon systems efficiency, and weakens an enemy's overall combat capability.[294]

In the information age, camouflage, stratagems, and high-tech means have been supplemented with virtual, voice, and other forms of deception. Electronics now can perform what appears to be magic on the battlefield in the opinion of some Chinese theorists. Electronic camouflage uses electromagnetic and thermal technological measures to simulate and duplicate the environment and make friendly targets blend in with their background. This "hides what is true" and "displays what is false" about specific targets. Such camouflage can help thwart enemy electronic attacks and protect one's own systems. Metal foil strips, angular radar reflectors, colored smoke screens, plasma, multifrequency-electromagnetic screens, photochromatic coatings, and optical bait are representative of such measures. For example, smoke camouflage now includes smoke made up of metallic chemical compounds and plasma which, when

---

[294] Zhang Shengyu and Shen Yueguo, "Informatized Warfare Challenges the Camouflaging of Military Targets," Jiefangjun Bao, 28 December 2005, p. 11, as translated and downloaded from the Open Source Center website, document number CPP20051230502001.

mixed with certain polymers in specific ratios, make smoke screens that can fluctuate to be consistent with the target and its background.[295]

With respect to information warfare, deception has several applications, two of which are written about frequently. They are the use of information-based stratagems and information camouflage, both of whose effects can be multiplied through their integration with high-technology equipment. Other applications discussed here include fooling reconnaissance systems and utilizing "information-hiding technology."

If national interests are at stake, one is not restricted by "righteous warfare" as the <u>Chinese Military Encyclopedia</u> entry for deception indicates. Any means of scheming and deception are acceptable. Deception can include disguising one's troops as enemy troops; taking secret actions; manufacturing, distorting, and fabricating facts; escaping unnoticed; luring the enemy from his base; harming someone through the hands of another; making troops appear disordered when they are in order; making troops seem hungry although they are well-fed; making troops seem poorly equipped when they are well-armed; making troops appear massed when they are scattered; and so on.[296] Deception can increase combat efficacy and achieve victory at a smaller cost. This is the essential principle of basing strategy and tactics on deception.[297]

To transform what is real and what is false, to transform passivity into initiative, and to change disadvantage into advantage requires scheming and deception. According to Zhang and Zhang, points to consider when deploying scheming and deception in campaign stratagems include:

- Coordinating movement with statis
- Exposing to the enemy an intention and situation opposite to one's actual intentions and conditions (polarities such as weak/strong, urgency/rest, false/real, open/hidden, etc.)
- Affirming the enemy's intentions and, at times, doing what the enemy expects to fool him as you make alternate plans
- Integrating what is false and what is real (for example, pretend to attack at many points to hide the real target)

---

[295] Dai Qingmin, <u>Direct Information Warfare</u>, National Defense University Publishing House, 2002. Translation credit belongs to Senior Chief Bart Zobel of the Navy Reserve Navy Information Operations Command.
[296] Zhang and Zhang, pp. 76-77.
[297] Ibid., p. 77.

- Attending to differences in personality among commanders (quality, knowledge, experience, personality, psychological makeup, endurance, and adaptability). The personality and psychology of the commander is the priority and objective of "strategizing" today according to the authors.[298]

Chinese commanders, in addition to these points, have a new challenge before them in the information age. That challenge is finding a way to integrate new technologies into their campaign stratagems. Commanders must develop integrative methodologies if they hope to keep pace with advancements made in other armies.

One of the sections of the book <u>Campaign Stratagems</u> focuses on the implications of forces being either real or virtual. Here virtual means both "digital" as it does today as well as things or situations that are contrived or fake. For example, an army could display its real force posture or a fake (virtual) posture to appear strong either via electrons or via a real force posture. A real force, one with imposing strength, could utilize virtual aspects of force (attacking a sector with a force that appears strong but is only a virtual or fake force) together with real force to win a battle. Or a weak army, unable to show a strong force posture, could attempt to use a virtual posture (contrived or fake show of force, for example) to convince another side that they possess a real strength posture. Force postures will also vary depending on the speed at which units advance. There could be time and space gaps that make a real force appear virtual (if it becomes fragmented) or a virtual force appear real (if gaps do not appear and an opponent thinks a force is larger than it really is). Further, not only material but moral strength could be real or virtual.[299]

Three sections follow that amplify this discussion of deception in the information age. They are a discussion of Chinese camouflage techniques, a discussion of Chinese high-technology reconnaissance, and a discussion of the stratagem-technology link designed to induce deception.

Camouflage and Deception

Camouflage is closely related to deception (hiding something enables deception!) and is the focus of this section. There are many definitions in the <u>Chinese Military Encyclopedia</u> that concern the term "camouflage." For example, Chinese military professionals write about strategic, tactical, and thermal camouflage. Listed below are truncated definitions for strategic and

---

[298] Ibid., pp. 78-82.
[299] Ibid., p. 61.

tactical camouflage taken directly from the <u>Chinese Military Encyclopedia</u>. These definitions will be followed by some recent opinions of Chinese camouflage experts.

Strategic Camouflage: Strategic camouflage is measures taken to deceive or confuse the enemy so as to conceal strategic intent and actions. Strategic camouflage is an important part of strategic support and an important measure in the struggle against strategic reconnaissance. Strategic camouflage includes the use of political, diplomatic, military, and scientific and technological measures to hide the truth and display what is false, to combine real and fake, to employ openness and secrecy together, and thus conceal a side's strategic intent, strategic disposition, strategic actions, and strategic goals. It makes the enemy misperceive the situation and make mistakes in judgment, and in so doing protects one's own side and creates conditions favorable for achieving strategic surprise. The plan for strategic camouflage is drafted, organized, and executed by the supreme headquarters.

The methods of strategic camouflage are numerous. Advanced camouflage materials and devices can be used for disguising military targets and economic targets of national importance, for changing the external appearance and characteristics of such targets, and for making it difficult for the enemy to determine the nature of the target quickly and accurately. This technique can also be combined with the use of false targets to make the enemy mistake them for real targets. To conceal strategic actions and intent, a side can spread false information, leak false intelligence, carry out diplomatic activities, shape public opinion, minimize signs of military activity, step up reconnaissance, and, depending on the situation, carry out electronic camouflage, deception, and feints. It can also have a small unit pose as a main-force unit in "a feint to the east but an attack to the west" scenario.

The main requirements for strategic camouflage are:
1. Make full preparations and tight-knit plans, have centralized and unified direction, and get everyone involved with the plan to coordinate as one.
2. Make strategic camouflage extend throughout the war from start to finish. The enemy will conduct frequent reconnaissance before and during a war, and so strategic camouflage must be implemented continuously throughout the entire course of the war.
3. Research the opponent's mental state and psychological weaknesses, focus efforts to confuse and deceive the enemy, make the enemy misperceive and be caught unprepared, and force the enemy into a passive position.

4. In camouflaging strategic targets and strategic actions, be flexible and use various methods, suit measures to conditions at hand, combine various measures, make various measures supplement each other, do not reveal weaknesses, and use measures which are feasible and effective.
5. Take strict measures for secrecy.

The struggle between strategic camouflage and strategic reconnaissance will become more intense. It is even more difficult to completely camouflage strategic intent in warfare under high-tech conditions. Strategic camouflage is not only applied on the vast battlefield but also in the use of political, diplomatic, and high-tech measures where it will receive even more emphasis.[300]

Tactical Camouflage: Tactical camouflage utilizes measures taken by combat formations, units, and elements to conceal themselves and deceive the enemy. Tactical camouflage is a combat support measure.

Tactical camouflage normally focuses on concentrations of military units, forces on the move, axes of movement, force dispositions, the main axis of attack or the main axis of defense, fighting positions, firepower systems, fortifications and obstacles, and other tactical targets, to include their locations, status, and use as well as other activities undertaken by military units.

The basic requirements for tactical camouflage are: conform to the tactical intent of the commander and coordinate with unit actions; fully exploit terrain, weather, and materials; integrate the use of various camouflage measures; and take the initiative and never stop the camouflage effort. The main content of tactical camouflage includes plans for simulations or feints, implementation methods, measures to be taken, allocation of materials, camouflage discipline and requirements, and so on.

The main measures of tactical camouflage are: fully exploit terrain and other surface features, bad weather, darkness, and other conditions providing concealment; use camouflage patterns and smokescreens; exploit vegetation, use manmade screens, and acoustic and light concealment; conceal one's own units and their combat actions; use mockups, noise-making devices, smoke generators, and other camouflage materials and construction techniques to set

---

[300] Chinese Military Encyclopedia, Academy of Military Science Press, Volume 3, July 1997, p. 726. Entry by Wang Peikun and Ye Teng.

up decoys, create fake battle positions and areas laid out as decoys; simulate the combat actions of units and elements; use a part of a force to execute a feint, a feint by firepower, or an electronic feint to confuse the enemy, pin him down or rouse him into action; and maintain strict discipline, block the leakage of information, and prevent the disclosure of military secrets.

In future warfare, with the extensive use of high-tech reconnaissance measures and precision-guided weapons, the place and role of tactical camouflage will be even more prominent. The organization and execution of tactical camouflage will be more complex, and technical measures will develop in the direction of integration, multi-functionality, and high effectiveness.[301]

PLA Camouflage Experts Speak Out

These two definitions of strategic and tactical camouflage offer an official but rather dated military interpretation of camouflage. As might be expected, there are other Chinese experts on camouflage that, through their positions as instructors or advisors to military officers, provide a more current view on the topic. One of them is Li Xinguang, a Professor at the PLA's General Staff Headquarters. Li states that the objective of informatized strategic camouflage is to "win an 'informatized war' by employing all the scientific and technical measures available to deceive and confuse the enemy based on the characteristics and patterns of an informatized and digitized battlefield."[302] He believes that if a country can hide its strategic targets, activities, and intentions, it will be able to accomplish its military objectives. To that end the Chinese must be good at hiding the true and displaying the false. The manipulation of another side's cognitive tendencies is imperative. Strategic camouflage can be turned into a weapon that enables friendly forces to achieve strategic superiority and "make the enemy do what we want them to do."[303] Thus, Li Xinguang seems to echo once again the words of Li Bingyan regarding the cat and the pepper.

Strategic camouflage involves many processes according to Li. For example, if a country wanted to portray an atmosphere of peace and tranquility, it might engage in diplomatic maneuvers, propaganda campaigns, cultural events, or political actions. Such actions can help paralyze an enemy force and enable surprise blows against it.[304] [Author: Li's use of peace proposals as an

---

[301] Chinese Military Encyclopedia, Academy of Military Science Press, Volume 3, July 1997, p. 742. Entry by Zhang Zuhui.
[302] Zhang and Bie.
[303] Ibid.
[304] Ibid.

element of deception through diplomatic camouflage is disturbing and lowers international trust in Chinese diplomatic pronouncements. Suspicion is raised over the true objective of such proposals.]

Today high-technology surveillance accounts for over 90% of intelligence acquired on a high-tech battlefield. However, it does have its deficiencies and Li mentions four. They are: the inability to get a complete picture of an event at a specific moment in time; surveillance is dedicated to detection and identification; intelligence gathered by surveillance is usually biased; and surveillance is susceptible to interference.[305]

Li mentions five types of new stealth materials in his discussion. They are:

- Nanometer Stealth Material: It has unique electromagnetic, optical, thermal, and chemical characteristics along with good wave absorption capability.
- Multiband, Multifunction Stealth Material: These materials simultaneously absorb visible, near-, mid-, and far-infrared light and millimeter radar waves.
- Intelligent Stealth Material: It contains built-in sensing and information processing capability.
- Transparent Stealth Material: It is transparent to electromagnetic waves and neither reflects nor absorbs radar waves. It lets radar waves penetrate right through.
- Chameleon Material: This is an electric field-induced, color-change thin film. Once an electric field is applied the polymer film can change its color (to blue, gray, or white). An aircraft could thus change its color to blend into the background of the sky.[306]

Li also paid attention to active stealth technology in this 2005 article. This is a new technology that employs active means to evade detection by sound, light, electromagnetic waves, and heat. Li also discussed the effects of plasma and bionic stealth technologies. Plasma technology is important. Sometimes called the fourth state of matter, plasma technology is an electrically conductive material. It can lower radar detection to below 1%. It can even change the frequency of reflected radar waves to let the enemy acquire the wrong data for target position and speed. Plasma has a wide absorption bandwidth and is highly absorptive. Bionic stealth refers to "unique physiological and structural

---

[305] Ibid.
[306] Ibid.

characteristics of an animal to achieve informatized bionic stealth of a strategic target." For example, Li notes, the volume of a bee is less than one one-hundredth of a sparrow. Yet the radar reflection cross section of a bee is sixteen times that of a sparrow. Studying these peculiarities can enable the development of bionic technologies.[307]

All of these methods require innovation on the part of scientists involved with the projects. Scientists must focus on control over information throughout the entire process of strategic camouflage. The most important objective of strategic camouflage is to win the information war.

Another Chinese camouflage expert is Li Xiaoqi, director and professor of the Disguise Research and Teaching Group at the Command College of the Corps of Engineers. Li seeks to turn his students into disguise experts, and he uses such devices as audio and photo-electric technology to use disguise as deception. He has compiled national military standards for "disguise requirements for electronic targets" and has worked on projects such as "protection and disguise for urban targets" and "disguise and protection for large transportation hubs."[308] Here disguise and camouflage are synonymous.

Wang Xiangwei, head of the sixth office of a research institute (unidentified) under the Second Artillery and a deputy head of the All-Army Specialty Group on Camouflage, offers another expert opinion. He teaches students that it should be a source of pride when camouflage they develop can pass for the real thing (camouflage battlefield deception) and when they can detect flaws that exist in a camouflage setup (deception detection operations). Most interesting about this article was the deception techniques described during a Red Force on Blue Force confrontation in training. First, the Blue Force (the US) could not detect the Red Force (China) because the latter was using camouflage so well. When the Red Force suddenly switched on its wireless communications system, which had remained silent, the Blue Force immediately took it out. After a 30 minute Blue Force attack, Blue returned to its base. During the return route, Red silently shot missiles at the force and the force's airstrip and missile emplacements. It turns out that the Blue attack had been against false targets set up by Red. The Red Force had also "changed the

---

[307] Ibid.
[308] Li Kaituo and Li Xiaofeng, "Li Xiaoqi, Dedicated to Raising 'Disguise Experts,'" Jiefangjun Bao Online, 31 July 2008, p. 9, as translated and downloaded from the Open Source Center website, document number CPP20080801710007.

deception patterns of several of its important military targets, which had again disappeared without a trace."[309]

Camouflage paint is another means China is using to neutralize surveillance from space and the air. Differences exist when viewing objects on the ground and from the air, explained Lu Xuliang, the Director of the Camouflage Material Research Office of the Engineering Corps Engineering Academy. There are four such difference, which are: different colors, different degrees of brightness, different shapes, and different textures. Lu's team first collected background image information on a large area around a target that required camouflage protection. Then they calculated "comprehensive indexing data from the digital images for all sorts of colored spots in the background area."[310] Second, design personnel used special design software to process the data, using computer software to design the pattern, colors, brightness, and texture of the camouflage paint. Finally the selection of coating materials was the determining factor in whether the camouflage project would succeed or not.[311]

Camouflage paint does have its shortcomings, however. It can crack or peel. It must have a strong pressure-proof property to enable it to withstand constant rolling. It may not be allowed to fade, and it must resist ultraviolet light. All of these shortcomings indicate that surfaces must be repainted frequently. Lu's team reportedly developed a camouflage paint that can be applied to concrete and sandy mud. The paint seeps .5 to .7 millimeters into the concrete or sandy object which prevents peeling or color fade up to ten years.[312]

High-Tech Reconnaissance and Deception

The PLA Daily makes it clear that China's armed forces must learn to conduct deception and employ camouflage measures under conditions of a "complex electromagnetic environment." There are excises held nearly every week or month by units somewhere in China under these conditions. In this

---

[309] Wang Tie, Wu Yanbing, and Qu Chen, "Expert on 'Concealment and Deception'—Profile of Wang Xiangwei, PLA Second Artillery Corps Outstanding Member of the Communist Party of China," Jiefangjun Bao, 21 September 2005, p. 6, as translated and downloaded from the Open Source Center website, document number CPP20051004318001.
[310] Ma Shengwei, Lu Zunhou, and Wang Ping, "While the Means of Reconnaissance Are Changing, Camouflage Techniques Must Also Change," Jiefangjun Bao, 21 February 2006, p. 11, as translated and downloaded from the Open Source Center website, document number CPP20060221510006.
[311] Ibid.
[312] Ibid.

environment, units learn how to counter reconnaissance activities of foreign armies and how to counter or deceive opponents with the use of signals and the electromagnetic spectrum. Special paint, decoys, deceptive radio signals, hiding among civilians (to include moving in civilian traffic), distorting the shape or appearance of important infrastructure sites, and other passive techniques receive the most attention. Active measures can include signal disruption or, as Defense News reported, blinding US satellites and thus preventing them from acquiring information.[313]

High-technology reconnaissance includes flat-plane reconnaissance as well as multi-dimensional reconnaissance from the air, on sea, underwater, and from space. Reconnaissance is also conducted by sound frequency and by microwave, infrared, laser, and other frequency bands thus providing multi-dimensional, multiple-frequency high-technology reconnaissance. The weak side in a high-technology war will not be at a complete loss, however, since it can use civilian identities or hide in civilian installations. Residing among civilians will remain a trump card by which the weaker side can defeat the enemy.[314]

Creating a counter surveillance capability to work against such technologies is a priority for all armed forces. In China, the focus is on implementing a strategic deception plan to interfere with surveillance capabilities. This will include transmitting a large volume of false and useless information that will draw an enemy force into making an incorrect or contradictory judgment.[315] Establishing a competent counter surveillance force requires much practice in peacetime. For China, this can mean countering an enemy force's use of unmanned aerial reconnaissance vehicles, satellites, or Google Earth.

More recently Chinese innovators have examined ways to fool Google Earth although the methods are not truly revolutionary to a Westerner. A Jinan Military District Red Army Corps commander thought about ways to do this

---

[313] Vago Muradian, "China Tried to Blind US Sats with Laser," Defense News, 22 September 2006, p. 1.
[314] Cao Jiang, Wang Shengliang, and Peng Wei, "The Informatized Battlefield is More and More Transparent; How Do We Manage Modern Camouflaging?" Jiefangjun Bao, 12 April 2007, p. 12, as translated and downloaded from the Open Source Center website, document number CPP20070412710006.809
[315] Huang Shan, "China Studies Four Counter Surveillance Measures Owing to Intensified Collection of Information by Western Countries," Huanqiu Shibao, 17 January 2003, as translated and downloaded from the Open Source Center website, document number CPP20030122000059.

after viewing photos on Google Earth of his unit. He took these photos to his party committee meeting and then instituted new security means at the next troop exercise. With resolution now reaching .6 meters to 1 meter from regional satellite photos, Google is now working with the same level of resolution as that possessed by military satellites just ten years ago. The results of his innovations (not described in the article) proved to be successful. Google Earth did not find his unit during the next exercise due to the camouflage methods he practiced, at least not on the pictures he downloaded for his unit.[316]

With regard to other measures to protect a unit from observation or to deceive an opponent, one of the best sources of historical information is the 1998 book High-Tech and Modern Warfare. Chief Editor Li Yuankui includes a section on jamming and deception, regarding both as effective methods to deal with missile weapon attacks. Jamming radar guidance systems, jamming against infrared guidance systems, and jamming against laser guidance systems are the main technical approaches advocated by Li. Camouflage protection includes concealing targets, reducing the exposure of targets to cause guidance systems to lose targets, and utilizing decoys. Natural obstacles (buildings, terrain, etc.), antiradar protective screens, antiradar camouflage coating materials, and releasing antiradar smoke screens were suggestions to help attenuate the transmission of enemy radar waves and thus hinder the detection of friendly targets.[317]

In late 2006, Bingqi Zhishi published an interview in which experts expressed their views on countering reconnaissance satellites with jamming and camouflage. Hua Rong, a reputed expert on the topic, was asked if the US EP-3 aircraft could pick up dialects and accents. Hua stated that the voice intercept system on the EP-3 has the ability to conduct electronic spoofing and use identical tones to distort the content of communications. Another expert, Zhao Feng, was asked if camouflage is still the primary means for countering reconnaissance satellites. Zhao stated that camouflage nets are now one and the same as the equipment itself and that nets can reduce detection by up to 90%. Furthermore, wide area smoke screen shielding is used for targets on large surface areas such as roads, bridges, loading zones, and assembly areas. The

---

[316] Jiefangjun Bao, Internet Version, 14 June 2007, as translated and downloaded from the Open Source Center website, document number FEA20070628207266.
[317] Li Yuankui, editor, High-Tech and Modern Warfare, Military Yiwen Press, January 1998, as translated and downloaded from the Open Source Center website, document number CPP20061220320004.

smoke must contain traces of counter-laser control and guidance and counter-electronic control and guidance.[318]

To camouflage cars, tanks, and ships on the move, spotted cloth was recommended with two different sides and with inset insulation stickers. There is also what Zhao referred to as water fume defilade camouflage. Water fumes have a strong attenuating effect on visible lights, near infrared, intermediate infrared, and lasers he notes. Ferrous sulfate, potassium sulfate, and other additives will increase the absorption of infrared and radar waves. Nano-ceramics and fire resistant composite materials can be used in place of traditional steel or aluminum structures to reduce radar signals as well. Low temperature camouflage paint can lower the temperature of some surfaces by 10 degrees Celsius or more. A heat sensitive bio-camouflage material turns red at 28 degrees Celsius; blue at 33 degrees; and black at low temperatures.[319]

When satellites track large targets, creating false appearances is a good technological solution. This can involve camouflaging with colors, changing shapes, creating false targets, covering buildings and equipment with camouflage, or camouflaging using shrubbery.[320]

The Stratagem-Deception Link

The Chinese PLA Officer's Handbook offers a link between stratagems and deception in defining the science of military stratagem. The definition notes that

> Strategic science, campaign science, and tactical science research the general principles of war guidance; however, the science of military stratagem researches how to flexibly apply these general principles in war. If the former's research focuses on the 'positive path,' then the latter focuses on the 'deceptive (or scheming) path'; if the former's research focuses on the 'constant,' then the latter focuses on the 'variable…'[321]

---

[318] Lan Bai, interview with Hua Rong and Zhao Feng, "Confronting Satellite Reconnaissance," Bingqui Zhishi, 1-31 December 2006, pp. 20-24, as translated and downloaded from the Open Source Center website, document number CPP20070111465001.
[319] Ibid.
[320] Ibid.
[321] Chinese People's Liberation Army Officer's Handbook, Qingdao Publishing House, June 1991, p. 197. Translation support for the term "science of military stratagem" was provided by Dr. John Tai, an expert on Chinese affairs. Dr. Gary Bjorge of the Combat

The stratagem-deception link is universal in China's military literature. For example, the Chinese authored book <u>On the Chinese Revolution in Military Affairs</u> has several intriguing sections of value regarding strategy, stratagems, and deception. An example is a statement by Major General Li Bingyan, a stratagem specialist, regarding the flood of information available to modern analysts:

> In the information age there is information excess, information overload, information surplus, information inflation, and information overflow, and that is a new factor of war friction. One philosopher said that absolute light and absolute darkness have the same effect—we cannot see anything. With information overflow, the modern battlefield is more richly colorful and an area for cunning and deception.[322]

That is, you can turn the lights out and be blind with no information; or you can shine xenon lights in someone's eyes and blind them with too much information. In either case deception is easy to induce with too much or too little information on hand.

To Li, deception is deeply embedded in strategy. He adds that high-technology warfare has hastened the appearance of many new characteristics of military strategy and, therefore, opportunities for deception. Six new features are most prominent:

- Methods are new.
- Information is abundant.
- Content is vast.
- Summaries are strong.
- Preplanning is detailed.
- Resolution is quick.[323]

Information technologies also allow deception theories to be tested in the lab.

Studies Institute of Fort Leavenworth, Kansas made his <u>PLA Handbook</u> available for use.

[322] Li Bingyan, "Applying Military Strategy in the Age of the New Revolution in Military Affairs," <u>On the Chinese Revolution in Military Affairs</u>, ed. Shen Weiguang, New China Press, 2004, pp. 2-31.

[323] Ibid.

Li's most intriguing example of the combination of strategy and deception is his hypothetical question "How do you make a cat eat a hot pepper?" His answer was as follows: "You can stuff the pepper down the cat's throat (the most difficult), you can put the pepper in cheese and make the cat swallow it, or you can grind the pepper up and spread it on the cat's back. The latter method makes the cat lick itself and receive the satisfaction of cleaning up the hot pepper."[324] The cat is oblivious to the end goal. This is strategy imposed by deception. Li thus indicates that when a successful strategic move is implemented, the person or nation responding to the move is unaware of its overall impact and significance.

Li's example reminds one of a scene in the movie "The Usual Suspects." In the scene, Verbal, a cripple who is really the notorious killer Keyser Soze, dupes the police into believing he is a pitiful accomplice and bystander with little purpose in life. When the police interview Verbal, he appears fearful of Soze's exploits and indicates that Soze is always able to disappear in an instant. In describing Soze's exploits Verbal states that "the greatest trick the devil ever pulled was to make us believe he does not exist." That is exactly what Verbal did to the police, using the strategy of deception by appearing to be something (a cripple) he wasn't. He made the police believe he (Soze) didn't exist. The police made fun of him and set him free. This type of deception, forcing the opposing side to do what you want while making it appear that they are holding the winning hand, represents the type of deception present in Li's cat and hot pepper example.

Li explains later in <u>On the Chinese Revolution in Military Affairs</u> that he defines IW differently than most IW specialists. He defines it as the use of information networks or informatized weapons to attack an enemy's cognition systems. Cognition systems include knowledge systems plus belief systems. Knowledge systems refer to decision-making systems that understand or observe verifiable phenomena and change the phenomena into perceivable reality. Belief systems refer to systems that carry out guidance for testable empirical information and for information and awareness that cannot be tested or is difficult to test.[325] In this case, attacking cognitive systems that observe phenomena or test information can be successful if it introduces deceptive material and thus alters the output of knowledge and belief systems according to Li.

---

[324] Ibid.
[325] Ibid.

Information (and therefore cognitive) supremacy allows for what Li terms "control power." One must prevent the enemy from understanding your information while you know everything about the enemy's situation. However, caution must be exercised here. The side with information inferiority can also control a situation. To do so, it must send information it wants the superior side to know and thereby influence it. If the inferior side sends nothing but misinformation to the superior side and the latter collects and acts on it, then the superior side is basing its next moves on bad information. Or the inferior side could use strategy to control an opponent. In this case, the inferior side would use information misdirection[326] (make it appear a force is attacking from one side when it is attacking from another) to control how an information superior force can gather information at will but make bad decisions if the information isn't credible. This is increasingly a deception method.

LTC Liu Aimin, a staff officer in a General Staff Department of the PLA, adds to this idea. He writes that deception warfare is rising quietly on virtual battlefields. By this he means the insertion of simulated information into an enemy's command and control system. This could cause an enemy to mistake what is false for what is true, or it could throw an enemy command and control scheme into chaos. Liu concludes that "network deception will become an important combat measure on the future virtual battlefield."[327]

Another IW writer who emphasizes deception is Dai Qingmin, former head of the Chinese General Staff's Fourth Department (electronic warfare). Two deceptive aspects of the information age that he stresses are network psychological warfare (NPW) deception and using deception to attain information supremacy.

Dai states that deception is an element of NPW. NPW is an operational activity that uses the theory of psychology, has computer networks as its carrier, and uses measures such as psychological propaganda, psychological deception, and psychological deterrence to break down the spirit of the enemy's military and people.[328] NPW combines traditional psychological-warfare thinking with modern network-information technology. This type of warfare can influence people's awareness and feelings about politics, economics, culture, and military affairs via propaganda, intimidation, deception, enticement, bribery, and deterrence.

---

[326] Ibid.
[327] Liu Aimin, "The Characteristics of Informationized War," Zhongguo Junshi Kexue (China Military Science), 1 August 2001, pp. 69-72, as translated and downloaded from the FBIS website on 20 November 2003.
[328] Dai Qingmin, p. 142.

Virtual deception is of particular concern as a network psychological technique. Technology can edit or piece together different visual scenes and environments to create a picture or incident that confuses truth with falsehood. Information can be published under any name. Most important, NPW is extremely timely. It can take place literally minutes after an event. This can make the substance of the material appear more pertinent, reliable, and effective without the benefit of a proper timeframe to check out the facts. In turn this has the potential to enhance psychological panic or create social chaos.[329] Thus virtual deception can produce immediate strategic results.

Dai continues by noting that in joint operations under high-tech conditions, in order to achieve information supremacy, a difficult series of steps must be initiated. Each of the two sides must use all capabilities to include information deterrence, information interdiction, information deception, and information contamination. This makes the substance of command and coordination extensive and complicated.[330] Dai's reasoning is that an adversary's attainment of total information supremacy can be contaminated and made counterproductive with the proper insertion of information that is deceptive and misleading.

In a later work in which Dai served as a co-editor with Xu Genchu, he continues to focus on deception. He and Xu write that to exert control over enemy personnel and weapon systems, it is necessary to use information deception and information obstruction.[331] Deception plays a key role in both strategic IW and battlefield IW.

Authors Zhou Yun, Zou Zhenning, and Yang Zhiqiang, writing in Yangzhou Jianchuan Dianzi Kuikang, discuss a deception technique that China appears to be applying to computer network warfare. They write that information-hiding technology (another term for steganography) can be applied to a friendly C4ISR system in the form of text, digitized audio and images, or some other means in order to conduct the covert transmission of secret battle command messages "in order to prevent leaking information and forfeiting a

---

[329] Ibid., p. 143.
[330] Ibid., p. 172.
[331] This author reviewed the Table of Contents and selected terms from Editor Xu Genchu and Director Dai Qingmin's Study Guide for Information Operations Theory, 2005, Academy of Military Science Press. Translation support was provided by a private company.

chance for combat."[332] Information-hiding refers to the means to hide specific information instructions, orders, resolutions, situation maps, and so on in a digitized information-related host such as text, digitized audio, graphic images, video frequency signals, and meteor burst communications.[333]

Deception techniques can be used in both strategic IW and battlefield IW. Strategic information warfare's main features include a broad scope, the involvement of special forms (psychological warfare, public opinion warfare, deception warfare, and media warfare) and targets (especially cognitive ones), and specialized personnel. The personnel involved in strategic warfare are not necessarily soldiers but may include civilian computer experts, international criminal groups, hackers, or terrorist organizations with ulterior motives.[334] Some Chinese theorists believe that the US uses strategic deception quite often. They site the use of the media and political declarations in regard to the war with Iraq as well as US actions in Kosovo as prime examples. They also often state that US descriptions of the China threat are strategic deception measures designed to get more money for the defense budget.

Battlefield information warfare is information warfare occurring within battle or combat space. It includes comprehensive countermeasures in warning, detection and reconnaissance, information transmission and processing, weapons control and guidance, operations command and control, camouflage, deception, interference, and military stratagems.[335] The creation of information power is a PLA battlefield goal. This can occur with the use of electronic camouflage, electronic deception, network deception, and "virtual reality warfare." The goal is to conceal what is real and reveal what is false and to confuse, deceive, and arouse the enemy. This causes the enemy's information to be false and judgments and decisions to be mistaken.[336] Deceptive defensive methods include the combined use of technical means and tactical measures of information deception such as signal source deception, signal channel deception, and information (content) deception.[337]

---

[332] Zhou Yun, Zou Zhenning, and Yang Zhiqiang, "Application of Information Hiding Technology in Computer Network Warfare, Yangzhou Jianchuan Dianzi Duikang, 1 February 2005, pp. 7-11, as translated and downloaded from the Open Source Center website, document number CPP20050819000214.

[333] Ibid.

[334] Xu and Dai, p. 82.

[335] Ibid., pp. 82-83.

[336] Ibid., pp. 85-87.

[337] Ibid., pp. 88-90.

112

Other Chinese authors who wrote on deception and stratagems are Niu Li, Li Jiangzhou, and Xu Dehui in an article titled "Planning and Application of Strategies of Information Operations in High-Tech Local War." They recommend applying deceptive schemes simultaneously or consecutively according to strategic or operational intentions. Actions taken should be coordinated and corroborated with one another to ensure the enemy will have no suspicion.[338]

These deceptive schemes and stratagems must interfere with, damage, or destroy listening and anti-listening measures, camouflage and anti-camouflage devices, reconnaissance and anti-reconnaissance measures, and stealth and anti-stealth measures in the planning phase of an operation. Stratagems may be included in information flows to sever channels of communication while keeping friendly flows of information secure. The processing phase requires stratagems that, in addition to their transmission task, include misleading and anti-misleading efforts targeting the enemy's information processing system to cause the enemy to make decision-making errors.[339]

Finally, Zhou Min, in a paper for the Sixth International Seminar on Sun Tzu's Art of War, notes that information warfare attack technologies include "information deception technology" which transmits false information to the enemy's information systems, various sensors, and media. This includes various deception and camouflage technologies and stealth technology, and it causes the enemy to make erroneous decisions when the information is received.[340]

Conclusions

China's long history has been embedded with references to deception since the time of Sun Tzu. Deception is used to achieve objectives and enhance concealment. The concept is now finding new uses through the addition of information technologies. Denial and deception techniques, countermeasures (anti-reconnaissance, anti-radar, anti-deception satellite systems, etc.), camouflage, and disinformation are major areas in which the Chinese focus their efforts. Jamming unmanned aerial vehicles and other surveillance assets

---

[338] Niu Li, Li Jiangzhou, and Xu Dehui, "Planning and Application of Strategies of Information Operations in High-Tech Local War," Zhongguo Junshi Kexue (China Military Science), Number 4 2000, pp. 115-122, as translated and downloaded from the FBIS website on 9 November 2000.
[339] Ibid.
[340] Zhou Min, "The Basis for the Psychological Warfare Planning of Sun Tzu," paper from the Sixth International Seminar on Sun Tzu's Art of War," November 2004.

are being researched. So are technologies designed to alter the outlines of friendly equipment. When utilized in conjunction with stratagems and camouflage, information technologies become very powerful allies for deception efforts.

Stratagems induce cognitive mistakes into an enemy force, particularly into an opponent's decision-making. "Killing with a borrowed sword" was originally used by feudal bureaucrats to cheat or outwit one another in a political sense. When extended to the military realm, it was used to divide and demoralize an opponent or to use a third party to defeat an enemy.

The stratagem makes use of another person or country to rid one of an adversary and enables the person "behind the stratagem" to avoid dealing directly with the person or country. One can also induce two enemies to fight against one another via stratagems without either side realizing they are being used for such purposes.[341]

The same emphasis on stratagems is apparent in Chinese military thought today except that it is updated to include the use of advanced information technologies. Using advanced surveillance equipment to obtain a top-down image provides a "vision" for stratagem developers to work from and with. Stratagem designers provide input for computers which then develop more strategic options. This requires sophisticated commanders who understand the most recent scientific and technological breakthroughs and how to integrate them with stratagems. Subjective initiative thus remains a key element for commanders to possess. Commanders must practice, master, and utilize stratagems as needed. Chinese deception practitioners realize that stratagems are no longer enough, that stratagems must be combined with technology to enable the optimum level of combat efficiency on the information age battlefield. Thus, proficiency is required in the use of techniques such as using electronic feints, camouflage, and jamming; virus attacks; and space satellite jamming and deception in order to lead the enemy to draw the wrong conclusions and enable friendly forces to attain the goal of strategic deception.

When reading Chinese deception theories, especially with their focus on innovation, it becomes obvious that high-tech means such as new camouflage technological advances will be used in conjunction with

---

[341] Liang Shoulei, "Kill with a Borrowed Knife—Third of the Thirty-six Stratagems," Guofang, Issue 5 2008, pp. 79-80, as translated and downloaded from the Open Source Center website, document number CPP20080819563003.

stratagems. Old means will also be used. Knowing that surveillance satellites are watching their every move, Chinese force deployments and maneuvers will inject abnormalities and ambiguities into their formations and advances to fool high-tech means much as they once fooled enemy reconnaissance agents on the ground. Speed of movement, hiding forces that appear only at the last minute, and other such techniques can be used to fool high-tech means by "showing the false and hiding the true." But that is not all. These same actions will be used in conjunction with political, diplomatic, and economic activities to affect other areas of the battlefield, such as finance and logistics. Integrating these issues introduces huge questions into the mind of the opponent as he tries to determine the where, when, and why of Chinese military actions.

There are, of course, risks associated with the use of stratagems and camouflage in the information age. One risk is whether one's advance contingency planning is accurate and complete and doesn't end up backfiring on the plan's developer. A second risk is the increased ability of satellite reconnaissance to uncover camouflage and other deception-type activities. A final risk is that enemy forces may be able to quickly identify and then annihilate friendly forces working camouflage issues.[342]

Another cognitive method to deceive but not discussed in this chapter is the use of online fake news. According to a report in Huanqiu Shibao, there is all sorts of fake news floating around China. Some of the news is produced by people who are concerned about China's military prowess and inflate news reports to make the military appear strong. Other reports are simply fake news that creates suspicion. Fake news confuses public opinion in China not to mention the violations of the professional ethics of news reporting. Fake news can also add fuel to the fire with regards to the China threat theory since, authors Jiang and Wang note, certain Western countries continue to trumpet threat theories.[343]

Thus, Sun Tzu's admonition that "all warfare is based on deception" continues to have digital legs into the twenty-first century. The danger is that in an age of high-precision weaponry, huge explosive power, and influence over financial flows, the consequences of deception operations gone bad are hundreds of times more dangerous to nations in particular and mankind in general. China is treading on this dangerous path with its reputed/alleged cyber

---

[342] Zhang and Shen.
[343] Jiang Xueqing and Wang Haifeng, "China Entangled in Fake Military News," Huanqiu Shibao (Internet Version), 7 July 2006, as translated and downloaded from the Open Source Center website, document number CPP2060905465001.

incursions, using deception devices, into other nations' computer network systems and equipment.

CHAPTER FIVE: INTEGRATING HIGH-TECH INTO CHINA'S CAMPAIGN STRATAGEMS

This chapter summarizes key points from editors Zhang Xing Ye and Zhang Zhan Li's 2002 book <u>Campaign Stratagems</u>. The focus of the chapter is the integration of high-technology systems and stratagems.[344]

The source of stratagem is knowledge.[345]

Introduction

When US planners gather to make decisions for an upcoming operation, they generate courses of action. A commander then examines his options and decides which course of action provides the best chance for success. Joint Publication 1-02, <u>Department of Defense Dictionary of Military and Associated Terms</u>, defines a course of action as

> 1. Any sequence of activities that an individual or unit may follow. 2. A possible plan open to an individual or commander that would accomplish, or is related to the accomplishment of the mission. 3. The scheme adopted to accomplish a job or mission. 4. A line of conduct in an engagement. 5. A product of the Joint Operation Planning and Execution System concept development phase and the course-of-action determination steps of the joint operation planning process.[346]

When Chinese planners gather to make decisions, they generate potential stratagems for use by commanders instead of courses of action. A stratagem is designed to mislead an enemy's perception, thinking, and emotional processes. By definition, it is designed to fool an enemy force whereas a course of action is designed to take advantage of a situation or, as the definition states, the scheme adopted to accomplish a mission. These definitions have been used for years but they differ in intent.

---

[344] This author reviewed Zhang Xing Ye and Zhang Zhan Li's <u>Campaign Stratagems</u> and credits the content, concepts, and ideas to the book's editor and authors of the individual chapters. The content of their book is reviewed based on translated material. Translation credit belongs to the Translation Doctors. Page numbers listed are those from the translation, not the original Chinese text.

[345] Zhang Xing Ye and Zhang Zhan Li, <u>Campaign Stratagems</u>, National Defense University, 2002, p. 249.

[346] Joint Publication 1-02, <u>Department of Defense Dictionary of Military and Associated Terms</u>, 12 April 2001 (as amended through 19 August, 2009), Internet version located at http://www.dtic.mil/doctrine/dod_dictionary/index.html.

Today, one factor that courses of action (COA) and stratagems share is a reliance on information technology (IT) components. Due to rapid advances in science and technology, the Chinese see IT as a valuable asset and feel that "the contents of the stratagem are continuously changing and renewing; the methods of stratagem are becoming more comprehensive; the space encompassed by the stratagem is multi-directional; and the technological contents in stratagem methods are unique."[347] Stratagems thus remain an effective way of planning for engagements with an opponent and for manipulating your opponent's reactions. A key factor is that stratagems are changing with the times and generating electronic campaigns to fool or mislead opponents.

To win with stratagem in the information age, the People's Liberation Army (PLA) believes that a strategist must link technology, strength, and stratagem to control victory. A good strategist is a good thinker who is innovative, creative, and flexible in his use of stratagems. A good stratagem performs a host of cognitive tricks, to include deceiving, controlling, inducing, arousing, creating, innovating, or manipulating another person or an entire staff.

There is a methodology for developing a good stratagem. The methodology requires the close study of an opposing force's field manuals, their wartime lessons learned, and their military philosophy. In the information age, this includes studying another nation's cyber plans and field operation procedures under high-technology conditions. Such study exposes preferred actions or defenses associated with electronic means that stratagems can exploit.

Some Chinese writers openly state that the primary battlefields of future stratagem will be computer networks.[348] Several nations (India, South Korea, Japan, Canada, Germany, England, Australia, and the US) have suggested that China may be getting a head start in this regard. They believe China has been harvesting information through the use of Internet reconnaissance stratagems. It is suspected that Chinese reconnaissance performs two functions: to expose an opposing force's military plans and to study the conditions and vulnerabilities that lead to the successful use of Internet attacks.

---

[347] Zhang and Zhang, p. 249.
[348] Ibid., p. 255.

The editors of the 2002 book Campaign Stratagems (a book published by China's National Defense University Printing House), Zhang Xing Ye and Zhang Zhan Li, note that "the side being in a strategically superior position, planning first and fighting later, winning through strategy, is able to fully promote high-tech superiority..."[349] A human's control over high-tech weapons and his or her ability to integrate weapons with stratagems makes one maximally effective.[350]

The focus of this chapter is on three aspects of Zhang and Zhang's book: the elements, factors, and features of campaign stratagems; creative ways to integrate high-technology and stratagems; and ways to manipulate the thought process of enemy commanders. The chapter ends with a description of how the new battles of wits between opposing commanders will involve the integration of high-technology equipment, virtual deception, and stratagems. These stratagems will reduce the accuracy of an opponent's analytical capabilities and his chances of success.

The Concept of *Moulue*

The editors of Campaign Stratagems state that in the Chinese language, *mou* is idea and stratagem while *lue* is plan and stratagem. Together, *moulue* is stratagem, trick, and/or tactic. The concept is adaptable to decision-making, subjective initiative, and deception, and it is applicable to politics, the economy, international affairs, and military affairs.

Elements, Factors, and Features of a Campaign Stratagem

Elements

Strategic stratagems are different than campaign stratagems. They operate on the highest level and are able to exert influence via politics, the economy, and international and military affairs. Campaign stratagems are more closely related to military affairs.[351] While deception and campaign stratagem are closely related, deception was and remains a subset of campaign stratagem. Deception is a means to manipulate an enemy force. However, the editors of Campaign Stratagems feel deception is the most important element of campaign stratagem.[352]

---

[349] Ibid., pp. 4-5.
[350] Ibid., p. 5.
[351] Ibid., p. 17.
[352] Ibid., pp. 16-17.

Li Qi writes in <u>Campaign Stratagems</u> that a campaign stratagem is when "the commanding officer, on the basis of certain strength, fully performs his subjective initiative, and manipulates and drives the enemy in the confrontation of intelligence, so as to create a situation that is favorable to his own troops but unfavorable to the enemy."[353] The goal of campaign stratagem is to achieve higher efficiency and to move away from a situation of simple static strength.[354] This requires taking advantage of differences in troop morale, topographical and meteorological conditions, and troop distribution and combat methods. The transformation from static strength to operational efficiency requires the exploitation of friendly campaign strength, enemy campaign strength, and the campaign environment. This analysis is commonly referred to as uncovering *shi*, the sum of all the factors that impact on the performance of the respective operational efficiency of two sides in a general confrontational situation.[355] Campaign stratagem aims at creating a situation unfavorable to the enemy and favorable to the friendly side. Planning and creating this situation is an element referred to as the "core of campaign stratagem application."[356]

A main element of campaign stratagem is the battle of wits. With action verbs such as manipulate, deceive, trick, and control, this is understandable. Editors Zhang and Zhang list three features of the battle. First is the competition of contradictory interests between two sides. Second is the manner in which decision-makers interact and attempt to influence one another. Knowing the decision-making process of one's opponent allows for the manipulation of that process. Third is the commander's personality and how he or she reacts under pressure in an uncertain environment. A study of hobbies, weaknesses, and flaws is "the best breach point for stratagems."[357] This implies that the Chinese conduct intense data-gathering on the personalities and interests of foreign commanders and leaders.

There are three campaign stratagem methods. The first method is to "break up and unify," changing the balance of static strengths of both sides in terms of time and space. The second method is to use special and regular forces, applying general concepts in irregular ways. The third method is to use deception and real actions (alternating between them). Integrating these three methods can improve chances of success. The editors periodically mention

---

[353] Li Qi, "Introduction to Campaign Stratagems," in Zhang Xing Ye and Zhang Zhan Li, <u>Campaign Stratagems</u>, National Defense University, 2002, p. 9.
[354] Ibid., p. 10.
[355] Ibid., p. 11. See Appendix Two for a detailed description of *shi* and some present day variants of the 36 stratagems.
[356] Ibid., p. 12.
[357] Ibid., pp. 12-14.

these three methods throughout the text. When applying these methods, creativity and flexibility become the soul of a campaign stratagem's "battle of wits" since stratagems are the primary means for the creation of a situation.[358]

Factors

Ancient Chinese history is flooded with examples of the use of stratagems. From their use, several factors have emerged. Those serving as the strongest factors for the development of campaign stratagems are the political environment, military thought and strategies, campaign development, military heritage and culture, and a commander's character.

First, a liberal and active political environment, from a Chinese point of view, encourages commanders to utilize their subjective initiative to the utmost. Such environments offer the use of the full range of creativity and flexibility instead of a passive, mechanical approach to stratagem which marks a corrupt and rigid political environment. Second, military thought has a significant impact on campaign stratagems. Advanced or new modes of thinking are required for stratagems to flourish, to employ flexibility, and to overcome enemy thinking. Third, campaigns develop when they take into consideration context and time, be it at the level of development of weapons and equipment, science and technology, or key operational methods. Most important for this work is that the development of science and technology offers many new innovations for the means and methods of campaign stratagem, where a combination of technology and stratagem is stressed. Simultaneously, the weaknesses and limitations of an enemy's high-tech equipment must be exploited.[359]

The fourth factor is culture and military heritage. The editors believe that differences exist among Chinese and foreign stratagem experts due to objective conditions, each nation's operational environment, and various cultural and military heritages. Under various conditions the concept of risk, for example, would be treated differently. Zhang and Zhang note that the PLA stresses being active and steady, pursuing certain victory, engaging in prudent early engagement (cyber reconnaissance?), encouraging reasonable risk-taking, and avoiding unfavorable decisive battles. PLA thought processes based on dialectical materialism introduce the alternating patterns of breakup and unity, the coexistence of special and regular forces, and a transformation between fake and real actions. In the opinion of the editors, Western armies use common sense as the primary component of their stratagem thought process along with

---

[358] Ibid., pp. 14-15.
[359] Ibid., pp. 44-46.

systems theory, information theory, control theory, images, intuitional thinking, associative thinking, and psychology and behavioral science.[360]

The fifth factor is the character of the commanding officer. Since stratagems are the product of creative thinking by the commander, he or she will be the subject of stratagems from the opposing side. His or her personal qualities help determine success or failure. Knowledge structure, modes of thought, and psychology determine what stratagems he or she will introduce or to which ones a commander will be susceptible. The editors cite Zhege Liang here, who noted that "if a commander has no knowledge in meteorology, geology, forecast, and yin and yang or he does not read dispositional plans and has no information about the entire campaign, he will be a very poor commander."[361] The most important element is the commander's mode of thinking, and commanders must master the dialectical method, logical thinking, thinking in images, three-dimensional thinking, unconventional thinking, and associative thinking if they want to make a proper analysis. These types of thinking enable a commander to comprehend the essence of a situation and apply the proper stratagems.

Features

Editors Zhang and Zhang listed six major features of campaign stratagems. The first, which has been mentioned already, is the battle of wits. In a battlefield situation there will be an intense struggle among commander's strategies, stratagems and counter-stratagems, and deceptions and counter-deceptions. Second, there will be a desire on both sides to speculate since there are few truly advantageous situations where a commander totally understands the battlefield situation in front of him or her. This requires speculation and the adoption of the best alternative. This also requires "profound knowledge of dialectical principles" and a familiarity with the thirty-six stratagems of war.[362]

Craftiness is a third feature of campaign stratagem. By craftiness is meant the use of ruses and manipulation. A fourth feature is innovation which is usually fused with craftiness. Innovation represents the vitality of campaign stratagem since it has no fixed form and is always changing.[363] A fifth feature of campaign stratagem is higher effectiveness. A stratagem's use lowers an opponent's operational efficiency and enables higher efficiency and thus higher effectiveness on the part of friendly forces. A final feature of campaign

---

[360] Ibid., pp. 46-47.
[361] Ibid., p. 47.
[362] Ibid., pp. 18-19.
[363] Ibid., pp. 20-21.

stratagem is risk. The danger in taking a risk is that if the enemy sees through a deceptive scheme then they can use it to lure friendly (Chinese) forces into a trap. Caution is urged as well as ambition.[364]

Creatively Integrating High-Technology and Stratagems

Wang Yungming, writing in Campaign Stratagems, notes that high technology developments such as precision-guided weapons, global-positioning systems, electromagnetic decoys, technologically advanced camouflage means, and advanced night vision equipment can be used to produce illusions (both real and virtual) and thus impact the development and use of campaign stratagems. These material developments induce change and result in new means to apply strategy. New battles of wits and improved wisdom and strategies are thus on the horizon. The soul of these revolutionary changes lies in the PLA's ability to innovate and apply information-based creative thinking.[365]

Two chapters in Campaign Stratagems focus on the development of stratagems under high technology conditions. Dr. Li Qi wrote Chapter Eight titled "Campaign Stratagem Application under High-Tech Conditions" and Colonel Liu Xubing wrote Chapter Nine titled "Demands on the Campaign Commander's Qualities When Applying Stratagems under High-Technology Conditions." Both authors, according to the postscript to the book, appear to work at the National Defense University's Campaign Research Office.

Li believes that the development of technology has opened up more avenues for the use of campaign stratagems. He develops his argument by offering both the positive and negative aspects of high technologies. First, he discusses the challenges that high technologies introduce. These are: the transparency of the battlefield offered by real-time intelligence transmission which offsets surprise and concealment; the rapid reaction capability that technology offers, making it difficult to take advantage of stratagems; and the high lethality of high-tech weapons, making operations more procedural and difficult to include the application of stratagems.[366]

---

[364] Ibid., p. 21.
[365] Wang Yungming, "Campaign Strategy and Objective Conditions," in Zhang Xing Ye and Zhang Zhan Li, Campaign Stratagems, National Defense University, 2002, pp. 181-182.
[366] Li Qi, "Campaign Stratagem Application under High-Tech Conditions," in Zhang Xing Ye and Zhang Zhan Li, Campaign Stratagems, National Defense University, 2002, pp. 215-217.

In spite of these challenges, Li feels there are many opportunities for the use of stratagems. He states:

> Under high-tech conditions, the expanded campaign space, the diversification of campaign forces, the proliferation of operational modes, and the complexity of engagement relationships have led to an increase in the number of uncertain factors in campaign operations, making campaign command more flexible. This in turn creates more opportunities for stratagem application in campaigns, opens up larger thinking space for strategizing, and provides more means for stratagem execution.[367]

Since the entire strategic depth is now open for exploitation, this creates more flexibility in target selection and the employment of stratagems. Engagement relationships are more complex due to the uncertain mix of symmetrical and asymmetrical operations.[368]

High technologies have enhanced the ability to cover and conceal forces as well as to expose them. On today's battlefield, reconnaissance and surveillance technologies must battle against camouflage and deception technologies. Also possible is the surprise introduction of new technologies on the battlefield that may play a decisive role in attaining success. Perhaps most important of all, high technologies have greatly assisted in the enhancement of command and control organization and, thus, future stratagem planning. The end result is that technology is now assisting stratagems to become more useful and contemporary.[369] Li Bingyan also stressed this point in On the Chinese Revolution in Military Affairs.

Li Qi writes that an understanding of "disposition" is crucial to stratagem application. This is similar to the concept of *shi* mentioned earlier and examined in Appendix Two. By disposition he is referring to force composition, battlefield environment, and campaign engagement methods. The concept of a force/superiority also has changed from concentrating forces such as troops and weapons to concentrating capabilities based on issues such as information mobility and long-range firepower. Capability superiority consists of the "mobile dispersal of entities (forces and weapons) and mobile concentration of capabilities." As an example, Li used the Kosovo conflict where forces were dispersed all over Europe, the US, and space, yet operational

---

[367] Ibid., p. 217.
[368] Ibid.
[369] Ibid., pp. 219-220.

capabilities were focused on an area to form theater superiority in what the US termed "global force integration." Long-range firepower and information mobility do not require the time or the infrastructure that ground troops require to concentrate assets on an area.

Li advocates the creation of a favorable battlefield posture that accounts for all dimensions (air, sea, land, electromagnetic, space, cyber, and psychological) and new developments (battlefield robots, smart unmanned strike platforms, laser weapons, electro-magnetic pulse weapons, smart weapons, and so on). Li pays special attention to the creation of information superiority by bringing into play high-tech systems. He notes that:

> It is particularly true when the military information system as represented by C4ISR systems integrates into an organic whole various departments such as command, control, communications, intelligence, operations, and support units, troops at different levels, various weapons and equipment and facilities, and various operational and support actions. Such a military information system optimizes the structure of campaign force systems, their functions and operational modes, and strengthens their collective operational capabilities…information superiority is also a precondition for seizing the initiative of the entire campaign and for winning the final campaign victory.[370]

Superiority in the air and outer space battlefields must be attained as well. They are closely linked with information superiority since "aerial-spatial integration and space informatization have linked air and space battlefields closely with information fields."[371]

Li considers the basic operational mode under high-tech conditions as the system-to-system contest. When analyzing enemy forces, then, it is necessary in Li's opinion to

> focus on disrupting enemy forces' systemic structures, breaking down their coordination and balance, and degrading their collective operational capabilities so as to create a favorable posture with our collective power trained against the enemy's local power, our

---

[370] Ibid., p. 223.
[371] Ibid., p. 224.

126

coordination against the enemy's confusion, and our balance against the enemy's imbalance.[372]

It is also important to match a campaign stratagem with the overall political, economic, and diplomatic situation. Only in this way can an enemy be convinced of an action, when the stratagem matches the strategic situation.[373] Perhaps this is similar to Wang and Qiao's concept in Chapter One of creating the proper moment in time or destiny.

Degrading an Enemy's High-Tech Intelligence and Reconnaissance Capability

In order to effectively utilize campaign stratagems, friendly forces first must neutralize or manipulate the enemy's intelligence, surveillance, and reconnaissance (ISR) assets. Then friendly forces must adapt to the characteristics of a battlefield informatization environment and correctly employ stratagems such as the divide-concentrate strategy to move the enemy, the use of direct-indirect strategies to surprise the enemy, or alternating the use of feints and real strategies to deceive the enemy. Finally, Chinese forces must find weaknesses in enemy high technology systems and exploit them.[374] Weaknesses can include blind spots in battlefield coverage (based on area coverage capabilities, time, or resolution), frequency or environmental constraints of certain systems, analysis constraints or bottlenecks (based on acquisition, transmission, and processing factors) of various military cultures, self-protection mechanisms or system stability factors of certain assets, and, most important of all, limitations on the decision-making capabilities of commanders. This latter point includes decision-maker problems such as understanding an enemy's true intent and resolve, being oversaturated with information so that analysis cannot be promptly or properly developed, and an overdependence on technical measures that ignores other sources of information. Each of these factors could limit the subjective creativity and innovation of a decision-maker who becomes paralyzed in the decision-making process.[375]

Li feels that there are several flexible means that make it hard for enemy ISR to collect information. They include the use of mobile targets, disguising real targets and creating fake targets, creating countermeasures, and exploiting weaknesses in an enemy's rapid reaction capability. One must study enemy reconnaissance patterns and learn to control blind spots, to deploy in a

---

[372] Ibid.
[373] Ibid., p. 228.
[374] Ibid., p. 229.
[375] Ibid., pp. 229-232.

dispersed manner to avoid detection or make deceptive shows of force, to mix false information with true information (to include exploiting the news media and computer networks to spread false information), to create information pollution and other forms of interference with an opponent's systems, and to imitate the features of real targets. The overall goal is to reduce the accuracy of an opponent's analytical capabilities.[376]

New technological breakthroughs could affect campaign stratagems in several ways. These include the achievement of surprise or placing an opponent in a very passive position where negotiation or destruction would appear to be the only options available. Technologies include super high-speed equipment such as planes that can outrun missile defenses, smart or unmanned technology that can operate in polluted or alien environments, laser or high-powered microwave equipment that could dispose of an opponent's space systems or electronic equipment, or digitized information technology that can offer better decision-making or knowledge options to the user. Developed during peacetime these technologies could catch an opponent unprepared.[377]

Creative operational methods put uncertainty in the minds of an opponent and this curtails their reaction time. Using multiple points of engagement along with irregular and non-linear forces and structures, respectively, also induce uncertainty. Friendly (Chinese) forces must take advantage of a quickened operational pace to throw an opponent off balance and to control battlefield initiative. They must select times and places most beneficial to friendly forces to strike weak points as appropriate. Network attacks, special operations, and strikes against an enemy rear area serve as indirect attacks in support of direct attacks.[378]

Manipulating Adversary Commanders

One section of <u>Campaign Stratagems</u> (perhaps the most important) is HOW to manipulate enemy commanders. The section opens by stating that not only high technologies, but also control theory, information theory, psychological theory, organization and behavioral theories, and the methodology of system engineering science are required to guide a campaign stratagem's planning and execution. This includes rationally selecting campaign objectives and, most important of all, deductively devising stratagem

---

[376] Ibid., pp. 233-234.
[377] Ibid., pp. 235- 236.
[378] Ibid., pp. 237- 238.

information to control the "intelligence-judgment-decision" process of the enemy.[379]

Li states that there are two ways to set campaign stratagem objectives. The first is to determine what kind of battlefield posture one intends to create through stratagem application. This is a core element of stratagem application. A battlefield posture should be developed in accordance with the needs of an operational method to enable its realization. This type of posture is different from an initial campaign posture and a final campaign posture. The second way to set objectives is to manipulate an adversary commander's judgments and to decide which judgments and decisions to use to control the enemy. This objective posturing includes one's own targets, enemy targets, and environmental targets. Targets are controlled (that is, deceived or manipulated) via the following models:

- Fortified control targets—support original judgments and decisions of enemy commanders
- Transforming control targets—shake original judgments and develop new judgments and decisions for an enemy commander under one's control
- Fuzzy control targets—increase fuzziness through excess information or contradictory information so that enemy commanders have trouble making correct judgments
- Compound control targets—use fortified-fuzzy types or transforming-fuzzy types together.[380]

To deductively devise stratagem information requires the meticulous preparation of special information. An information developer's application of a stratagem requires the creation, transmission, receipt, and processing of information as the developer intends. Stratagem information is based on the development of specific information for different control targets. Fortified-fuzzy control targets require three things: supporting information to affirm the correctness of an enemy's judgment; interfering information of an independent or contradictory nature; and the blocking of key information concerning friendly intentions. For transforming-fuzzy type control targets one should alter enemy commanders' original judgments. They must be fed negative information, supporting information, interfering information, and, as with fortified-fuzzy targets, key information must be blocked.[381]

---

[379] Ibid., pp. 239- 240.
[380] Ibid., p. 239.
[381] Ibid., p. 240.

There is a recommended procedure to follow to prepare special information. First, enemy commanders must be convinced of the truthfulness and rationality of stratagem information. To do this the following process must be followed:

- Stratagem information must conform to the current situation and overall campaign posture.
- Supporting, interfering, negative, and other information categories must be logical and support one another.
- Information coming from different angles pointing to one judgment will enable a commander to draw a clear conclusion.
- Deceptive information should have 80-90% true information.[382]

Second, the developer of a stratagem must do everything possible to control the enemy's method of intelligence analysis and processing. This will put the stratagem developer in sync with the enemy's "intelligence-judgment-decision" process and induce the enemy to make decisions as one would expect him to do. The stratagem must consider the following points:

- Take into consideration an enemy's belief system, formed from knowledge structures, subjective leanings, method of thinking, and personality to meet concerns and needs and influence judgments.
- Take into account the enemy's decision-making organizational mechanisms. Anticipate distortions and insert redundancy of key information. Influence the basic characteristics of key individuals and links such as the intelligence processing procedures of the enemy.
- Take into account when sending out the first batch of stratagem information that it should be highly seductive and influential, followed by supporting information.
- Take into account political, superior/boss, and environmental pressures and their impact on decision-making.[383]

The proper means to create and transmit stratagem information must be developed and coordinated. Stratagem information should reflect the coordination among various deployments, actions, or intentions that the information represents. Actual conditions must be used, and the location and timing of stratagem information must be coordinated. Stratagem development

---

[382] Ibid., p. 241.
[383] Ibid., p. 242.

and other campaign actions must also be coordinated to fit into an enemy commander's comprehensive view of the battlefield.[384]

Transmission channels must be carefully controlled. Those channels that China controls completely, partially, or not at all are called white, gray, and black respectively. If black channels uncover friendly stratagems, then the stratagems can be used against friendly forces. This is the worst of outcomes, to fall into a counter-stratagem trap. The use of white channels that the enemy considers as reliable is the best for transmitting information. Further,

> We [China] must pay a lot of attention to the cultivation and development of reliable channels during peacetime so as to develop enemy trust in these channels and to transmit stratagem information during war time. Under high-tech conditions, a strong enemy tends to highly trust, and heavily rely on, high-tech intelligence reconnaissance means. Therefore we must pay close attention to the characteristics of the enemy's high-tech reconnaissance means and study effective deceptive measures.[385]

Invariably, Li adds, some stratagem information will be distorted or lost due to an inability to properly predict certain subjective or objective responses. As a result multiple channels must always be utilized. In addition, feedback channels must be established to monitor the success or failure of the stratagem and to avoid having a counter stratagem developed by an enemy.

Friendly forces must keep track of stratagem conditions concerning their execution; enemy reactions; and external interference. This requires setting up proper review and reporting mechanisms, establishing a battlefield environment monitoring system, and creating channels to monitor and control enemy reactions. This latter point concerns both direct and indirect feedback channels. Direct feedback channels include:

- Cracking of enemy core secret codes through technical means
- Penetrating enemy core information networks allowing access to confidential communications
- Special agents who have penetrated the enemy's senior ranks
- Defectors from enemy core agencies.[386]

---

[384] Ibid., p. 243.
[385] Ibid., p. 245.
[386] Ibid., p. 246.

Indirect feedback channels refer to knowledge concerning enemy reactions via active intelligence and reconnaissance activities, which requires meticulous analysis to allow information extraction and prevent counter-manipulation. Exploratory, special, and firepower reconnaissance are other indirect methods.[387]

Adjustment and control measures should be in place to measure and adapt to feedback. Based on perceived deviations in enemy reactions, adjustments should be made if the enemy has not received stratagem information, the enemy is not paying enough attention to stratagem (information channels utilized are not valued highly by the enemy, etc.), the enemy rejects stratagem information (conflicts with other information, etc.), the enemy misunderstands the stratagem (information doesn't conform with the intelligence-judgment-decision process, etc.), or the enemy sees through a friendly stratagem.[388]

One control measure that Li recommends is the development of an authoritative institution that answers directly to the campaign commander and carries out the unified organization and coordination of campaign stratagem actions. This institution would plan stratagem application, de-conflict campaign stratagem actions and other campaign actions, organize stratagem's execution, and take responsibility to coordinate with relevant departments regarding stratagem application.[389]

High-Tech Stratagem Applications: Commander Characteristics

The author of Chapter Nine of Campaign Stratagems, Liu Xubing, writes that an army general must understand all types of connections and be knowledgeable in many fields. Otherwise he cannot be a wise general and implement stratagems. He adds that a reasonable/rational knowledge foundation is formed from two layers. The first layer is basic science, which includes the philosophy of Marxism, the basic culture of science, and the basics of military affairs. The second layer is the expertise layer, which includes the theory of tactics, the science of military leadership, and the theory of military stratagem.[390]

---

[387] Ibid.
[388] Ibid., p. 247.
[389] Ibid., p. 248.
[390] Liu Xubing, "Demands on Campaign Commander Quality When Applying Stratagems under High-Tech Conditions," in Zhang Xing Ye and Zhang Zhan Li, Campaign Stratagems, National Defense University, 2002, p. 261.

Knowledge is respected in China as reflected in the maxim that "the source of stratagem is knowledge." The military campaign is the most stringent test of a general's knowledge, strategies, and dispositions. Campaign stratagem is a highly creative thought process that tries to deceive an enemy's electronic eyes and ears. Instead of relying purely on the human brain, commanders now must rely on both human brains and computers. The computer allows commanders to control information after gathering, analyzing, and storing it.[391]

A sound stratagem is equated with half of the success of a campaign in Liu Xubing's opinion. Computers and the Internet further enhance chances of success of the "advanced technological stratagem."[392] Advanced technological knowledge, in particular information theory and system theory, has added wings to campaign stratagems and increased the reliability, accuracy, and timeliness of the application of stratagems. Stratagems use the scientific way of thinking, which is a way "to analyze, design, research, manage, and control such a complicated system and provide the most optimized ways and methods."[393] It is first necessary to defeat an enemy by thinking and only later by action.[394] Simultaneously, what is termed "psychological position exchange" must be accomplished. This means making a parallel comparison with the opponent's thought processes in order to imagine what he would do and think, that is to put yourself in your opponent's shoes.[395]

Conclusions

The use of a stratagem indicates that a force understands what the other side is about and how it thinks. The Chinese believe that new battles of wits are on the horizon, battles which involve high-technology equipment, virtual deception, and stratagems. New technological breakthroughs can impact the overall goal of a campaign which is to reduce the accuracy of an opponent's analytical capabilities. Operational stratagems may be pitted against strategic stratagems or an integrated operational/strategic stratagem may evolve that attempts to fool an opponent's analytical capabilities at each of these levels. The overall goal will be to control an opponent's "intelligence-judgment-decision" process. The Chinese are aware that the US, for example, relies on high-technology reconnaissance means and thus an effort will be made to influence them.

---

[391] Ibid., pp. 249-253.
[392] Ibid., p. 255.
[393] Ibid., p. 263.
[394] Ibid., pp. 263-264.
[395] Ibid., p. 265.

The use of high-tech stratagems in combination with other measures is something that US officials must be prepared to confront. According to Zhang and Zhang, the PLA is developing institutions to prepare and monitor the use of stratagems. The PLA actively studies the analytical processes of foreign militaries to apply the proper stratagem techniques against them. Stratagem techniques enable the PLA to create a situation that is favorable to them. They are preparing for future "battles of wits" now in peacetime.

Before stratagem techniques can be applied there must be a proper analysis of adversary decision-making processes and an in-depth knowledge of adversary culture and thought. It also requires an acquaintance with several types of thinking to include dialectical, logical, three-dimensional, unconventional, and associative thinking. An understanding of force disposition, or the force composition, battlefield environment, and campaign engagement methods of an adversary, is also crucial to stratagem application along with an understanding of wartime capabilities.

The three steps involved with utilizing campaign stratagems are neutralizing an enemy's ISR assets, adapting stratagems to the informatization environment, and finding weaknesses in enemy high-technology systems and thought processes. Five elements associated with successful campaign stratagem development are speculation, craftiness, innovation, high effectiveness, and risks. Deceptive techniques remain the most important for stratagem implementation. They put uncertainty in the mind of adversary commanders and thus curtail reaction time.

It is important that US national security personnel understand that these military capabilities can be applied to political, economic, and other fields of study. There may well be Chinese institutes in existence now that are involved in the study of campaign stratagems to manipulate US financial flows or to create other disruptive situations. The US and its allies must prepare now for such eventualities.

CHAPTER SIX: THE SICHUAN PROVINCE EARTHQUAKE: CRISIS MANAGEMENT AND INFORMATIZED WAR

This chapter summarizes the PLA's crisis management response to the May 2008 earthquake in Sichuan. This response was termed a non-war military action that practiced informatized-war concepts.

To develop informatized troops, thinking must not be conservative, troops must master diversified tasks, issues should be viewed from a strategic viewpoint, problems must be anticipated, and failures and mistakes should be immediately summarized and learned. Innovation will continue to drive the PLA.[396]

Introduction

Crisis management has long been a topic of interest to US analysts. For a host of reasons explained below, China's interest in and approach to the topic has been slow, sporadic, and unusually secretive. The Chinese weekly journal Liaowang published an article addressing the country's inadequate approach to crises in 2003:

> A crisis is an emergency condition created by unusual events. For the longest time, a crisis has frequently been regarded as a kind of partial and random phenomenon, and the majority of them have been handled by methods of monitoring; but what is lacking is the necessary advance attention, preventative monitoring, and control along the entire length of the process. If we are not able to consider the problem of crises in terms of strategic national security, the result will be that some emergency incidents, that originally could have been avoided or controlled, will ultimately and regretfully evolve into one series after another of social or even national crises.[397]

It is ironic that this article was published on the same day (May 12) but five years before the 2008 Sichuan earthquake.

---

[396] Editorial Department, "A Great Historic Responsibility—Written When Major Phased Victory in Anti-quake Operation is Achieved," Jiefangjun Bao, 4 July 2008, p. 1 as translated downloaded from the Open Source Center website, document number CPP20080707710001.

[397] Qiao Liang and Wang Xiangsui, "Controlling Crises—Expanding the Strategic Vision of National Security," Liaowang, 12 May 2003, No. 19, pp. 23-25, as translated and downloaded from the Open Source Center website, document number CPP20030522000092.

Today domestic challenges in the form of natural disasters (floods, chemical spills, earthquakes, and nuclear accidents) and social and religious unrest have served as motivators for China to rework its crisis management system, which they have done. A prime example is the 2005 "Regulations for Military Participation in Disaster Rescue" that outlined precisely what was expected of the People's Liberation Army (PLA) in times of emergency. Another motivating factor was information age capabilities which have improved the PLA response mechanism. Simultaneously, however, the information age has enabled average citizens to receive images of a disaster or news instantaneously via text messaging or cell phone videos, thus prohibiting government secrecy in its prior form and further motivating a reform of China's crisis management system.

Currently the Chinese appear to view crisis management as a type of non-combat operation that has links to informatized warfare. This is because non-war military tasks possess a "high degree of similarity and commonality with informatized war. Only by possessing the core military capability of winning local wars under informatized conditions will there be an abundant capability foundation for completing other military tasks."[398] Some of the core military capabilities referred to are satellite technology, GPS systems, and other high-technology devices that have enabled the PLA to become a modernized, high-tech force. These same assets enable the PLA to combat natural disasters in a high-tech fashion. Such advances allowed for a high-technology response to the Sichuan earthquake and enhanced information security preparations for the Olympic Games. Further, the conduct of military non-war operations associated with disaster management enhances military preparedness.

This chapter will look at the development of China's crisis management regulations and activities over the past few years. It will begin with a short historical perspective on the topic and then proceed to outline China's adjustments to its crisis management system in the recent past. It will conclude with a look at China's military response to the Sichuan Province major earthquake (also referred to as the Wenchuan earthquake, the county in which major damage occurred) of May 2008 and to the information age technologies that supported it.

---

[398] Jie Zhengxuan, acronym for the PLA General Political Department's Propaganda Bureau, "Engrave Loyalty to the Mission on the Earthquake-Fighting and Disaster Relief Battlefield," Jiefangjun Bao, 3 July 2008, p. 6, as translated and downloaded from the Open Source Center website, document number CPP20080703710001.

Studying China's crisis management system is important. It provides insights into the organizations, rules, and thought processes that the US will have to cooperate or contend with during a US-Chinese incident or over issues related to Taiwan. The study of the Sichuan earthquake crisis management incident, a remarkable PLA achievement for which the armed forces should be rightly proud, revealed that recent crisis management adaptations appear to be working. On the other hand, there remains a strong propaganda overtone to the Chinese understanding of transparency during such operations. Some old traditions live on.

A Short Historical Perspective

For over 50 years now, the US and China have faced off over Taiwan. This means that crisis management in one form or another has played a role in both sides' negotiating strategy for many years. However, China has been slow getting off the mark with a crisis management system and organization that is visible and consistent.

Xia Liping, Director and Research Fellow at the Center for International Strategic Studies, Shanghai Institute of International Studies, wrote an interesting article on US and Chinese crisis management techniques in 2003. Xia explains how the US and China might work together in the crisis management field. He outlines five categories that require a good crisis management mechanism, categories into which crises might be divided:

> The first category includes crises that arose from conflicts in China's periphery. One example is the Korean War. The second consists of crises ignited by the Taiwan question, such as the Taiwan Strait crises of 1955, 1958, and 1996. The third category is made up of crises caused by incidents such as the plane collision incident of 2001 and the embassy bombing incident of 1999. The fourth category consists of crises that arose over a domestic matter within China, such as the June 4 incident of 1989. The fifth category includes crises that arose over disputes involving the prevention of the proliferation of nuclear weapons.[399]

Since China and the US differ widely in culture, values, strategy, policy, and decision-making mechanisms, it is difficult to imagine a process

---

[399] Xia Liping, "Theory and Practice of Crisis Management in the United States—Sino-US Relations as Example," Beijing Meiguo Yanjiu, 5 June 2003, No. 2, pp. 73-86, as translated and downloaded from the Open Source Center website, document number CPP20030715000184.

acceptable to both countries. However, Xia believes important issues to consider in handling crises can be divided into three areas: first, that neither side humiliates the other or sets one's ambitions too high. The other side's vital interests must be accommodated when possible; second, that signals must be clear and interpreted correctly; and third, a crisis management mechanism must be developed amenable to coordination and proper information transmission. A set of decision-making procedures, rules of operation, and contingency plans must be put in place to serve as an information communication mechanism between China and the US.[400] In short, China and the US need to develop a crisis co-management system. However a crisis co-management system was not possible in 2003 when Xia wrote his article. China had no crisis management mechanism in place. Now two and a half years later China has started developing the organizations, mechanisms, and legal apparatus appropriate for crisis management discussions.

A turning point regarding formalizing the natural disaster and crisis management relationship appears to be the 2003 Sixteenth National Congress of the Communist Party of China. It was decided that China needed a comprehensive mechanism of warnings and emergency responses. The actual building of these systems, mechanisms, and laws would begin in 2003. In May 2004 the General Office of the State Council directed that the provinces must formulate their own master plans for emergencies. In July 2005 the State Council held a national emergency management conference. The first draft of the Law for Emergency Incidents and States of Emergency was developed as well.[401]

Chu Xiaobo was a Professor at the School of International Studies at Beijing University when he wrote on crisis management in 2005. He discusses why China needs an updated crisis management system. He believes that China has entered a period of social crisis fostered by four issues: the convergence of old and new systems; an accelerated pace of development; the requirement to synchronize Chinese actions with the globalization movement; and the recognition of crisis consciousness apathy on the part of government officials and the people. As a result China can no longer be passive in responding to crises nor can it address crises as they occur. A warning, response, and recovery system must be established.[402]

Chu believes a crisis is identified in the following way:

---

[400] Ibid.

[401] Chu Xiaobo, "An Urgently Needed Crisis Management System for China," China and World Affairs, No. 1, 2005, pp. 140-141.

[402] Ibid., p. 140.

Only events which threaten the fundamental construct of society, its values and its regulatory structure, and which occur when people must make critical decisions during periods of great temporal stress and uncertain circumstances such as natural disasters, disastrous accidents, public health incidents, and social security incidents.[403]

Crisis management, on the other hand, Chu notes should

not only entail responding to emergencies after they occur but should be a complete operational mechanism for the various stages of an emergency prior to an incident, the onset of an incident, during the progression of an incident, and following an incident. It should specifically involve a series of issues, such as gaining precise control over crisis prevention, prediction and warning, crisis information reporting and dissemination, situational control, and reducing losses; post crisis revival and reconstruction; and the summation of experiences and lessons learned.[404]

These new systems and laws are being enacted, it should be pointed out, while China is changing from autarky to an integration philosophy with world markets; and from being a peasant-based society to a large-scale urbanized society. In the past the compartmentalization of government agencies made it more difficult for people to organize themselves and get correct guidance. Without organization people become apathetic and difficult to motivate, leaving crises for the government to handle.[405]

This situation requires that China's leadership recognize the need for further improvements and additions in the powers and responsibilities between government and local government, among government agencies, and between the government and the people. Procedures must be public and transparent, Chu underscores, and supervision and assessments need to be evidence-based. These various realms of crisis management must be legally regulated as well from the perspective of the rule of law to help avoid abuses of power.[406]

According to Chu China needs to place its emphasis on the following areas: more emphasis on academic research; more individual government agencies working openly; more references available to individual government

---

[403] Ibid., pp. 141-142.
[404] Ibid.
[405] Ibid., pp. 144-145.
[406] Ibid., p. 149.

140

agencies and regions; and more lessons learned from different national realms. The need for a crisis management database organized at the national level is also mentioned. A keen watch on new crisis management trends should also be maintained.[407] Chu believes that with the experiences of the Olympics in 2008 in Beijing and the World Expo in 2010 in Shanghai that China will have a structural, legal, and mechanistic framework for crisis management in place within ten years, or by 2015.[408]

In February of 2006 China established a National Control Center for Coordinating Disaster Operations. The center has five functional departments and it intends to work out contingency plans for various potential accidents. The center hopes to publicize proper steps to take in case of large-scale accidents and thus help the self-protection capabilities of ordinary citizens. In 2005 in China there were 803,571 reported accidents resulting in 136,755 deaths. Traffic accidents were the leading cause followed by coal-mining deaths.[409]

Also in February of 2006 it was announced that the television program "24 Hours" would return for a second season. The show is dedicated to crisis management and shows how staff at the Emergency Management Center (EMC) teaches people to escape natural disasters and overcome crises. The TV series highlights fictional stories based on real life.[410]

Recent Crisis Management Measures

Events of the recent past have brought crisis management situations into sharp focus for the Chinese leadership. The severe acute respiratory syndrome (SARS) epidemic of 2003, combined with the benzene spill in the Songhua River in 2005, frequent coal mining disasters and floods, and recent social unrest all have enhanced the importance of the topic. However, the information age has also played a key role in promoting changes to China's crisis management system since technology has made it more difficult to keep crises secret. China's citizens want immediate answers from their leaders on developing situations that threaten their survival and that of their friends and relatives.

---

[407] Ibid., p. 153.
[408] Ibid., p. 156.
[409] Feng Yun, "Center Set Up for Disaster Operations," Beijing China Daily (Internet Version-WWW), 0019 GMT 22 February 2006, as translated and downloaded from the Open Source Center website, document number CPP20060222052020.
[410] "China's Ground-Breaking TV Series on Crisis Management Returns for Second Run," Beijing Xinhua, 1459 GMT, 9 February 2006, as translated and downloaded from the Open Source Center website, document number CPP20060209074025.

Zhong Kaibin, a Ph.D. candidate at Tsinghua University, wrote a very enlightening article on China's past and present crisis management system in the Winter 2007 edition of China Security. Focusing mainly on China's civilian crisis management system, it is without a doubt one of the best articles on the topic to date. Zhong lists ten problems with the system:

1. A lack of clarity about the roles that different levels and sectors should play
2. The persistence of self-interests among government players that place limitations on state actions where bureaucratic authority remains fragmented into horizontal and vertical power structures
3. Structural inefficiencies that result in an inability to create a clear crisis management system
4. A lack of clarity in the reporting process that discourages timely and accurate reporting
5. Legislative measures that inhibit effective communication both among government entities and with Chinese citizens (such as the over-classification of issues)
6. The failure to institute an atmosphere promoting accountability and transparency (officials reporting to superiors rather than to the people they govern)
7. The existence of power disparities and conflicts of interest between government and bureaucratic agencies
8. A lack of adaptability due to a dependence on an outdated national defense mobilization system
9. Tensions between a system designed to control and manage information and a society that is "wired" with access to more information than officials allow
10. The absence of an integrated command and control system, listed by Zhong as the predominant problem.[411]

As a result of these problems, China's responses to past crises have been wrapped in measures designed to deny or conceal them or to simply react without prior planning. Zhong notes that the former encourages the latter. If you don't have to deny incidents then there is less need to worry about planning for them. Instead of planning that could have included preemptive measures, simple reaction in secrecy was enough until the introduction of information age technologies to the citizenry. In fact, Zhong notes, the reactions became

---

[411] Zhong Kaibin, "Crisis Management in China," China Security, Winter, 2007, pp. 92-96.

propaganda opportunities for slogans such as "love the people—deliver water," exhortations of medical personnel as "angels in white coats," and the maintenance of an overall posture of "internal vigilance and outward calm."[412]

Government Inspired Change

However, change is underway. Chinese officials have recognized that the development of a sound emergency system is linked to the development of a harmonious society, the latter a necessity in any Chinese response. Several mechanisms have been put in place since 2003 following the SARS virus scare. In 2005, for example, the State Council created a national plan for emergency responses. Emergencies are graded according to severity and emergency levels. The latter is further subdivided into natural disasters, public health incidents, and social security crises.[413] In addition to this plan the government developed a national level Emergency Management Office (EMO) in December 2005 to help with planning and response mechanisms.[414]

Eight legal initiatives have also been implemented. The first initiative is an amendment to China's constitution that replaces the term martial law with "states of emergency." This allows the President to declare states of emergency and increases opportunities for state funding for specific crises. Second, legislation has enabled the creation of emergency management system procedures. Third, all national and provincial departments must have a news spokesperson. Fourth, natural disaster fatalities will no longer be classified at both the national and provincial levels. Fifth, emergency management issues are allowed on the government's official website as of 1 January 2006. Sixth, scientific research and technical training programs are undergoing revision. Seventh, measures for a more accountable and transparent government response in time of crisis have been created. Finally, more collaboration with the international community is encouraged.[415]

Zhong believes that China's new leadership is eager to introduce reforms and exert its authority to control crises. Much work still remains, however. Zhong notes that the government needs to shift its approach toward prevention issues and the development of a strong structural system. Further, China must continue to encourage collaboration between multiple levels of government and agencies, and China must promote a sound emergency response that builds better social capital (getting more citizens to participate

---

[412] Ibid., p. 97.
[413] Ibid., p. 98.
[414] Ibid., pp. 98-99.
[415] Ibid., pp. 99-100.

builds better social capital!). This latter point will require more interaction with non-governmental organizations (NGOs).

A Military Look at Crisis Management

The PLA has often been involved in the management and eventual solving of crises in China. Therefore it is no surprise that the Academy of Military Science's 2001 book <u>The Science of Military Strategy</u> devoted a small section to crisis control. A crisis, authors Peng Guangqian and Yao Youzhi note, is "a state of danger in which there is the possibility of confrontation or military conflict between or among nations or political groups."[416] It is also the outcome of the intensification of contradictions between two or more players. A crisis could turn into a war at any time. Therefore it is important to always strive for establishing and improving upon a nation's crisis control mechanism.[417] Internal crises were not mentioned in the book even though the PLA is a major support element for most internal crises.

US military joint publication 1-02, <u>Dictionary of Military and Associated Terms</u>, defines a crisis and crisis management as

> Crisis—an incident or situation involving a threat to a nation, its territories, citizens, military forces, possessions, or vital interests that develops rapidly and creates a condition of such diplomatic, economic, political, or military importance that commitment of military forces and resources is contemplated to achieve national objectives. (JP 3-0)[418]

> Crisis Management—measures to identify, acquire, and plan the use of resources needed to anticipate, prevent, and/or resolve a threat or an act of terrorism. It is predominantly a law enforcement response, normally executed under federal law. Also called CrM. (JP 3-28)[419]

In Peng and Yao's book, the term "crisis control" is used instead of crisis management. It is defined as "the control of tense political and military situations caused by the intensified contradictions of national interests." It is an

---

[416] Peng Guangqian and Yao Youzhi, editors, <u>The Science of Military Strategy</u>, Military Science Publishing House, Academy of Military Science of the Chinese People's Liberation Army, English version, 2005, p. 202.
[417] Ibid., pp. 202-203.
[418] <u>Department of Defense, Dictionary of Military and Associated Terms</u>, Internet version, updated through 30 May 2008, p. 141, located at http://www.dtic.mil/doctrine/jel/new_pubs/jp1_02.pdf.
[419] Ibid.

initiative taken by a crisis management subject to control various uncertain and unstable factors in the whole process of crisis.[420]

Peng and Yao note that a crisis is a dynamic process that goes through stages of inception, escalation, de-escalation, and termination. With regard to crisis control strategy, they list five aspects:

- Develop confidence-building measures in peacetime to prevent the emergence of a crisis (periodical meetings of high-ranking officials, notices of military exercises, regular meetings on border issues, and hot line links)[421]
- Increase transparency and information exchanges (make the following items public: diplomatic policy, military strategy, defense strength, troop buildups, and state of readiness figures that do not endanger national security)[422]
- Enhance personnel exchanges and contacts (hot lines, mutual visits, etc.)
- Develop joint disarmament and arms control mechanisms (maintain the strategic balance and control the arms race)
- Lay down regulations and set up supervisory organizations (develop scientific norms and supervisory organizations to ensure regulations are practiced).[423]

If all of these mechanisms fail and the crisis is inevitable, then negotiations must ensue to hold off the crisis, prevent its escalation, and promote its termination.[424] Principles of crisis control include finding an intersection point for the interests of both sides, compromising as appropriate without concession, keeping uninterrupted communication with each side open, and adopting coercive measures (weapon embargos, economic sanctions, and military blockades) as required to prevent negative influences.[425] In short, "dialogue is better than confrontation, political settlement is better than settlement by force or threat of force, and preventive controls are more desirable than coercive ones."[426] From a western point of view, most analysts would agree with Peng and Yao. US politicians would most likely hope that

---

[420] Peng and Yao, p. 202.
[421] Ibid., p. 203.
[422] Ibid., pp. 203-204.
[423] Ibid., p. 204.
[424] Ibid.
[425] Ibid., pp. 205-206.
[426] Ibid., p. 206.

145

such ideas are made part of both Chinese and US views of crisis management matters.

The 2005 Military Regulation on Disasters

In 2005 the State Council and Central Military Commission of China wrote a military regulation designed to better control crises. The "Regulations on Military Participation in Disaster Relief" serves both as a military statue and as a national defense mobilization law for the PLA. Composed of 18 articles, it represents the "first law that has been issued since the founding of New China to standardize the military's participation in disaster rescue efforts. The disaster rescue rules bring the military's fulfillment of its mission of disaster rescue onto the legal track."[427] The rules focus on the following four areas:

- Standardizing coordination between the military and civilian aspect of government when the military participates in disaster rescues
- Providing explicit stipulations on the power and the procedures for arranging military forces and a joint command between the civilian government and the military
- Providing explicit stipulations on guarantees regarding preparations, expenses, and supplies of materials and apparatuses for disaster rescue
- Providing a legal foundation for the establishment of an emergency mechanism for combating natural disasters.[428]

Three articles in the regulation are of particular importance and have direct applicability to the PLA's coverage of the Sichuan earthquake. First, the armed forces are directed to accomplish the following tasks in Article 3:

- Rescue, transfer, or evacuate stranded personnel
- Protect the safety of important targets
- Rescue and transport important goods and materials
- Participate in specialized emergency rescue work, including emergency road repair, marine search and rescue, nuclear-biological-chemical rescue, epidemic situation control, and medical relief

---

[427] "Legal Basis for Troops' Participation in Disaster Relief," Jiefangjun Bao, 21 June 2005, p. 1, as translated and downloaded from the Open Source Center website, document number CPP200506221000093.
[428] Ibid.

- Eliminate or control other significant dangers and disastrous situations and, if necessary, assist local people's governments in advancing reconstruction work after the disaster.[429]

An analysis of newspaper coverage of the earthquake (still to come in this chapter) offers a look at whether the PLA accomplished these tasks.

Second, the regulation notes in Article 12 that "the local people's governments and the troops carrying out disaster relief tasks shall share information about epidemic situations with each other and jointly undertake sanitation and epidemic prevention work."[430] Thus it appears that efforts to control information and state secrets are now less strict than in the past. In fact residents were told the opposite, to "share information."

Finally, in Article 15 of the regulation the following was reported:

The propagation and coverage of significant disaster relief operations participated in by the army shall be organized and implemented uniformly by competent authorities of the state and the army. News agencies conducting interviews and reports on disaster relief operations participated in by the army shall observe relevant regulations stipulated by the state and the army.[431]

Two Recent US-Chinese Military Crises

In addition to responding to natural disasters, China must have contingency plans prepared to respond to real world crises. Two such crises have arisen with the US, both coming before the implementation of the 2005 crisis management regulation. However the incidents remain important for lessons learned.

Writing in 2007, Chinese analyst Wu Xinbo discussed Chinese crisis management techniques against the US in two specific and fairly recent military incidents. Wu is a professor and deputy director of the Center for American Studies at Fudan University in Shanghai. He notes that China exhibited five features in its responses to two crises with the US: the US Air Force's accidental bombing of the Chinese embassy in Belgrade, Yugoslavia in

---

[429] Text of regulations provided by the "regulations" page of the Jiefangjun Bao website, translated and downloaded from Open Source Center website, document number CPP20061003325003.
[430] Ibid.
[431] Ibid.

May 1999 during the conflict over Kosovo; and the 1 April 2001 mid-air collision between a US EP-3 aircraft and a Chinese F-8 fighter over the South China Sea. The features China displayed were: paying attention to assigning responsibility for the crisis, emphasizing sovereignty and national dignity, appreciating symbolic gestures greatly, responding relatively slowly, and placing the Foreign Ministry in charge of crisis management.[432] (Wu used the term management instead of control in his article)

First, China attempts to find out who is responsible for a crisis. If China believes the other side is at fault, it will ask for reparations to fix the situation. Second, national dignity is very important to China since it was humiliated by the West and Japan during its recent history ("recent" is from the beginning of the twentieth century). Third, since national dignity is so important, Beijing may pay more attention to symbolic gestures than to substantive issues. Fourth, China's relatively slow response may be due to the slow flow of information within the Chinese system and the implementation of an ad hoc crisis management system for each new crisis. Finally, with regard to having a Foreign Ministry spokesman, there is good and bad news. The good news is that there is only one voice speaking. The bad news is that, due to the lack of a good coordination mechanism, the spokesman may not get all the necessary information he or she requires.[433]

Wu recommends in his conclusions that the US and China set up some channel of communication ahead of time to handle such future crises. He also recommends quiet diplomacy over public diplomacy and keeping in mind a broader picture of bilateral relations when dealing with one another in crisis situations, thereby avoiding any temptation by one side or the other to seek excessive near-term gains and causing irrevocable damage to Chinese-US relations.[434]

Also of interest for researchers and policy makers is Wu's listing of sources for further study. He cites the Center for Crisis Management Studies at China's Institute of Contemporary International Relations (CICIR) in Beijing, for example. Such centers should provide a nice meeting point for countries to carry out Wu's recommendation for developing channels of communication for further study of crisis management mechanisms.

---

[432] Wu Xinbo, "Understanding Chinese and US Crisis Behavior," The Washington Quarterly, Winter 2007-08, p. 71.
[433] Ibid., p. 72.
[434] Ibid., p. 74.

The PLA's Response to the Sichuan Earthquake of May 2008

The photos of the PLA's earthquake relief effort on the pages of journals such as <u>PLA Pictorial</u> or <u>National Defense</u> tell the story of an armed force dedicated to mission success. The officers and soldiers responded professionally to the earthquake in a very short time to rescue survivors, bury the dead, provide tents for the homeless, and clear away debris to begin the rebuilding process. Photography from the stricken region shows vividly the difficulties in terrain elevation and harsh weather conditions under which the PLA operated. Soldiers marched miles with food bags on their backs and formed human chains to move people from isolated areas to safety. Measures for medical care, the control of epidemics, and the maintenance of law and order were also worked out. China should be proud of the response of its military.

To US listeners of National Public Radio (NPR), it appeared that the Chinese press coverage of the Sichuan earthquake of May 2008 was a fairly transparent event that offered a look at a contemporary PLA crisis management operation. By chance NPR had reporters in the area when the earthquake struck, and these reporters had some access to local citizens. The Chinese press, on the other hand, did a good job of not just covering the stories of human interest but also in covering the PLA's high-technology response.

Before the Quake: Preparatory News Articles

Zhong Kaibin noted that the PRC has revamped its crisis management system and is working to improve its function and utility in several ways. The military did not fall behind in this matter and appeared to implement some of the 2005 "Regulations on Military Participation in Disaster Relief" in Sichuan. Here are some news reports in 2008 before the quake that support this fact:

1. On 18 February, <u>Zhongguo Guofang Bao</u> reported that the city of Ningbo had proceeded with its merger of military command centers and government emergency management centers. A combined military and civilian underground command center allows for sharing information among government offices, public security departments, and frontline troops. Reportedly the center has nine systems, to include a command automation system, a communication system, a closed-circuit television monitoring and control system, and a support system.[435]

---

[435] "Summary: Ningbo City Merges Military, Civilian Emergency Command Centers," <u>Zhongguo Guofang Bao</u> (Internet Version-WWW) in Chinese, 18 February 2008, as

2. On 18 February, <u>Jiefangjun Bao</u> reported that troop capabilities in anti-disaster and relief work were being honed. Reporters were told how troops had responded to the heavy snow and sleet that had hit southern China a few weeks earlier. They made maps for relief work and repaired communication lines or used back-pack satellite telephones while waiting for repairs. Units also established a disaster information system with civilian units in order to get real time information to disaster-stricken areas.[436]

3. Qiu Yanhan, a delegate to the March 2008 Communist Party Conference in Beijing, proposed the establishment of a Permanent National Command for Emergency Management at one of the sessions. Such an institution would have five parts: first, the Legislative Suggestion and Routine Management Center to command, coordinate, operate, and manage emergencies; second, the Command and Coordination Center to work out preplans for handling national emergencies and to impose a unified command; third, the Monitoring and Situation Prediction Center to conduct monitoring, prediction analysis, and risk assessment of emergencies; fourth, the Training and Supervision Center to provide guidance to ministries and commissions as well as emergency response training and examinations; and fifth, the Resources Planning and Management center to mobilize and organize social forces, arrange and store materials, conduct post-disaster recovery and reconstruction, and so on.[437]

China's Immediate Response—May 2008

In May 2008 the PLA's rescue and disaster relief organization swung into high gear. Movement of PLA forces and resources near Sichuan began on the day the earthquake struck (12 May) and some reached the region within 24 hours. Other forces from more distant regions began to arrive on the 13th and 14th.

---

translated and downloaded from the Open Source Center website, document number CPP20080221711004.

[436] Wang Yongxiao and Li Yongfei, "SAF Base Hones Troops' Capabilities in Anti-Disaster and Relief Work," <u>Jiefangjun Bao</u> (WWW-Text), 18 February 2008, as translated and downloaded from the Open Source Center website, document number CPP20080221702009.

[437] Qian Xiaohu and Yang Zurong, "Delegate Proposes to Establish a Permanent National Command for Emergency Management," <u>Jiefangjun Bao</u> (WWW-Text), 4 March 2008, as translated and downloaded from the Open Source Center website, document number CPP20080305702006.

On the evening of 14 May, the State Council deployed 70 helicopters and 30 transport planes to the disaster region. More than 1170 wounded were evacuated that day. On 15 May, as rain stopped in the earthquake area, air rescue units conducted operations that were reported to be the largest in Chinese history. The rescue operation utilized airborne troops, air drops, and helicopter landings. Some 4,000 paratroops were taken to the disaster region. The State Council announced that rescue units had reached all 58 towns and townships severely hit by the earthquake.[438]

One of the first reports about technological support referenced satellite repositioning on 16 May. The Xian Satellite Monitoring and Control Center shifted to its emergency response mode to "ensure the security of the operations of fifteen satellites of nine types."[439] It was reported that in the four days after the quake, the center input more than 10,000 emergency application orders to ensure continuous coverage.[440]

On 17 May it was reported that the PLA Quake Relief Command Group held its third meeting since the quake. Xu Caihou, Vice Chairman of the Central Military Commission (CMC), analyzed the current situation, made plans for future work, and instructed troops to follow Chairman Hu Jintao's instructions (following the latter's trip to the area). General Staff Chief Chen Bingde, head of the PLA Quake Relief Command Group, encouraged troops to stay well organized and efficient. The prevention of epidemics was highlighted along with opening blocked roads, performing logistic support work, and transporting supplies.[441]

Also on 17 May Zhongguo Xinwen She reported on eight new kinds of search and rescue techniques. These included vertical drilling, slant hole

---

[438] Hou Yongde, "Chinese Military Took Actions Simultaneously in Three Ways to Perform Air Rescue Mission on the Largest Scale in History," Zhongguo Xinwen She, 1217 GMT 15 May 2008, as translated and downloaded from the Open Source Center website, document number CPP20080515338016.

[439] Sun Haixia, "China's 15 Satellites of Nine Types Provide Support for Dealing with the Quake and Providing Relief to Disaster Victims," Xinhua Domestic Service, 0435 GMT 16 May 2008, as translated and downloaded from the Open Source Center website, document number CPP20080516716009.

[440] Ibid.

[441] Cao Zhi, "PLA Quake Relief Command Group Further Studied Rescue and Relief Work—Xu Caihou Attended the Meeting and Delivered a Speech," Xinhua Asia-Pacific Service, 1359 GMT 17 May 2008, as translated and downloaded from the Open Source Center website, document number CPP20080517136019.

digging, and crawlspace searches. The methods were developed by the Second Artillery Corps' engineering regiment.[442]

On 18 May the China Daily reported how China's Beidou-Compass Satellite Navigation and Communication System had helped the armed forces to navigate and how it had offered message communication services where other communication means had been destroyed. The first team into the area from Beijing (entering on 15 May) had 20 cell-phone-like terminals.[443] On 18 May a spokesman for the Chinese Ministry of Defense made his first appearance (ever) to announce information on what the armed forces were doing in the area. The spokesman's appearance indicates that China's legal announcement of improvements to the crisis management system (reported above by Zhong Kaibin that all national agencies must have a spokesman) is in fact being implemented. At the briefing, held by the State Council Information Office, reporters were briefed on the PLA's work in the area of the quake. Yao Yonzhu, a researcher at the Academy of Military Science, stated that the spokesman's appearance indicates that the armed forces are establishing an image of self-confidence and responsibility among the people.[444] On 20 May a reporter wrote that China's quick response indicated an increasing maturity in setting up an emergency management system. The transparent response has helped prevent widespread panic and maintain social order. Sending Premier Wen Jiabao immediately to the region also demonstrated the leadership's immediate focus on the problem area, the reported noted.[445]

Unofficial statistics indicate that by 1200 on 18 May, 113,080 PLA and Armed Police troops had been dispatched to the area; 1,069 aircraft sorties were flown; 92 military trains were dispatched; and 78,000 metric tons of materials were transported to the region. In addition, 21,566 people were pulled from the

---

[442] Xia Hongqing and Wang Yongxiao, "Second Artillery Corps' Creative Search and Rescue Makes Show of Force in Beichuan Earthquake Relief Effort," Zhongguo Xinwen She, 1317 GMT 17 May 2008, as translated and downloaded from the Open Source Center website, document number CPP20080517136015.

[443] Wang Xu, "Beidou Satellite System Delivers," China Daily (Internet Version-WWW), 0008 GMT 18 May 2008, as translated and downloaded from the Open Source Center website, document number CPP20080518968005.

[444] Hao Yalin, Chang Lu, and Wang Yushan, "Spokesman for the Chinese Ministry of National Defense Makes First Appearance at a News Briefing to Announce Information on the Armed Forces," Xinhua Asia-Pacific Service, 1403 GMT 18 May 2008, as translated and downloaded from the Open Source Center website, document number CPP20080518163008.

[445] Ding Yuanzhu, "Crisis Management Ideas Come of Age," China Daily (Internet Version-WWW), 0005 GMT 20 May 2008, as translated and downloaded from the Open Source Center website, document number CPP20080510968040.

rubble; 34,051 people were provided medical treatment; 205,371 earthquake victims and tourists were transferred to other locations; 301 metric tons of material were airdropped; and 557 kilometers of roads were repaired.[446]

On 19 May Zhongguo Guofang Bao reported that government bodies were to coordinate with national defense mobilization commissions (reserve forces) and the people's armed forces departments dedicated to help keep forces rolling into the area and supporting relief operations. Disaster relief troops from the Beijing, Nanjing, and Jinan Military Regions already on-station need this support.[447] That same day Senior Colonel Hu Changming, the Ministry of Defense spokesman, along with other General Staff Department chiefs, held a press conference in the State Council Information Office to brief the country on the earthquake relief effort. He noted that the Chengdu, Jinan, Lanzhou, Beijing, and Guangzhou military regions as well as forces from the Navy, the Air Force, the Second Artillery Corps, and the People's Armed Police Force had participated in the relief effort. More than 110,000 transportation vehicles and generators were transported to the region along with 115 medical teams and anti-epidemic and psychological emergency response teams. Over 3,319,000 pieces of clothing, food, warfare rescue medication, and tents were distributed.[448]

Apparently a four-tier response mechanism was established: the military earthquake resistance and disaster relief command center; the joint earthquake resistance and disaster relief command center in the Chengdu Military Region (MR); the command center for each jurisdiction; and the operational and disaster relief forces. Additionally, five jurisdictions were created. Ma Jian, deputy chief of the Operations Department of the General Staff Headquarters, briefed the military deployment for the earthquake. This was the first time one can remember the PLA providing such a briefing. Ma did so using a map that had five circles drawn for the five jurisdictions. The first jurisdiction covered the Wenchuan, Lixian, Maoxian, Yingxiu, and Dujiangyan counties and townships with 23,950 servicemen from Jinan MR and some from the Chengdu MR. The second jurisdiction covered Chongzhou and Pengzhou counties with 11,792 servicemen from the Jinan MR. The third jurisdiction

---

[446] Hao, Chang, and Wang.

[447] Shen Yan, "Provide Strong Support to Disaster Relief Troops," Zhongguo Guofang Bao Online, 19 May 2008, as translated and downloaded from the Open Source Center website, document number CPP20080626711002.

[448] China View News, "For the First Time China Releases its Military Deployment for the Earthquake Relief," Zhongguo Pinglun Tongxun She (WWW-Text), 19 May 2008, as translated and downloaded from the Open Source Center website, document number CPP20080519436001.

covered Shenfang and Deyang counties with 14,290 servicemen from the air force, marines, and some Chengdu MR troops. The fourth jurisdiction covered the Beichuan, Mianzhu, and Anxian counties with 8,838 servicemen from the Chengdu MR and the Second Artillery Corps. The fifth and final jurisdiction covered Pingwu and Qingchuan counties with 25,082 servicemen from undisclosed units covering an undisclosed area. The Armed Police reportedly had 25,770 people involved in the relief operation.[449]

Poor construction of the non-government buildings in the region caused intense criticism from concerned citizens. They felt that government buildings were better constructed than school houses, which led to the deaths of many students. Corner-cutting, corruption, and lack of government oversight were named as well. A suggestion for the future was to ensure that whoever was responsible for the construction of a building was identified as well as those who managed the construction. It was suggested that a plaque with the names of these responsible individuals be placed on each building.

On 22 May a Jiefangjun Bao report noted that the Communications Department of the General Staff, under the command of Chen Dong, ordered emergency-response plans to be activated shortly after the 12 May quake. This included the activation of satellite phones, faxes, and other data communication means. At 1520 on 12 May China Central TV opened a reserve image transmission channel in the Beijing-Chengdu direction. By 1800 on 14 May 3,000 hand-crank electric generators and 2,000 satellite phones had been issued to the Chengdu MR.[450]

Luo Yuan, deputy director of the World Military Research Department of the Academy of Military Sciences, and research fellows Li Xiaodong and Yu Xiaopeng discussed militarized rescue under conditions of a major natural disaster. They stated that the toughest challenge comes from meeting the demands for rapid, effective, and accurate fulfillment of various tasks. They noted that establishing quick response times, making correct decisions, and offering accurate information are as important as accumulating material supplies for victims.[451]

---

[449] Ibid.

[450] "Beijing Calling Wenchuan!" Jiefangjun Bao, 22 May 2008, as translated and downloaded from the Open Source Center website, document number CPP20080523088003.

[451] Bie Tuolun and Bao Guojun, "On Militarized Rescue in Major Natural Disasters," Jiefangjun Bao (WWW-Text), 1019 GMT 26 May 2008, as translated and downloaded from the Open Source Center website, document number CPP20080527705004.

In early June Chinese reporters began noting some of the PLA's achievements in restoring normalcy to the earthquake region, an area described as three times the size of Taiwan or some 100,000 square kilometers. The PLA transported the injured, repaired roads and bridges, participated in restoring electrical power and water supplies, cleaned up debris, performed disease-prevention work, erected tents, provided medical care to throngs of victims, set up temporary schools, and dispatched soldiers to be teachers among other duties. The reporters stated that the Western media was reporting positively on the PLA response and that the concern shown by the troops demonstrated the true meaning of the phrase that the military is made up of the "sons and brothers of the common people."[452]

Another staff reporter covered the equipment that the PLA utilized in the rescue effort. The Mi-26 multi-purpose heavy-lift helicopter was cited for its ability to transport the necessary machinery and supplies across the Yansai Lake on Tangshan Mountain. Winged paragliders were used to jump from heights of 5,000 meters. The Beidou-terminal of the satellite navigation system became the only method of transmission for some rescue units that did not have standard-issue maritime satellite phones. PLA aerial reconnaissance planes flew over the disaster zone to take photographs and measurements with one-meter resolution. The General Surveying Administration produced large-scale, three dimensional maps for command posts. An emergency response mobile communications vehicle, with a 14-meter high rotating surveillance camera and satellite receivers, was used to send pictures and to conduct videoconferencing. Medical field tents/containers treated and released, on average, one earthquake victim every eight minutes. Two blood transport vehicles shuttled between the front and rear areas, and more than 40 clean water trucks arrived in the disaster area.[453]

On 10 June CCTV-7's military-themed documentary program reported on the dispatch of several elite communication units from the Chengdu Military Region to the quake area. One of the eight-man teams was the first to reach Wenchuan on the morning of 14 May, and it established an observation and communications post. Staff officer Colonel Wang Kai stated that maritime

---

[452] He Liangliang, "Let the World Recognize the PLA," <u>Renmin Ribao</u> (Overseas Edition) (Internet Version-WWW), 6 June 2008, p. 1, as translated and downloaded from the Open Source Center website, document number CPP20080606710004.
[453] Bai Chanping, "Sophisticated Military Equipment Demonstrates Remarkable Abilities in Disaster Areas," <u>Jiefang Ribao</u>, 10 June 2008, as translated and downloaded from the Open Source Center website, document number CPP20080612066009.

satellite phones issued to the detachment did not work. The satellite dish worked only when a radio and satellite communications post was established three kilometers away from the magnetically charged conditions of the area.[454]

On 12 June a series of articles were published in the Chinese press about the context and response of the PLA to the earthquake. One article was devoted to two changes in the coverage of this type of natural disaster. First were the government and general public responses and second the coverage of the media. With regard to media coverage it was noted that the Tangshan earthquake of 1976, occurring as it did during the 1966-1976 Cultural Revolution, received only a short notice from the Xinhua News Agency. The agency reported only that a quake had taken place 180 kilometers to the west of Beijing. There were 240,000 killed in that quake. When the earthquake struck on 12 May 2008, media coverage had changed dramatically. Within ten minutes, CCTV started non-stop coverage of the disaster and relief work. Some 550 journalists, including 300 foreign reporters, converged on the area. China now has 221 million web surfers, the world's largest contingent and a huge number of cell phones conducting text messaging. Blogs, chatrooms, and image-sharing portals are prevalent everywhere. Through this network concerned citizens expressed their opinions and recommendations.[455]

The military command in Chengdu set up a command post ten minutes after the quake and the Central Military Commission started to coordinate its response three minutes later. Premier Wen Jiabao was on a plane headed to the area within two hours and President Hu Jintao braved aftershocks to visit shortly thereafter. The Red Cross of China invited the National Audit Office to supervise the distribution of funds. Nearly 6 billion US dollars worth of funds and goods were collected from factories and local citizens. Instead of refusing international assistance the government accepted military-use synthetic aperture radar images for disaster assessments. And, for the first time in history, flags flew at half-staff from 19-21 May in national mourning for quake victims, some 80,000 in all, and there was a moment of silence for them throughout the nation as well.[456]

---

[454] "Junshi Jishi Program," CCTV-7, 1203 GMT 10 June 2008, as translated and downloaded from the Open Source Center website, document number CPP20080704017001.

[455] Wang Aihua and Yu Zheng, "Interpreting the Sichuan Earthquake—A Different Picture from What We Used to See," Xinhua, 0222 GMT 12 June 2008, as translated and downloaded from the Open Source Center website, document number CPP20080612968118. It is now thought that one out of every two Chinese now has a cell phone, or some 650 million people.

[456] Ibid.

The date 12 June also marked the end of a four-part series in Jiefangjun Bao on "The Great Wenchuan Earthquake—Practice and Thoughts on Non-War Military Actions" that ran from 9-12 June. This theme was prominent in the wrap-up discussions of political organs in the July time period.

Part One of the series gives credit to the high-quality and efficiency of command organs "guided by informatization." The article notes that the all-army emergency–response command mechanism was turned on just 13 minutes after the quake occurred. This implies that the army has not lost its superiority after the introduction of informatization in many units.[457] Part Three of the series (Part Two could not be located) emphasized diversified capabilities. The PLA is now not just a defensive organization, the article noted, but one ready to assist with diverse security threats and military tasks. Specialized technical troops have new capabilities to contend with disasters.[458] Part Four of the series noted that the PLA activated an equipment emergency-response support mechanism that offered different types of technologies and equipment and high scientific-technical content. This included the Xian Satellite Observation and Control Center, which readjusted 15 satellites to map meteorological cloud photos and for geomorphology surveys and navigational services. Remote-sensing aircraft and unmanned aircraft flew to "information isolated islands" to rescue people. Finally, the National Development and Reform Commission activated its emergency equipment support plan and the Sichuan Province National Defense Mobilization Committee requisitioned engineering machinery.[459]

Also on 12 June a Xinhua article discussed the ten "firsts" of this natural disaster. These included:

- A top-grade emergency response (by the National Commission for Disaster Reduction)

---

[457] Wu Tianmin and Ding Haiming, "Key Lies in Building Core Military Capabilities, Jiefangjun Bao (Internet Version-WWW), 9 June 2008, as translated and downloaded from the Open Source Center website, document number CPP20080611088001.

[458] Wang Yongxiao, Hu Junhua, and Xia Hongqing, "Diversified Capabilities Needed to Accomplish Diversified Tasks," Jiefangjun Bao (Internet Version-WWW), 11 June 2008, as translated and downloaded from the Open Source Center website, document number CPP20080612088001.

[459] Yu Chunguang and Wang Weidong, "Innovative Mechanism Increases Equipment Support Efficiency," Jiefangjun Bao (Internet Version-WWW), 12 June 2008, as translated and downloaded from the Open Source Center website, document number CPP20080616088001.

- A large domestic and foreign donation of money and material
- A large volunteer effort
- The participation of foreign rescue personnel
- A national mourning for ordinary citizens
- The development of a post-quake reconstruction regulation (on 8 June)
- The impression that China's coverage of disasters was now more transparent. The mobilization of other provinces to help in the reconstruction effort
- A gigantic quake-formed lake was drained
- It was the first use of a large-scale airlift.[460]

At 1600 on 12 June the third news conference on the progress of the PLA in its disaster relief effort was held. PLA spokesman Senior Colonel Hu Changming said the military was moving and settling the masses, rescuing and treating the wounded, guarding against secondary disasters, carrying out sanitation and epidemic prevention measures, rendering psychological intervention services as required, helping the masses resume production and school students resume classes, and assisting local governments in maintaining social order.[461]

A 16 June report by the PLA's Political Department was typically Marxist in nature and only of propaganda value. The article stated that the fundamental guarantee for succeeding in disaster rescue was the wise leadership of the Party Central Committee, the Central Military Commission, and Chairman Hu Jintao. Furthermore citizens were instructed to serve the people wholeheartedly and believe in a sacrificing and dedicated spirit. Core values of military personnel must be taken as the contemporary topic in political work. Party building in military units must continue and ideological work is encouraged.[462]

---

[460] "'Factbox': the 'Ten Firsts' that Follow China's Massive Quake," Xinhua 1618 GMT 12 June 2008, as translated and downloaded from the Open Source Center website, document number CPP20080612968312.

[461] Li Jingpo, "Ministry of National Defense News Spokesman Briefs Chinese, Foreign Reporters on Situation of Earthquake Control, Disaster Relief by Liberation Army, Armed Police Force," Jiefangjun Bao (Internet Version-WWW), 12 June 2008, p. 4, as translated and downloaded from the Open Source Center website, document number CPP20080611271001 1.

[462] "Carry Forward the Disaster Relief Spirit, Promote Military Force Building in All Aspects—Learning from the Disaster Rescue and Relief Actions for the Political Work in the Armed Forces," Qiushi Online, 16 June 2008, as translated and downloaded from the Open Source Center website, document number CPP20080619710003.

The success of the military effort in neutralizing many of the consequences of the Sichuan earthquake prompted the most interesting article with strategic significance for Western countries. Author Zhao Zongqi wrote that building the core military capabilities of the PLA should translate into a capability to win local wars under informatized conditions and that the PLA should work to be able to deal with two strategic tasks and two major crises simultaneously. Reform measures will accelerate this improvement in capabilities. This will ensure social stability and the neutralization of threats from the West to split China. Chinese overseas investments and the potential need to evacuate persons living abroad require China to adjust its force deployment with intensified monitoring and control of strategic passageways and a strengthening of China's sea mobilization and escort capability.[463]

Another area in which the PLA played a significant role was psychological counseling. The PLA, since May 20, assigned 360 psychological experts to the quake area. By 22 June the Joint Logistics Department of the Chengdu Military Area Command said it had offered face-to-face counseling to over 5,000 people affected by the quake. The psychological counseling included what was termed "affection and peace exchange phones" and established "expert psychological consultation stations." Materials for psychological treatment were distributed and crisis intervention counseling was offered to people suffering from fear, anxiety, and depression.[464]

On 26 June it was reported at an unmanned aerial vehicle (UAV) convention in Beijing that UAVs had been used in several surveillance operations over Yansai Lake during relief operations. This provided important information for emergency disaster relief teams who were involved in draining the lake. However, the exact type of UAV used in the operation was not mentioned. Some characteristics of the relatively new "Dark Sword" UAV model were described for convention participants.[465]

---

[463] Zhao Zongqi, "What Kind of Capabilities Do We Need to Accomplish Diversified Tasks," Jiefangjun Bao, 17 June 2008, as translated and downloaded from the Open Source Center website, document number CPP20080623088002.

[464] Guo Xi, "Chengdu MAC Assigns 360 Psychological Experts to Quake-Hit Areas," Jiefangjun Bao, 0930 GMT 24 June 2008, as translated and downloaded from the Open Source Center website, document number CPP20080625705005.

[465] Lu Desheng, "Approaching 'Winged Scout' and Examining the Development of China's Unmanned Aerial Vehicles," Jiefangjun Bao, 26 June 2008, p. 12, as translated and downloaded from the Open Source Center website, document number CPP 20080626710006.

In another 26 June technical report, repair vehicles were highlighted. The Second Artillery Force's rescue and relief troops utilized two types of repair vehicles. First, reporters described the optical cable rush repair vehicle, with cutting-edge hi-tech equipment for monitoring and testing optical cable failures and maintenance. It can identify failures and provide information on the wear and tear of optical cables, offering repair methods as well. Troops were able to unblock up to 100 kilometers of cable within three hours. Second, reporters described the communication and command support vehicle. It earned the nickname of "clairvoyant" and "clairaudient" in the quake rescue and relief operations. The vehicle has the ability to transmit voice, data, fax, and images, and it can map out scenarios, receive information, and offer technological diagnosis and inquiries.[466]

Another 26 June article noted that political workers from the Jinan MR used text messaging to relay information and conduct propaganda and agitation work. The political officers also formulated a "basic flow of daily grass-roots political work," and officers installed phones for troops to call home.[467]

A final 26 June article stressed both the value of the Internet and the need to self-govern it with morality and respect for the law. Hu Jintao stated that the Internet is the key channel for people to get information. It serves as a link for the party and the government to keep in contact with the people. In this regard the Internet played a very important role during the Sichuan earthquake, as the network media produced propaganda and open and transparent situational reports. Timely reports had a psychological calming effect on the population. These government reports were the first since the enactment of the "Regulation on Information Publicity" of May 2008. Media networks need to guide public opinion and build networks of trust. One Internet user posted "10 prohibitions" as a means for developing a User Self-Governance Convention on the Internet. This convention can become the key for network management the

---

[466] Xia Hongping, Zhang Qi, and Guo Yichuang, "New Equipment Excels in High Efficiency in Quake Rescue and Relief," Jiefangjun Bao, 26 June 2008, as translated and downloaded from the Open Source Center website, document number CPP20080627702005.

[467] Yang Jilong, Meng Bin, and Huang Kunlun, "Becoming Fast, Solid, and Flexible— Experience and Enlightenment of Several Political Workers at the Earthquake Fighting and Disaster Rescue and Relief Front," Jiefangjun Bao, 26 June 2008, as translated and downloaded from the Open Source Center website, document number CPP20080704088002.

article noted. The Internet "should not and cannot free itself from the restraints of law and morality."[468]

On 27 June the PLA Air Force noted that it was producing three-meter wide and fifteen-meter long aerial photographs displaying the seismic belt of Longmen Mountain. To date the air force had taken 1,850 aerial photographs, produced 16,550 objective maps, and 431 copies of photographic interpretation reports. Four aircraft were used for aerial monitoring.[469]

Cleaning Up After the Damage—July 2008

The General Political Department reported the majority of the PLA's lessons learned from the earthquake experience in the July timeframe. It was obvious that several themes were being pushed by the propagandists. On 1 July it was reported that maritime satellite telephones were issued to publicity departments of the political departments of some major military units. This device is a mobile satellite communication device that covers the entire world and is used by all major media in their news reporting. It can perform real-time transmission of information in writing, photograph, voice frequency, or visual frequency.[470] Also on 1 July, the Communist Party's journal Qiushi Online discussed the PLA's ability to conduct diversified tasks. The authors were Li Shiming, the Commander in Chief of the Chengdu Military District Joint Earthquake Relief Headquarters and Commander of the Chengdu Military District, and Zhang Haiyang, Secretary of the Party Committee for the Chengdu Military District Joint Earthquake Relief Headquarters and Political Commissar of the Chengdu Military District. Therefore the article has a specific propaganda overtone but also one of first-hand knowledge of the situation.

Li and Zhang's article stated that by 17 June the PLA had transferred more than 1.34 million victims and rescued over 3,336 survivors. This effort

---

[468] Ji Guilin and Zhang Feng, "President Hu Jintao's Important Speech on Intensifying Construction of New Media and Elevating Statuses and Functions of Network Media to a New Strategic Height—Historically Sacred Missions and New Development Chances Request Us to Intensify Construction of Network Media and to Form a New Pattern for Guiding Public Opinions," Jiefangjun Bao, Online, 26 June 2008, p. 11, as translated and downloaded from the Open Source Center website, document number CPP20080626710004.

[469] Zhang Jinyu and Li Jianwen, "PLA Air Force Puts Air Survey Means into Service in Quake Rescue and Relief," Jiefangjun Bao, 27 June 2008, as translated and downloaded from the Open Source Center website, document number CPP20080630702002.

[470] Zheng Wanxuan, "GDP Issues Information Transmission Equipment to Quake Rescue Troops," Jiefangjun Bao, 1 July 2008, as translated and downloaded from the Open Source Center website, document number CPP20080702702002.

moved the people to shouts of "the PLA has come" and "the Party's forces are here" according to their reporting. More than 20 specialized rescue, chemical defense, engineering, medical and epidemic prevention, reconnaissance, and communications branches were employed during the relief operation. More than 643 million square meters of polluted areas were purified and sterilized. Initially, 25,805 civil-military reserve personnel were utilized and by 17 June the number exceeded 48,000. The army and armed police mobilized 4,696 helicopters and dispatched 96,800 medical personnel.[471] With regard to high-technology equipment it was reported that

> Radar life-detection instruments, hundred-ton hydraulic jack devices, special rescue helicopters, naval satellite phones, data terminal communications, and other high-tech equipment were used in great quantities in the rescue operations. The army activated 15 satellite measurement and atmospheric charts of nine different types, implemented satellite communications, conducted general surveys of the earth's surface, provided navigation service, and promptly provided the disaster area's important information to headquarters. Satellite networks were employed for long-range diagnosis and treatment of wounded.[472]

On 3 July the PLA's General Political Department (and in particular it's Propaganda Bureau), praised the PLA's relief efforts. Typical Communist Party propaganda verbiage was used to describe the soldier's achievements. The soldiers worked with "resolve," carried out a "sacred mission," wrote a "historic chapter of loyalty to the mission," drew "ideological and political nourishment" from the relief struggle, and carried on the "excellent tradition of obeying the Party's commands." The soldiers forged a combat spirit that showed no fear, the propagandists continued. Soldiers had the "hot blood of heroism" flowing in their bodies, they wholeheartedly served the people, and they served as the "sons and brothers of the people." The Propaganda Bureau added that manifest in mission execution is the PLA's excellent tradition of listening to and obeying the Party's commands, serving the people, and heroically putting up a good fight generation after generation.[473]

---

[471] Li Shiming and Zhang Haiyang, "Vivid Earthquake Rescue Efforts Illustrate the PLA's Ability to Complete Diversified Military Missions," Qiushi Online, 1 July 2008, No. 13, as translated and downloaded from the Open Source Center website, document number CPP20080703710009.
[472] Ibid.
[473] PLA General Political Department's Propaganda Bureau, "Engrave Loyalty to the Mission on the Earthquake-Fighting and Disaster Relief Battlefield," Jiefangjun Bao

The Political Department noted that the PLA delivered battlefield awareness, information transmission, search and rescue, and medical treatment, and it integrated logistical support capabilities. Wind and Cloud, Resource, Beidou, and other such satellites provided continuous information support. The General Political Department itself organized psychological service expert groups to treat and guide victims of psychological stress. Finally, the department underscored the necessity of enhancing domestic public opinion and propagandizing to other countries. Military media in particular should be organized and capable of reporting on disaster recovery progress. Strategic arrangements of the Communist Party and Central Military Commission must be transmitted to settle the hearts of the people and encourage the morale of the officers and men.[474]

On 4 July the Jiefangjun Bao Online website (the website of the daily newspaper of the Central Military Commission of the PLA) produced an editorial that discussed the "phased" victory of the PLA's earthquake operation. It laid the groundwork for the discussion by reiterating Chairman Hu Jintao's mission for the PLA of "providing three things and playing one role." The army must provide a force guarantee for the Party to consolidate its governing status, provide a security guarantee for safeguarding this important strategic opportunity for development, and provide backing to safeguard national interests. The role the PLA must play is in preserving world peace and promoting common development. Building a diversified force allows the PLA to achieve its three historic missions: pushing forward modernization, accomplishing the reunification of the motherland, and safeguarding world peace. [475]

One way the PLA has done this, the editorial notes, is through boosting capabilities to conduct and win local wars under informatized conditions. Military training is conducted under informatized conditions, high-tech weaponry has been developed, and a new type of military personnel cultivated. These types of soldiers are needed not only to fight natural disasters but other non-traditional threats as well, such as terrorism, secessionism, and extremism. During the relief operation, command, information, mobilization, and support

---

Online, 3 July 2008, p. 6, as translated and downloaded from the Open Source Center website, document number CPP20080703710001.

[474] Ibid.

[475] Editorial Department, "A Great Historic Responsibility—Written When Major Phased Victory in Anti-quake Operation is Achieved," Jiefangjun Bao, 4 July 2008, p. 1, as translated and downloaded from the Open Source Center website, document number CPP20080707710001.

capabilities were important conditions to meet in order to accomplish non-military operations. These operations had characteristics of informatized warfare. To develop informatized troops, thinking must not be conservative, troops must master diversified tasks, issues should be viewed from a strategic viewpoint, problems must be anticipated, and failures and mistakes should be immediately summarized and learned. In this manner innovation will continue to drive the PLA.[476]

On 8 July it was reported that the military transportation system of the PLA distributed information-based equipment such as the dynamic monitoring system, the Beidou satellite command system, and onboard intercommunication equipment to relief troops to enhance command and control capabilities of commanders.[477]

On 12 July, in an article on the current situation in Sichuan, it was noted that there were nearly 70,000 people dead, 18,000 still missing, and five million people homeless. Temporary housing was projected to be available for all of the homeless by 1 August. Farmers complained that their land was "borrowed" by the government and they fear it would not be returned to them. One Beichuan villager, pointing to shelters on farmland, criticized the PLA for flattening their land to build temporary shelters with no explanation of what would happen afterwards. This was one of the very few criticisms of the PLA. Seismologists were also blamed for not providing prior warnings, and some media were banned from discussing the issue of poorly constructed schools (termed "tofu buildings").[478]

With regard to political work, a 16 July report in Qiushi Online (the semimonthly official journal of the Communist Party of China's Central Committee) discussed what types of propaganda the Air Force's Propaganda Department utilized in the response phase of the Sichuan earthquake. First, an information and propaganda center was established that launched mobilization, propaganda and education, and "on-site inspiration." The department promoted slogans such as "heart to heart, breath to breath, live and fight together" and "carry forward the spirit of a sharp knife and compete to be a vanguard in earthquake resistance." The department also performed the following tasks:

---

[476] Ibid.
[477] Zhang Cheng and Fan Juwei, "Quake Relief Transportation Troops Create Traffic Safety Records," Jiefangjun Bao, 8 July 2008, as translated and downloaded from the Open Source Center website, document number CPP20080709702001.
[478] Klaudia Lee, "Rubble and Strife," South China Morning Post Online, 0023 GMT 12 July 2008, as translated and downloaded from the Open Source Center website, document number CPP20080712968034.

- Edited short "endure the quake" and disaster relief messages
- Produced "endure the quake" and disaster relief posters and postcards that were distributed to relief personnel
- Organized professional production crews to go deep into the disaster zone for on-site interviews
- Compiled and distributed education outlines and manuals
- Organized psychological experts to go to sites for consultations
- Established a website called "All the People of One Mind, Strength from Unity"
- Distributed daily the "Situation Update of Political Work" and the "Air Force Newspaper."[479]

The article also noted that political cadres served as team leaders and they could be found everywhere, especially in the most dangerous locations. The article concluded by stating that comprehensive use should be made of modern media means, such as TV, radio, and networks to increase the information content and political work of propaganda units.[480]

On 16 July the military's earthquake-fighting and disaster relief command group held its sixth conference at which the results of the relief effort were discussed. The conference reported that they studied and implemented the intentions of Chairman Hu Jintao and the Central Military Commission (CMC) regarding how to carry out the relief action. The conference felt the military's emergency response mechanism was timely, as was the establishment of a disaster relief command group. Unit actions were well-planned as were logistics and ideological and political work. Since 17 June, when the fifth conference took place, the CMC has switched its core work to the "eight tasks" outlined by Chairman Hu. The conference speakers noted that

> currently, earthquake-fighting and disaster relief emergency-response and emergency-handling tasks have basically been completed, victim groups have basically been settled in, disaster area production order has progressively been restored, the social situation is stable, and gearing

---

[479] Ge Shanbin, Liu Jiguang, and Luo Suying, "Several Revelations from the Earthquake Resistance and Disaster Relief Battle with Respect to Strengthening Force Building," Qiushi Online, 16 July 2008, No. 14, as translated and downloaded from the Open Source Center website, document number CPP20080716710013.
[480] Ibid.

165

support to the needs and restoring and rebuilding are going exactly according to plan.[481]

The Chengdu Military Region Joint Headquarters issued an article on 22 July that stated the PLA established a joint command structure for the first time during the Sichuan earthquake relief effort. The lessons learned from this non-combat operation are that commanders must: grasp the objective of operations from an overall perspective; aim to link and implement central and unified command; establish clear and smooth relationships (cooperation and coordination) as the most important element in organization and command; and emphasize resolute decision-making and flexible command. It is also necessary to integrate several transmission methods to be effective, to include wired and wireless communications, satellite communications, meteorological survey support, navigation systems, and the command information networks of other military regions. These non-combat military operations must be incorporated into the legal track as soon as possible. To insure there are no communication problems, work must be accelerated on optical, short wave, satellite, and mobile communications-centered methods. Integrated information networks must be expanded and strengthened and all information must be capable of being quickly, stably, securely, and privately transmitted. Subjective hopes must be consistent with objective realities.[482]

On 23 July, a psychological service team of the Xi'an Political Institute of the PLA discussed its rescue and relief operation during the Sichuan earthquake. Its aim was to develop a psychological "protection mode" that would help troops operate when involved in rescue operations. The eight man team stated that there are six parts to the mission, and they listed three in the article: defining the basic task of psychological protection, improving the system of work for psychological protection, and improving the composition of the team that is to perform psychological protection.[483]

---

[481] Shi Yongcai, "Military Earthquake-Fighting and Disaster Relief Command Group Holds Sixth Conference—Chen Bingde Gives Speech," Jiefangjun Bao Online, 16 July 2008, p. 1, as translated and downloaded from the Open Source Center website, document number CPP20080716710001.

[482] Chengdu Military Region Joint Headquarters for Earthquake Relief, "Rigorously Improving the Ability to Organize, Command Non-Combat Military Operations," Jiefangjun Bao Online, 22 July 2008, p. 6, as translated and downloaded from the Open Source Center website, document number CPP20080722710007.

[483] Guo Jiangshan, "Quake-Rescue-and-Relief Subjects Study Carried Out," Jiefangjun Bao, 23 July 2008, as translated and downloaded from the Open Source Center website, document number CPP20080724702008.

Conclusions

There are several conclusions to be drawn from this short look at the PLA's crisis management system. Many of them are positive when viewed from the perspective of the history of crisis management in China.

First, it can be stated that the PLA has updated its crisis management mechanism in both its capabilities and its legal framework. Its capabilities have been enhanced through the introduction of information technologies especially satellite and communication assets. Its legal framework has been enhanced through updated regulations that apply to disaster and relief operations. In particular, the PLA fulfilled Articles 3 and 15, the former dealing with earthquake relief functions and the latter with the conduct of interviews on the situation in the earthquake zone. A Defense Ministry spokesman made his first appearance ever to announce information on what the armed forces were doing in the relief operation, and a General Staff spokesman from the Operations Department also addressed the progress of the operation and its parameters. In a November 2006 article, steps were also developed for some armed forces command elements to bypass a significant section of the chain of command in order to respond faster to emergencies and small-scale military conflicts. This move gives priority to the immediate release of information to people to help dispel rumors and irresponsible reporting.[484] However, these crisis management developments are still in their infancy. Much work remains to be done.

Second, it is clear that new organizations are being constructed to deal with disasters. The following are some of the organizations noted in this chapter that are connected with crisis management: an Emergency Management Office (2005), the Center for Crisis Management Studies at China's Institute of Contemporary International Relations (CICIR), the National Development and Reform Commission, the National Commission for Disaster Reduction, and a proposal for a National Command for Emergency Management (proposed at the 2008 Party Conference). During the earthquake, the following organizations were noted:

- The PLA Quake Relief Command Group
- The Chengdu Joint Earthquake Resistance and Disaster Relief Command Center
- A command center for each of the five jurisdictions noted in a General Staff briefing

---

[484] "China Shortens PLA Chain of Command in Emergency Response Plan," Beijing Xinhua, 0658 GMT 15 November 2006, as translated and downloaded from the Open Source Center website, document number CPP20061115968071.

- An operational and disaster relief force organization
- The Sichuan Province National Defense Mobilization Committee.

Li Shiming, head of the Chengdu Military Region, listed the following organizations in his article on the situation in the region: the Chengdu Military District Joint Earthquake Relief Headquarters; the Joint Command Party Committee; the government emergency response system, the military combat readiness system, and the national defense mobilization "dual response" system; and civil-military emergency response battalions of seven military sub-districts that participated immediately.

Third, the Internet was put to good use to spread information about the relief operation, to express remorse at loss of life, and to thank people for their efforts in the quake area. The Internet has turned out to be a way the PLA can keep the people happy by providing them with the information they need in crisis situations. Keeping people happy was done in other ways as well, such as rescinding for some areas of China the one child policy since so many families lost their only child in the earthquake, usually in a schoolhouse setting. China's leadership showed its interest in the people, being on the spot within hours of the quake.

Fourth, the PLA's relief effort showed its ability to conduct a myriad of tasks. The Communist Party praised the PLA for its ability to conduct diversified tasks and this point will be developed further in the coming months and years as an important result of the relief effort according to reports.

Fifth, it was clear from the summaries of officials who described the results and importance of the relief effort that this non-combat action served as a practice event for a war under informatized conditions. This issue was clearly a propaganda theme that the Political Department of the PLA was determined to publish. For example, the following reports emphasized this point in July 2008:

- On 1 July reporters noted that "on the basis of improving the ability to win a localized war under informatized conditions, it is essential to strengthen research of the characteristics and laws governing non-combat military operations, organize troops to arrange for stability maintenance, and so on."[485]
- On 3 July the PLA General Political Department wrote that local wars under informatized conditions put forth very high

---

[485] Li and Zhang.

requirements for multiple service branch joint operations and more often than not, non-war military tasks have multivariate participants and military-civilian joint actions.[486]

- On 4 July a Communist Party editorial noted that non-military operations represent a "whetstone" (knife stone) for sharpening armed forces' capabilities in winning local wars under informatized conditions.[487]

- On 16 July reporters noted that "At the same time as improving the capability of winning local warfare under informatized conditions, we must emphasize highly the work to improve the capability of carrying out non-combat military tasks…"[488]

- On 22 July the Chengdu military region headquarters wrote that aspects of non-combat military operations such as command organization, rapid mobilization potential, and mobility capabilities help form the potential to win localized wars under informatized conditions.[489]

Zhao Zongqi, who also covered the topic of winning informatized wars in a 17 June article, stated that Chinese society and the PLA must work together to deal with two strategic tasks and two major crises simultaneously. The PLA's work to handle the snow and earthquake crises of 2008 along with flooding and the Olympics indicates that it has successfully accomplished the latter half of this wish list. What Zhao meant by strategic tasks is unclear but hopefully they don't involve warfare.

Finally, China received higher marks than usual for its transparency during this natural disaster. Many foreign reporters were allowed into the area. However, Chinese reporters and the PLA's Political Departments cited no problems with the relief effort. Almost every report from the Chinese point of view was a positive report. It is very unusual for only positive reports to come out of a relief effort. Any country that has been engaged in a relief effort understands that unexpected problems always arise. The Chinese press was quiet on such matters. "Positive" transparency was achieved but perhaps not "total" transparency. They are two different things but then again the Chinese system is a different system from Western reporting and this is perhaps the best

---

[486] PLA General Political Department.

[487] Editorial Department.

[488] Ge Shanbin, Liu Jiguang, and Luo Suying, "Several Revelations from the Earthquake Resistance and Disaster Relief Battle with Respect to Strengthening Force Building," Qiushi Online, 16 July 2008, No. 14, as translated and downloaded from the Open Source Center website, document number CPP20080716710013.

[489] Chengdu Military Region Joint Headquarters for Earthquake Relief.

that we can get at the present time. Overall, the reporting was satisfactory. However, being prepared to conduct non-conflict activities and wartime activities are two different things. It is unknown how prepared the PLA is to conduct a wartime crisis management response but according to reports, the Sichuan earthquake gave them several leads on conducting informatized war under non-military conditions.

PART THREE:

Electronic Reconnaissance Applications, the Book Information War in China, and Taiwan on the PRC

CHAPTER SEVEN: CHINA'S LONG-RANGE ELECTRONIC PATROL

This chapter examines the active-defense and preemption/reconnaissance activities of the PLA that are targeted at multiple countries.[490]

The fiscal 2008 National Defense Authorization Act, passed yesterday by the House, contains a provision requiring the annual Military Power of the People's Republic of China report to include a new section on Beijing's "efforts to acquire, develop, and deploy cyberwarfare capabilities" in its assessments of China's "asymmetric" warfare capabilities.—Early Bird, 14 December 2007.

Introduction

Since 2005, Chinese cyber attacks against US systems have increased at an alarming rate. However, the term "attack" carries unwanted connotations; these unwarranted incursions are more likely reconnaissance missions to collect intelligence on US military systems, to spot vulnerabilities or plant trapdoors or viruses in our systems, and to ensure that China's People's Liberation Army (PLA) has an immediate advantage in the event of any war involving the US and China. If the incursions were "attacks" then our systems would be down and destroyed. Instead, these computer reconnaissance measures appear to conform to an old Chinese stratagem: "a victorious army first wins and then seeks battle. A defeated army first battles and then seeks victory." Reconnaissance via computer to spot vulnerabilities before the first battle fits the stratagem well.

The US, of course, is not the only country accusing the Chinese of unwarranted incursions. Germany, England, France, Japan, Taiwan, and Australia, among others, have also been Chinese targets. When one views these events in light of open-source accounts of Chinese information operations (IO) theory over the past several years, there is much circumstantial evidence to find China guilty as accused. The only actual forensic evidence, of course, is classified and located in the security agencies of the countries that China has electronically invaded.

This article explains Chinese military thought that supports their cyber reconnaissance/attack activities. While other articles focus on who was attacked and how many times, this article focuses more on the theory behind the attacks,

---

[490] This chapter first appeared as an article in <u>Military Review</u>, Nov-Dec 2008, pp. 47-54.

especially the PLAs use of electronic stratagems for their computer network operations (CNO) and the use of surrogates such as patriotic hacker groups. The article reviews Chinese incursions and utilizes a temporal approach based on open source assessments provided by some of the most important Chinese IW theorists.

The PLA has followed theory with practice. Computer network operations have become part of the peacetime strategic activities of the PLA. More worrisome is the purpose of these incursions. Is it reconnaissance? Or is the purpose of these incursions to place Trojan Horses or some other device into US and other partner systems to disable or destroy them in case of war? There is much to evaluate as one reads about Chinese IW developments and much to consider about Chinese potential intentions.

IW Units and the "Active Offense"

While the exact reason for China's cyber attacks is unknown, we can follow a cause-and-effect rationale in Chinese contemporary writings. The cause of China's attachment to new information technologies and the "informatization" of their force is the dramatic impact the technologies have had on military affairs, most notably US use of technology in Iraq. The effect of these technologies on Chinese military thought, as demonstrated below, is their belief that only countries that take the initiative in an information war or establish information superiority and control ahead of time will win. This requires reconnaissance and intelligence gathering before the first battle to set the stage for the use of cyber forces.

Historically, the PLA based its strategic philosophy on "active defense," meaning that China would never attack someone first but would be ready to respond if attacked. That philosophy has changed over the past few years with the advent of the cyber age. There has been a continuous stream of open-source descriptions of both cyber units and offensive cyber operations in the Chinese military and civilian press. The PLA's open recognition of a need for offensive operations reflects a significant break with traditional Chinese military thought. Further, the PLA has openly stated that US reliance on computer systems is a huge vulnerability ripe for exploitation. If the PLA hopes to offset America's huge advantage in the practical application of IO theory (in Kosovo, Iraq, and Afghanistan), it has to exploit that vulnerability. To understand this shift from defensive to offensive-minded operations chronologically, we must begin by looking at developments in 1999.

Nearly a decade ago, Chinese IO theorists were already discussing offensive actions. Zhu Wenguan and Chen Taiyi's Information War, published in 1999, contains a section called "Conducting Camouflaged Preemptive Attacks." The authors note that preemptive active offense is needed to disrupt and destroy enemy computer offensive forces.[491] A part of preemption appears to be network surveillance, which involves collecting information on the performance, purpose, and structure of systems related to C4I, electronic warfare, and weapon systems. The authors note that, in the broadest sense, computer information surveillance is a part of computer information attack. They state:

> To conduct computer surveillance, we can use computer information networks set up in peacetime and enter networks as different users to do the surveillance in an area broader than the battlefield. We can borrow the power of computer experts, especially hackers, to finish computer surveillance tasks…it can be seen that using hackers to obtain military information from computer networks is a very effective method. We should be familiar with network protocols and accumulate network intelligence.[492]

The authors add that the PLA established small brigades of offensive and defensive computer confrontation forces to conduct these attacks.[493] Offensive training includes how to design and organize virus invasions and how to enter the other side's computer networks. Offensive brigades must repeatedly study and analyze the enemy's performance parameters. They must also be able to sort truth from deception, to pinpoint enemy computer-control centers, and to jam in targeted ways.[494]

In November of 1999 a Liberation Army Daily (Jiefanguin Bao) article stated that China may develop an IW branch of service—a "net force"—to complement the army, navy, and air force. While the article stated that this development was very likely to become a reality, there is no evidence to confirm the creation of such a branch of service today. The force's task would

---

[491] Zhu Wenguan and Chen Taiyi, Information War, 1999, Chapter Five (Computer Operations). This chapter discusses offensive and defensive computer operations. No further information (publisher, etc.) was available.

[492] Ibid.

[493] Ibid.

[494] Ibid. At one point in the discussion, the authors state that "we need to observe our military's strategy of active offense and in computer confrontation training ensure both defense and offense are main partners…"

be to protect net sovereignty and engage in net warfare. Elements of net warfare include "offensive and defensive" technologies, "scanning" technologies, "masquerade" (deception) technology, and recovery technology. Masquerade technology would assist a person who wanted to dissemble as a commander and take over a net.[495]

2000

The idea of focusing on reconnaissance and stratagem activities arose as early as 2000. A Liberation Army Daily (Jiefanguin Bao) article notes that units at and above army level should focus their study on reconnaissance and early warning, command coordination, and the application of strategy.[496] An article substantiating this thought appeared in the PLA's authoritative journal China Military Science (similar in importance to Joint Force Quarterly). The latter article notes that stratagems should create opportunities and favorable times for releasing viruses.[497]

Another China Military Science article clarified the offensive posture described in 1999. In it, General Dai Qingmin opines that offense is at least as important as active defense, and notes "as the key to gaining the initiative in operations lies in positively and actively contending with an enemy for information superiority, China should establish such a view for IO as 'active offense.'" His view is that active offense is essential for maintaining information control, obtaining the initiative, and offsetting an opponent's superiority. Offensive information methods can help sabotage an enemy's information system.[498]

Dai, who became the head of the PLA General Staff's Fourth Department (Electronic Warfare), also notes that IO stratagems can be formulated before launching a war to serve as "a sharp sword" that sabotages

---

[495] Leng Bingling, Wang Yulin, and Zhao Wenxiang, "Bringing Internet Warfare into the Military System is of Equal Significance with Land, Sea, and Air Power," Jiefangjun Bao (Liberation Army Daily), 11 November 1999, p. 7 as translated and downloaded from the FBIS website on 15 November 1999.

[496] Fan Changlong, "Stand in the Forefront of the New Military Revolution in Deepening Troop Training through Science and Technology," Jiefangjun Bao (Liberation Army Daily), 4 April 2000 p. 6 as translated and downloaded from the FBIS website on 6 April 2000.

[497] Niu Li, Li Jiangzhou, and Xu Dehui, "Planning and Application of Strategies of Information Operations in High-Tech Local War," Zhongguo Junshi Kexue (China Military Science), Number 4 2000, pp. 115-122 as translated and downloaded from the FBIS website on 9 November 2000

[498] Dai Qingmin, "Innovating and Developing Views on Information Operations."

and weakens a superior enemy while protecting or enhancing China's fighting capacity. IW can serve as a type of invisible fighting capacity to evade combat with a stronger enemy.[499] If a future IW goal is to defeat strong forces with weak forces using stratagems, then such methods are one of China's asymmetric means to combat US high technology.[500] Stratagems in this sense would be one of the "magic weapons" that Chinese strategic culture is always stressing.

Finally, Dai's August 2000 article in China Military Science discusses the use of electrons as stratagems and the development of an integrated network-electronic warfare capability. When combined with the active-offense concept, this article represents one of the most important IW articles written in China.

Other less notable publications also discuss offensive operations. In a March 2000 Internet version of Computer and Information Technology, analysts at the PLA's Electronic Engineering Institute at Hefei discuss the need for network confrontation teams and the requirement to conduct both defensive and offensive operations.[501] In September 2000, the journal Guangjiao Jing noted that the PLA had recently established IW departments within its headquarters organizations.[502] Thus, the idea of offensive operations was not limited just to Dai.

2001

The 2001 book Science of Strategy, published by China's National Defense University, includes a section on offensive IW operations. It states that strategic IW should "use offense as a main strategy but be prepared for both offense and defense." Further, it states "we should use the strategy of the preemptive strike and seize the initiative. Actively launching an information offensive is the key to seizing information superiority and the initiative on the battlefield."[503] In this sense, the thinking appears to apply mainly to wartime and not peacetime preemptive actions.

---

[499] Ibid.

[500] Ibid.

[501] Yang Jian, Zhang Youhua, and Lu Zhankun, [no title], Jisuanji Yu Xinxi Jishu (Internet version of Computer and Information Technology), Anhui Computer Subscriber Association and the Anhui Computer Society, 16 March 2000 as translated and downloaded from the FBIS website on 18 April 2000.

[502] "China's IW Capabilities," Guangjiao Jing, Hong Kong, 16 September 2000.

[503] Ge Zhenfeng, Chapter 16, Section 4, p. 366. For translations of excerpts of this book, the author thanks Dr. Gary Bjorge, Combat Studies Institute, Fort Leavenworth, Kansas.

The Science of Strategy also describes the type of war to fight against networks. The book states that in a war of annihilation, nodes must be attacked to break up the network. Information and support systems must always be the first targets to offset operational balance followed by the stronger weapon systems. Science of Strategy notes that "after strikes to damage the net and continuous operations and persistent weakening of the enemy, then vigorously launch an annihilating attack." Ground information warfare facilities, transmission means, perception platforms, and information-flow capabilities should be destroyed in that order. This type of attack enables one to "take away the firewood from under the cauldron."[504] While this scenario appears to apply to wartime conditions, it can easily be adapted to peacetime conditions as well.

Information technology has thus stimulated Chinese strategic thinking; military academics now argue that those who do not preempt will lose the initiative in what may be a very short-lived IO war. In modern conflicts, they suggest, it is easier to obtain the objective of war through one campaign or one battle than at any other time in history.[505] This line of thinking provides further impetus for the PLA to conduct cyber reconnaissance activities in peacetime to "win victory before the first battle."

2002

An article from June 2002 states that PLA units were prepared to tamper "with information in terms of order, time, flow, content, and form; deleting information in parts, in order to create fragmented information; and inserting information to include irrelevant information in order to confuse and mislead each other."[506] The author adds that two sides in a computer confrontation may attempt to invade each other's information networks by transplanting computer viruses to downloadable software that can be activated when necessary in order to sabotage each other's computer systems.[507]

General Dai Qingmin wrote in 2002 that a priority for the PLA was to acquire offensive information operations equipment; and that the PLA must

---

[504] Ge Zhenfeng, Chapter 24, Section 6, p. 493.
[505] Peng and Yao, pp. 418-419.
[506] Wen T'ao, "PLA Bent on Seizing 'Information Control'," Hong Kong Ching Pao, 1 June 2002, Number 299, pp. 44-46 as translated and downloaded from the FBIS website on 5 June 2002.
[507] Ibid.

take and maintain the initiative.[508] Other publications weighed in as well on this point.

Liberation Army Daily (Jiefangjun Bao), for example, carried an article in August of 2002 about the forms of network attacks. These were listed as "premeditated" (i.e., a persistent computer virus embedded in software), "contamination" (aimed at the quality of information), "strong" (refers to the forced modulation of computer viruses into electromagnetic waves), and "fission" (the strong regeneration capability of a virus).[509] All are capable of being inserted in peacetime except perhaps the "strong" variety.

2003

At the 2003 10th National People's Congress, PLA representatives revealed that it would activate the first high-tech information warfare units (IWU) in Beijing that year. The report stated that the units would eventually be in all PLA armies. IWUs would be outfitted with high-tech equipment, have the ability to conduct network warfare on the Internet, and have the capability to transfer data via remote sensing satellites.[510] How this "first" IW unit differs from the IW brigades under discussion in the 1999 Chinese book Information War is unknown.

General Dai, writing in 2003, stressed once again the importance of carrying out information attacks.[511] Dai wrote that IW is "precursory" (begins before other operations) and "whole course" (runs throughout an entire operation). Perhaps the current emphasis on gaining the initiative and on short wars are the main reasons that Dai gives the impression that preemption via IW is a necessity in future war.[512] He notes:

> Actions such as intelligence warfare, psychological warfare, and campaign deception in advance of combat seem to be even more important to the unimpeded implementation of planning and ensuring war. For this reason, information warfare must be started in advance of

---

[508]Dai Qingmin, "On Integrating Network Warfare and Electronic Warfare," Zhongguo Junshi Kexue (China Military Science), Feb 2002, pp. 112-117 as translated and downloaded from the FBIS website on 24 June 2002.

[509] Fan Yongsheng, Wu Xinghan, "War on Networks: Modern 'Contradictory' Offensive, Defensive Warfare," Jiefangjun Bao (Liberation Army Daily), 14 August 2002, p. 11 as translated and downloaded from the FBIS website on 14 August 2002.

[510] "PLA to Organize First Information Warfare Units," Mingpao News, 12 March 2003, http://full.mingpaonews.com/20030312.

[511] Direct Information War, p. 170.

[512] Direct Information War, p. 169.

other combat actions before making war plans and while making war plans.[513]

It goes without saying that intelligence warfare includes surveillance.

Specific reserve units also engage in IW activities. For example, in late 2003 the monthly journal of the PLA Academy of Military Science, Guofang, gave specific instructions on network attack activities to reserve units. Author Li Mingrang states that information storm troop "fist forces" must be established from the talent of local communications, telecommunications, and financial departments; and from scientific research institutes and institutions of higher education. Stratagems must be developed to increase system survivability.[514] Li adds:

> There is no shortage of computer experts and network jockeys among them, any one of whom could become a network guerrilla who could open up a gunpowderless battlefield all by himself by harassing attacks on the network, namely by releasing large volumes of data from many directions concentrated on some enemy network station to jam up its network router and bring the network station to a standstill...and once there is a military requirement, either enter the network system to steal intelligence, or to activate viruses or detonate 'bombs' to achieve the combat target of destroying the network....[515]

Reserve forces are directed to work on offensive strategies.

In his 2003 book Deciphering Information Security, China's "Father of Information Warfare," retired Colonel Shen Weiguang, wrote about the development of an information security university with a military information security specialty. The specialty teaches, among some twenty plus topics, "A Study of Hacker Attack Methods," "Network Intrusion Detection and Defending against Attack," "Information Attack and Defense Tactics," "Computer Virus Program Design and Application," "Network Security System Structures," and "Scanning for Hidden Troubles in Networks."[516] Many of

---

[513] Ibid.

[514] Li Mingrang, "Develop the Advantage of People's War under the Conditions of Innovation and Informatization," Guofang, 15 November 2003, pp. 7-8 as translated and downloaded from the FBIS website.

[515] Ibid.

[516] Shen Weiguang, Deciphering Information Security, Xinhua Publishing House, July 2003, pp. 127-241.

these topics would fit the definition of the PLA's peacetime computer network operations incursion activities.

2005

In the 2005 book Study Guide for Information Operations Theory, General Dai and his associates defined 400 IO related terms, many related to preemptive or reconnaissance activities. Only computer network warfare is described here.

> Computer network warfare is composed of computer network reconnaissance, computer network attacks, and computer network defense. Operations mainly involve the use of armed and equipped network warriors. The means of operations include various types of viruses, logic bombs, and chip weapons developed from computer technology. Computer network warfare will act as both a deterrent and a means of warfare, and it can have a large and profound impact upon the enemy's politics, economics, and military. It is also an important means of battle for a less well-equipped military against one with formidable strengths in high technology.[517]

Dai also discussed the importance of the conduct of warfare, focusing on information deterrence as a concept to consider and develop further at the strategic level. Other who have written on the topic of information deterrence include Shen Weiguang and the editors of the book Science of Military Strategy (an entire chapter in the book was devoted to the topic). It is thought that information deterrence (intimidating someone by demonstrating one's information power or might) can help achieve national and military strategic objectives. Deterrence methods include information technology, information weapons, and information-resource suppression. According to some Chinese authors, counter-information deterrence theories must also be considered.

In Warfare Strategy Theory (2005), Yao Youzhi asserts that strategy has developed to the point where technological considerations dominate and the use of technology has become strategic. Any strategy that distances itself from focusing on high-technology weapons has no useful value, according to Yao. This also means that China must develop sound counterstrategies.[518] He writes:

---

[517] Ibid., p. 211.
[518] Yao Youzhi, Editor-in-Chief, Warfare Strategy Theory, Liberation Army Press, 2005, pp. 475-476.

It is necessary to be proficient at utilizing the information superhighway, creating misleading information, spreading the fog of war, and jamming and destroying the enemy's strategic awareness, thereby using strategy to control the adversary. It is necessary to be proficient at using electronic feints, electronic camouflage, electronic jamming, virus attacks, and space satellite jamming and deception, leading the enemy to draw the wrong conclusion and attaining the goal of strategic deception.[519]

While designed for wartime use, several of these techniques work as peacetime preventive and preemptive measures as well.

In "stovepipe" structured commands of the past, a force calculated its strength by adding together all of its parts. Today, Yao notes, a force's combat strength is a product of operational elements where information technologies factor into a potentially exponential multiplication.[520]

Yao writes that informationized warfare has changed the traditional significance of "attack, capture, control, and defend" because precision attacks have made possible the destruction of the enemy's entire war system. The primary attack target has become an enemy force's strategic information system. All activities now revolve around gaining battlefield supremacy, and information supremacy is the foundation of battle supremacy. Directly destroying an enemy's will has supplanted the annihilation of an enemy's military capability. This focus on information invites completely new methods in future wars.[521]

2007

Author Zhang Zhibin notes in a 13 March 2007 Liberation Army Daily (Jiefanguin Bao) article that the dialectical relationship between offense and defense in network warfare must place equal emphasis on each. A network deterrence theory implies that both capabilities are necessary, offense to scare any potential enemy force, and defense to thwart any attack. Zhang says:

Only by doing a solid job of positive defense can China ensure winning the initiative in network warfare. Thus, China should make unremitting efforts to seek such preemptive opportunities through developing

---

[519] Ibid.
[520] Ibid., pp. 346-349.
[521] Ibid., pp. 99-101.

network technology and systems and making corresponding network defensive operations research and implementation.[522]

Other articles from 2007 stress a need for PLA action to gain network control, including access, if possible. Two books on Chinese IO by this author, Dragon Bytes and Decoding the Virtual Dragon, mention this focus on control.

Probable Chinese Computer Attacks against the US

Over the past several years, Chinese IW and IO capabilities have become more visible and troubling. China has used these capabilities not only against the US but reportedly against Japan, Taiwan, Germany, England, and Australia as well. Due to the nature of CNO, exactly how many Chinese IW reconnaissance or offensive events have transpired or the actual intent of these incursions remains unknown. Those episodes that have leaked into the public domain include the following:

- Espionage conducted against the US Department of Defense (DoD) computers, reported in Time magazine. The report concerned a Chinese cyber espionage ring that federal investigators code-named Titan Rain. Its target was DoD computers.[523]
- Chinese attempts to blind a US satellite, reported in Defense News. The report discussed high-powered Chinese laser attacks on a US satellite.[524]
- Chinese hacker attacks on the US Naval War College's net capability, reported in Federal Computer Week. This attack purportedly originated from China and took systems off-line.[525]
- The Chinese destruction of an old Chinese weather satellite with an anti-satellite missile, reported on National Public Radio. The report cited a Beijing People's University commentator. He noted "satellite

---

[522] Zhang Zhibin, "Offense is Not Necessarily the Best Defense—Preliminary Study and Thinking on the Dialectical Relationship between Offense and Defense in Network Warfare," Liberation Army Daily, 13 March 2007, as downloaded from the Open Source Center web site on 9 April 2007.

[523] Nathan Thornburgh, "The Invasion of the Chinese Cyberspies," Time, 29 August 2005, downloaded from http://www.time.com on 23 January 2007.

[524] Vago Muradian, "China Tried to Blind US Sats with Laser," Defense News, 25 September 2006, p. 1.

[525] Josh Rogin, "Network Attack Disables Naval War College," Federal Computer Week, 30 November 2006, downloaded from http://www.fcw.com.

killing technology is logical in the development of missiles and an IW capability."[526]

- A sophisticated computer attack on Tennessee's Oak Ridge National Laboratory in October and November 2007. The assault was in the form of phony e-mails which, when opened, allowed hackers to penetrate the lab's computer security.[527]
- Hacker attacks against Japan and Taiwan, reported in the Japanese and Taiwanese press.[528] The reports noted that these attacks were retaliations for Japan's anti-Chinese interpretations of history and for Taiwanese claims for independence.

On 5 September 2007 the Kansas City Star carried an article in which China denied cyber-attacking any country. Foreign Ministry spokesman Jian Yu noted that "the Chinese government has always opposed an Internet-wrecking crime, including hacking, and cracked down on it according to the law."[529] He dismisses accusations of Chinese attacks on Pentagon computers as "groundless." A Pentagon spokesman refused to say if the perpetrator was China, but Britain's Financial Times quotes an unidentified senior US official as saying the source had been traced to the PLA.

A week earlier, Germany's Der Spiegel magazine reported that the PLA had infiltrated Germany's government computer systems. The report said the "hackers" had been traced back to Guangzhou and Lanzhou.[530] Thus circumstantial evidence continues to grow. It is difficult to believe that Germany, Australia, Japan, Taiwan, and America are all conniving to indict China and portray it as a new threat. Indeed, through unprovoked cyber operations, China seems to have indicted itself without anyone's assistance.

China's Use of Surrogates

One of China's stratagems is to "attack with a borrowed sword." Perhaps the use of patriotic hackers fits this stratagem in a preemption and

---

[526] Anthony Kuhn, National Public Radio, 19 January 2007, interview with Beijing representative.

[527] "Oak Ridge National Lab Reports 'Sophisticated' Cyber Attack Netted Personal Data on Visitors," The Associated Press, 6 December 2007, as downloaded from http://www.iht.com/bin/printfriendly.php?id=8626732.

[528] "Chinese Hackers Attack Taiwan Military Computers," Taipei P'ing-kuo Jih-pao (Internet Version) 15 May 2006, as reported in Open Source Center report CPP20060516310002.

[529] Tim Johnson, "China Denies Cyber-Attack," Kansas City Star, 5 September 2007, p. A5.

[530] Ibid.

intelligence collecting way. A recent article in Time magazine discussed the use of the Network Crack Program Hacker (NCPH) group initiative to accomplish this goal. The article stated that the PLA had developed a competition for hackers and that the winner would receive a monthly stipend from the military. It noted that the NCPH group not only won the competition and received the stipend, but the PLA also used the NCPH to teach techniques and procedures to other members of the PLA's cyber warfare team. A US branch of VeriSign, iDefense, has noted that China's NCPH created 35 programs to implant Trojans (which take partial control of computers) and that these programs attacked US government agencies. VeriSign's iDefense accused the NCPH of siphoning off thousands of unclassified US documents. Such activity would fit the PLA's preemption focus.[531]

The concept of "People's War" also fits nicely with so-called patriotic hacking. "People's War" in the cyber age means that citizens get involved with hacking or cyber attacking an enemy's systems. Presently over 250 hacker groups operate in China.[532] In this sense, quantity could create a quality all its own with the variety and intensity of incursions they could conduct. None could be traced directly to the PLA if hacker groups or private citizens are involved (or for that matter, military members or military reservists conducting cyber operations from their home computers). Again, circumstantial evidence is all that one has to go on, but that evidence is becoming overwhelming.

Conclusions

Chinese CNO theory over the last several years from even open source material indicates that China wants to become proficient in the active-offense, cyber reconnaissance, cyber-stratagem, and computer exploitation activities in case the PLA has to go to war. If China feels it can gain the initiative by obtaining information superiority or by preventing cyber strikes, then the coming years may involve challenges from that sector. While it remains easy to measure the intent of steel in the form of a tank, it is much harder to measure the intent of a Chinese electron. Is it inserting a virus, conducting reconnaissance, or disabling a system? The world will move into uncertain territory as nations attempt to conduct responses to and develop consequence management actions for truly disruptive electronic intrusions.

---

[531] Simon Elegant, "Enemies at the Firewall," Time, downloaded from http://www.time.com/time on 19 December 2007.
[532] Conversation with Mr. Scott Henderson, whose book Dark Visitor is probably the best open source work on Chinese hackers.

The Chinese note that IO tactics and techniques allow more emphasis on the principle of offense than on traditional methods of warfare. A weaker force, for example, can inflict much damage on a superior force with a properly timed and precisely defined asymmetric information attack. China portrays itself regularly as the weaker side of the US-Chinese relationship. It thinks that offensive operations such as information deterrence, information blockade, information power creation (electronic camouflage, network deception, etc.), information contamination, information harassment, nodal destruction, system paralysis, and entity destruction are key to victory in a modern conflict with America.

One should remember that this analysis stems only from open-source information and public comments from the PLA, and that China's understanding of the intersection of strategy and information technology, especially as it relates to actual conflict, is not extensive in a practical sense. The Chinese have little recent experience with conflict. Their forces have not fought an actual war in decades. From a theoretical perspective, however, China has written extensively on the use of information technology and information preemption and given both much thought. Chinese cyber intrusions indicate that the Chinese are gaining a lot of practical and theoretical experience in peacetime.

The PLA's open-source comments can be interpreted either as an attempt to work with the West or to vigorously oppose it. Perhaps the PLA is being very open and transparent in its cyber strategies, perhaps more open than in any other area of military operations. (The PLA appears more open with its IW thinking, for example, than Russia). If the PLA's intent is to oppose the West, it may in fact be concealing rich information warfare concepts in PLA "rules and regulations" (the PLA's equivalent of doctrine) within the general staff directorates and research institutes. China's IW rules and regulations are not available to other nations, while unclassified US doctrine is available to anyone on the Internet. The PLA keeps its rules and regulations close to its chest. In this case, lack of doctrinal transparency introduces unwanted ambiguity. America and other nations under threat of PLA incursions may react harshly to some scenarios developed by the Chinese and, thus, unintentionally set off a conflict.

How and when China might use its active-offensive concepts for purposes other than reconnaissance is unclear, but, as general concepts, they are worrisome. It does not bode well for future cooperation and stability if Chinese theorists really do believe (as they openly state) that China can offset an opponent's information superiority only if China strikes first. China will no doubt continue to use technology in conjunction with innovative stratagems to try to deceive our high-tech systems or perhaps even to force errors in the cognitive processes of US decision-makers. We must continue to be on the lookout for these attempts.

CHAPTER EIGHT: A CRITIQUE OF THE BOOK INFORMATION WARFARE IN CHINA

This chapter highlights key aspects of the thinking of several important information warfare specialists in China, looking at both theory and technology.[533]

The core for a real update to our ideas lies in a transformation to our way of thinking.[534]

Introduction

In 2005, Shen Weiguang, the father of information warfare (IW) in China, edited a book titled Information Warfare in China.[535] Shen collected chapters from some of the most prominent writers in China on IW issues. Among them were Li Bingyan, master strategist; Wang Baocun, expert on the revolution in military affairs and foreign IW; and Wang Pufeng, a former director of the PLA's Academy of Military Science's Strategy Research Department. The ten authors in the volume focused solely on IW-related issues, to include: IW theory; changes in the nature of warfare; computer network operations (CNO); IW definitions; attacks on thought and spirit in peace and war; organizational development; information security; counters to adversary IW; innovative thinking; and the education of IW personnel.

This chapter discusses each author's thoughts. The chapter is divided into two parts. The first part describes theory-related input from specialists. The second part describes technical-related input. Authors are identified along with their chapter titles.

---

[533] This author reviewed Shen Weiguang's book Information Warfare in China and credits the content, concepts, and ideas to the book's editor and authors of the individual chapters. The content of their book is reviewed based on translated material.
[534] Feng Yi, "Considerations Regarding Information and Network Security for the Chinese Military," Information Warfare in China, Xinhua Publishing, 2005, New Military Affairs Reference (Special Edition), pp. 100-115.
[535] Shen Weiguang, Editor, Information Warfare in China, Xinhua Publishing, 2005, New Military Affairs Reference (Special Edition). *About page references in this chapter*: after a reference to the inclusive pages wherein a chapter is found in the original Chinese text, additional citations and quotes taken from the chapter are listed as "ibid." A translation was utilized for this chapter and therefore it is not possible to identify the exact page where the citation can be located in the original text, only the chapter pages.

Part One: Theory

IW Theoretician Shen Weiguang: Shen writes that information warfare is encouraging a revolution in military philosophy. This revolution would be marked by a leap from tangible to intangible warfare, the latter being a war fought in invisible space and capable of being conducted without bloodshed.[536] IW is making humanity seek ideal wars with minimal destruction.

During IW, Shen adds, groups are pitted against one another to contest for control over information space and to contend for information resources. Wars would seek to attain control or a balance point on behalf of one's interests. Strategically this involves destroying an adversary's will to fight. Battles would involve upsetting an adversary's decision-making process. Tactics would involve paralyzing an adversary's system of strength. Fights over the information frontier would be of the following types: invasion, confusion, deterrence, and destruction.[537]

In the 2000 book Ideal War, Shen proposed the establishment of an Internet Nation, an information factory, an information gendarme, and information-based armed forces. Ideal war, the least destructive form of war, reflects a country's comprehensive national power and the latest achievements in science and technology. Robot war, clone war, leader war, star wars, virtual war, ideological war, media wars, and cognitive wars all reflect the features of ideal war.

Other books by Shen include The Third World War: Total Information Warfare in 1990 and Cognitive Warfare in 1993. In these works he proposed that the real significance of IW lay in the methods to attack thought and spirit.[538] This is because there is no dividing line between war and peace when it comes to propaganda wars. There are always attempts to influence the emotions, motivation, judgment, and decision-making of the masses. Developed countries with access to broadcasting, television, and computer networks expand their information frontier through the dissemination of political will and political values abroad. The only defense against these actions is People's War where the people's spirit fights an intangible war to defend China's information sovereignty and information frontier.[539]

---

[536] Shen Weiguang, "The Profound Impact of Information Warfare on Civilization and Strategic Countermeasures," Information Warfare in China, Xinhua Publishing, 2005, New Military Affairs Reference (Special Edition), pp. 258-295.
[537] Ibid.
[538] Ibid.
[539] Ibid.

External threats to China (such as Shen's belief that the West intends to interfere with China's information security) and internal threats such as hackers and organized crime are daily events to monitor, in Shen's opinion. He is particularly concerned with internal threats, noting that local and regional problems could be disseminated over the Internet and thus become national problems. Chinese people have at times recklessly engaged in propaganda online which could incite a chain reaction of discontent. Perhaps most important, however, is that information strategies, policies, and rules and regulations have lagged behind progress in the incorporation of information technology in China. Many Chinese now possess information tools that are not regulated.[540]

Master Strategist Li Bingyan: Li's chapter was titled "The Framework of the Informationization Buildup of China's Armed Forces." His main thesis is that information technology can narrow the digital divide between the information-haves and have-nots among nation-states. This would be accomplished, Li notes, by presenting precise requirements for information age force purchases. Li writes that he is "anxiously awaiting the establishment of something on the order of a 'Government Agency for the Design of Future Operations'" and a discipline called the "science of demand."[541]

The focus of friendly information systems in Li's opinion should be to gain control of an adversary's command and control system. Chinese systems must be reliable and properly designed before being put to use. This requires, first of all, determining the PLA's strategic goals. Future information-based battlefield environments and the nature of capabilities required to win future wars must be clarified. It is vital to study history and avoid mistakes made by others if a system's developmental stage is to be shortened. Modes of thinking need to change as well. Second, introducing new systems requires the shattering of mechanized forces so that an information-based force can evolve. Forces, management, and operations are all equally important in this transformation.[542]

Li emphasizes that the change from an industrial to an information society is not focused solely on technology. He states that China must be careful not to neglect the changes to culture and philosophical methodologies that an information society produces. An all-round ideological revolution is

---

[540] Ibid.
[541] Li Bingyan, "The Framework of the Informationization Buildup of China's Armed Forces," Information Warfare in China, Xinhua Publishing, 2005, New Military Affairs Reference (Special Edition), pp.15-37.
[542] Ibid.

required, one that takes the human aspect into account. He notes that the US had produced such a revolution, replacing Newtonian theory with chaos and complexity theory.

Other recommendations for building an information-based military include learning how to solicit bids for orders based on operational demands, in particular how to work with civilian information-technology experts; learning how to continually update software; and learning how to select personnel for IW at the local level "as early as possible. We need to get our hands on them while they are little."[543] Thus, in addition to setting up networks, a knowledge system must be constructed that teaches people how to adjust their thinking to the information age. Outdated obstructions from another era, such as mechanized ways of doing business and dated cultural tendencies, must be eliminated as information technology is incorporated into the PLA's way of life and equipment.[544]

Li observes that all military activities are either movement activities or cognitive activities. Information technology activities are located principally in the cognition domain of soft warfare. Instead of counting divisions to weigh military capabilities, information technology "calculates competencies and communication capabilities."[545] He noted that technology and hardware can be purchased on the market, thereby "leapfrogging" over industrial age developments, but this cannot happen in education. Habits of thought and cultural developments are inherited and cannot be skipped over. Li is confident that in the next three to five years the number of personnel in the Chinese military graduating from institutions of higher learning may surpass the number graduating from similar institutions in developed countries.

Finally, Li envisions a melding of military cultures in the East and the West based on factors such as the East's craving for science and technology and the West's search for wisdom and knowledge; and the fact that warfare is undergoing a change from destroying the enemy to "controlling the enemy and looking out for your own interests."[546] Li summarizes his thoughts by noting that "the incorporation of information technology in the military requires placing emphasis on technology, but also upon wisdom and strategy."[547]

---

[543] Ibid.
[544] Ibid.
[545] Ibid.
[546] Ibid.
[547] Ibid.

Strategy Expert Wang Pufeng: Wang writes that theory is the guide for action and thus he begins his discussion with a look at IW theory. He defines IW using the 1997 edition of Military Terms, a Chinese military book. The definition states that

> IW is confrontational actions in the information realm performed by two hostile parties. They primarily contend for information resources, gaining the initiative in the production, transmission, and processing of information, and destroying the enemy's information transmission, as a means of containing or winning the favorable terms created by the war.[548]

Wang only considers wartime IW in his comments. Wartime IW includes electronic warfare, missile warfare, intelligence warfare, psychological warfare, and command and control warfare, which Wang believes is the core component of IW. The key to any action in war, Wang notes, is to gain information supremacy or to control information that can lead to control over another force's information initiative. IW, which is an operational term to Wang, is integrated into hard and soft warfare and into technology and tactics. It also includes aspects outside of military operations such as war mobilization and information confrontation actions in areas such as politics, diplomacy, economics, and science and technology. IW, due to its importance, could become an independent form of military operation or an independent stage of warfare or an independent act of warfare.[549] This is a most important development in Wang's opinion.

Further, Wang stresses that the battle for control and for the information initiative is key. Wang writes that controlling information is defined as "the volume of information acquired within a defined domain of time or space that is far greater than that of an opponent. One's flow of information must also be greater than that of an opponent."[550]

To gain control over an enemy, "three links and five measures" must be followed. The three links are that information acquisition capability determines information volumes; that information transmission capability determines information flow; and that information processing and utilization capabilities determine the value of information. The five measures are reconnoitering an

---

[548] Wang Pufeng, "My Views on a Number of Matters Pertaining to the Study of Information Warfare," Information Warfare in China, Xinhua Publishing, 2005, New Military Affairs Reference (Special Edition), pp. 36-47.
[549] Ibid.
[550] Ibid.

anti-reconnaissance site; interfering with anti-interference; destructing an anti-destruction site; annihilating an anti-annihilation site; and controlling an anti-control site.[551]

Command and control warfare in future wars will be reflected in the scientific and artistic nature of a commander's strategic intent and operational programs. These programs will include the development: of a good information infrastructure on the battlefield; of operational secrecy and military deception; of unobstructed communication links; of electronic warfare, network warfare, psychological warfare, and physical destruction; and of special operations.[552]

Wang concludes stating that China must innovate or it will fall behind. It must improve battlefield reconnaissance capabilities, put effort into network warfare, and develop precision weapons. It must pay attention to quantum and optical computer developments; micro-nano technologies; gene technologies; supersonic technologies; ion invisibility technology; unmanned platform technology; and developments in directed energy technology.[553] The revolution in military technology has produced a corresponding revolution in military thinking, operational methods, and structural organization to which the PLA must adapt according to Wang.[554]

RMA and IW Expert Wang Baocun: The basic goal of the informatization buildup of the Chinese armed forces, according to Wang, is the comprehensive integration of mechanized forces "materials and energy" with informatized forces "information and knowledge."The development of C4I systems, the integration of early warning and interdiction systems, and the development of command and control and precision strike systems are priority items that enable structure and function to be integrated.[555]

There are several ways that talent will be developed for this task. They are the development of new courses in IW and information technology, the increased use of attack and defend options in IW exercises, and the development of new military organization. Wang advocates a "one objective, two paths, and five pillars of support" methodology for China's informatization buildup. The objective of the buildup is to enhance China's information

---

[551] Ibid.
[552] Ibid.
[553] Ibid.
[554] Ibid.
[555] Wang Baocun, "A Limited View of the Informationization Buildup of China's Military," <u>Information Warfare in China</u>, Xinhua Publishing, 2005, New Military Affairs Reference (Special Edition), pp. 116-153.

195

capabilities to allow information and knowledge to serve as the main factors in combat power. The two paths are comprehensive integration and the use of virtual reality environments. The five support pillars are "information technology, informatized weapons and equipment, informatized military personnel, a structural organization amenable to the rapid flow and use of information, and completely new military theory with informatized war theory at its core."[556]

Informatized war occurs in strategic space's six spectrums, those being in Wang's view land, sea, air, space, information, and knowledge. In these spaces information is more likely to control firepower and mobility than at any time in history. Informatized weaponry offers the promise of greatly increased survival rates for planes, tanks, and ships.

There are six principles that will ensure the buildup of the PLA's forces. All are well-known to US analysts and leaders. They are:

- The principle of being guided by information. Without information one cannot strike accurately or implement concepts such as an information monopoly, protection, attacks, support, or umbrella, all of which provide an advantage over an enemy.
- The principle of comprehensive integration. Multiple systems must be integrated into one major system, as Admiral William Owens proposed years ago. Computer information processing technology will be the foundation for this integration.
- The principle of virtual practice. This principle allows nations to simulate future battlefields and future training and indicates when and how a force may face trouble. Combat laboratories accelerate the informatization buildup and enable operational theory and equipment to turn quickly into informatized operational capabilities.
- The principle of the integration of proximal and distal. This means being constantly ready for both immediate and long-term potential threats, since the latter can materialize quickly in the information age.
- The principle of concurrent push and pull. Military theory is pulling from the front. High technology is pushing from behind. These two factors keep the buildup moving.
- The principle of using the commercial world to promote the military. The civilian sector is driving the military sector more than

---

[556] Ibid.

at any time in history. China's strategies of national informatization and the nation's information infrastructure should guide the PLA's military buildup.[557]

Wang then provides his advice on methods to accelerate the informatization buildup of the PLA. First, he recommends strengthening macro-control and establishing organizations to lead the effort. Elements of this organizational aspect were accomplished, he notes, with the 1993 Joint Conference on National Economic Informatization; the 1996 Leading Group for Informatization under the State Council; and the 2001 Leading Group for National Informatization. Still, a decision-making body with authority, an implementation body for the informatization buildup, an advisory body of experts for the buildup (to include senior experts in information theory and technology), and leading groups for the buildup composed of leaders primarily from the Communications Departments of the war zones need to be developed.[558]

Second, unified planning at top state levels must be strengthened. A "gold combination" of comprehensive electronic systems should become the main element of combat power. In particular, systems integration must be standardized. This includes basic frameworks, port technology, upgrading and updating capabilities, and various types of software platforms and test standards. There must be a method established for demonstrations and assessments.

Third, there must be major theoretical innovations. Information network structures; information operations "fist" forces that test digitized departments and units; future war problems (such as digital blockades in the early stages of a conflict); a tactical framework that supports critical directions in preliminary planning; the cultivation of high-caliber personnel; and an investigation into the characteristics and use of People's War ideology, along with joint topics, must be developed.[559]

Fourth, a focus should be put on informatized war requirements for the future as the military's organizational structure is reformed. What is important today are structural adjustments, optimized and enhanced technical content, and an increase in the number of technical units, especially those for computer network warfare. Information security defense and electromagnetic frequency

---

[557] Ibid.
[558] Ibid.
[559] Ibid.

197

management forces are very important. Aerospace units must undergo enhanced research.[560]

Fifth, Wang recommends the creation of a mechanism for producing military personnel that is really people-centered since new personnel are the carriers of knowledge and information. Sixth, the focus must be on accelerating the buildup, especially for informatized systems and equipment as these are priority tasks. China must concentrate its development on communication systems that expand network coverage, on deception systems, and on the fusion of communication systems with other systems. Otherwise comprehensive control will not be possible. Reconnaissance, command and control, intelligence, electronic countermeasures, and early warning detection systems are other points of interest. Additional major developments include aerospace countermeasure weapons, destructive computer viruses, and directed energy and electromagnetic energy weapons.[561]

Mei Jun: To construct the proper military reform and have a chance to succeed in future wars requires an in-depth understanding of future war's nature, according to Mei. The RMA is really a revolution of the informatization of warfare. The goal of past wars, which was to strike enemy personnel, has changed slightly. Now the goal may be to force people to give up through a demonstration of technological might and control over events that perhaps don't even occur on the battlefield. Once control over willpower is lost an enemy force can become paralyzed and his combat capabilities decline drastically. Gaining control involves not just control over the carriers of information but also of the "meaning and effectiveness of information."[562]

The two major aspects of information warfare are information attacks and information defense. Informatized war, as distinct from information warfare, is characterized by high precision firepower. Information warfare includes electronic warfare, psychological war, and network warfare. Cognitive issues include "disrupting the effectiveness of information, especially the disruption of the understanding and use of information by the human brain." Such activities can be directly effective because they bypass many technical difficulties. Mei accuses the US of using laser holographic technologies during the Gulf War to concoct such a cognitive attack.[563]

---

[560] Ibid.
[561] Ibid.
[562] Mei Jun, "Understanding and Considerations of the Buildup of Information Warfare," Information Warfare in China, Xinhua Publishing, 2005, New Military Affairs Reference (Special Edition), pp. 217-228.
[563] Ibid.

Mei states that the search continues to transform IW into a "trump card" (Mei defines an IW trump card as "something involving a new mechanism or concept; it can be strategic, offensive, targeted, extremely effective, or acting as a deterrent."); to make use of the successful experiences of foreign militaries; and to seek out asymmetrical developmental solutions for an IW buildup. The buildup will be on two levels: the strategic battle force that implements the task of gaining information superiority during battle; and the combined armed forces that support and cover tactical forces in combat.[564]

The main task of IW in battle, in addition to achieving information superiority, is to disrupt the strategic electronic information goals that the enemy relies upon for support and means. This requires a concentrated buildup of IW forces, concentrated means of control, and the concentrated use of strategic battle power. With regard to electronic destruction capabilities, "trump cards" must receive priority development. Intensive microwave interference equipment, electromagnetic pulse weapons, and laser anti-satellite equipment represent three types of such weapons. The idea behind this concept is to achieve a new strategic advantage (or *shi*).[565]

Mei writes that whoever achieves an advantage in the fight for network space will possess the strategic initiative in the twenty-first century. A paralyzed network will cause losses to the national economy, create social chaos, and reduce combat capabilities among other consequences. Two fronts will be at work, a strategic network warfare front based on the Internet that focuses on political and economic networks; and a battlefield network front that focuses on the closed and local interconnected networks on the battlefield. The latter are usually isolated from the Internet. More importantly, "if viruses have already been planted in battlefield networks beforehand, then various means of triggering them can be employed at the right time in order to conduct attacks."[566]

Part Two: Technology-Related Issues

Kong Lingtong: Kong states that network attacks are an entirely new combat means that will impact the outcome of future wars. The goal of war now is to control the enemy instead of annihilating him. Making an enemy become incapacitated means influencing the thinking and will of people's ability to make decisions about war, to push an enemy into a dark box so that

---

[564] Ibid.
[565] Ibid.
[566] Ibid.

199

adversaries cannot "know the enemy" or "know thyself" which prevents them from converting war potential into war capability. Network platforms are special because they are not restricted by time, space, peace, or war.[567]

It will be necessary to mobilize people quickly during future network wars, Kong adds, and this will require new information-related developments in People's War theory. Civilians will provide not only a new impetus to network conflict but also offer political, military, and technical advantages. Higher education focused on the sciences is a must if China wants to encourage and protect its talent, especially in the area of software. China must develop its own operating systems. Then Kong (in a rather disturbing revelation from a US perspective) quotes Zhu Qingshi, president of the University of Science and Technology of China and academician with the Chinese Academy of Sciences. Zhu states that he had visited Silicon Valley and all he saw were former students. Turnover for these types of people, he notes, is like giving someone else an atomic bomb.[568] [Author: US analysts would view this comment with alarm. It can also be interpreted as the Chinese bleeding Silicon Valley dry of important information technology data.]

Kong adds that China must not let others lead it around. Instead China must prepare asymmetric responses to counter foreign advantages. China must "design programs which coerce the enemy into playing according to our rules." The US is still weak in network administration, countering attacks by hackers, and understanding the risks of electronic commerce. China must make multiple preparations to exploit these weaknesses and to construct retaliatory operations. This includes the use of Special Forces to destroy enemy network centers and information nodes. Controlling these centers and nodes and establishing an invincible position are dependent upon one's power of understanding and how alert and resourceful one is.[569] Such thoughts feed into the PLA's new mode of thinking.

Feng Yi: Feng writes, like others, that whoever controls information controls the initiative. To do so and to thwart the IW threat against China posed by Taiwan and other countries requires four things. First, China must decide upon the major focus of its development for short-term and long-term information security. Second, China must unify planning and implement development programs for IW technology and equipment. Third, China must

---

[567] Kong Lingtong, "Network Warfare and Our Strategies in Response," Information Warfare in China, Xinhua Publishing, 2005, New Military Affairs Reference (Special Edition), pp. 89-99.
[568] Ibid.
[569] Ibid.

intensify its development of defensive IW technology. Finally, China must accelerate the strengthening of its comprehensive IW capabilities in the PLA. To make these changes requires a revolution in China's military thinking, particularly at the highest level of leadership.[570]

Network-based modes of thought will eventually be integrated into cognitive networks. This means that an understanding of an issue, the cognitive side, must be in sync with technological achievements if new systems are to experience their most positive efficiency. This is not a short-term process as the issues before us are often difficult to compute, Feng notes, such as how much network security is required for systems to be safe and how to prepare for the increasing variety of network attacks. Attackers are often anonymous; they can strike civilian facilities before military ones; and they may attack decision-makers as well as computers. Determining the scale of the requirements to construct an effective defense is a very complex process due to the rapid advance in commercial products that can be used to attack systems.[571]

To strengthen China's military defenses in the digital realm, the following principles should be followed. First, there must be a synchronized buildup of network security systems. Second, the management structure should be based on the "top-down and regional" principle. Third, there must be a sound legal and regulatory system for information security. Finally, network security objectives must include such actions as prepare and protect, monitor and respond, and stabilize and develop. Only with dedicated management can China's security organizations be effective.[572]

China's information space must be closely analyzed. Feng believes specialists should look at the conditions present in information space, examine what detection methods are available to monitor information space, develop defensive anti-deception capabilities for information space, and develop a survivable system structure for China's information space. These conditions are actually reconnaissance, detection, and deception mechanisms. The latter mechanism is the trickiest since it is designed to create success in the mind of an enemy force when in fact his actions have failed. For example, the enemy force could believe that he is in your system when he is actually in a virtual system where his perceptions are monitored, manipulated, or disrupted.

---

[570] Feng Yi.
[571] Ibid.
[572] Ibid.

Input into China's network space perception system is examined by sniffers, login documents, protocol traps, infiltration detection systems, user databases, system messages, threat databases, and operational commands distributed in network equipment. Output includes the determination of the infiltrator's identity, threat sources and malicious activity assessments, classification of threats, rates of attack, evaluation of an attack's efficiency, and decision-making support and simulations. Data fusion and data mining are the two types of technology most often depended upon for "network space posture perception."[573]

Computer Expert Ma Yexi: Ma's chapter was titled "Computer Network Warfare: Functions, Means, and Developmental Trends." Ma writes that information networks are a prime target for attack during an information war, especially those associated with C4ISR systems, national transportation centers, and communication centers. Successful attacks on these targets can affect an adversary's strategic decision making.[574]

Ma defines computer network war (CNW) as "the general term for various types of computer network attacking and defending operations conducted throughout network space using advanced information technology."[575] Such attacks on national strategic command and control networks, communication networks, intelligence networks, and various civilian networks have a direct impact on national politics, the military, the economy, and diplomacy.[576]

Computer network warfare is hard to trace and its intent is hard to determine. The functions of CNW include deterrence, reconnaissance, disruption, deception, and protection. CNW's ability to distract an adversary or enable superiority (and convince an opponent that capabilities and advantages lie with friendly forces) can cause CNW to become a "network deterrent" that forces opponents to respect the rules of the game. Reconnaissance of military networks allows friendly forces to steal military intelligence. Once passwords are acquired, programs can be configured to steal data and preconfigured programs can steal information. Adversary systems must also be monitored for information leaks. Ma writes that in the US the authority for, legitimacy of, and target selection for the use of network warfare have yet to be clearly

---

[573] Ibid.
[574] Ma Yexi, "Computer Network Warfare: Functions, Means, and Developmental Trends," Information Warfare in China, Xinhua Publishing, 2005, New Military Affairs Reference (Special Edition), pp. 229-257.
[575] Ibid.
[576] Ibid.

demonstrated. [Author: Perhaps this is a main reason why China attempts to conduct so many reconnaissance operations against the US.]

Disruption includes the use of viruses, hacker attacks, and information interference or physical destruction to either keep systems from working properly or to paralyze or destroy them. Deception involves the use of false electronic intelligence, false electronic resolve, and false electronic deployments to entice an opponent into making erroneous judgments or to take an action beneficial to friendly forces. Finally, Ma adds, the protection of friendly systems can involve attacking adversary systems to improve the defensive capabilities of one's own computer networks. Strikes should be made against important nodes of adversarial networks. Other defensive means to preserve the normal acquisition, transmission, and processing of information include camouflage, confidentiality, hardening, and backups.[577]

The basic form of CNW, Ma notes, is attacking and defending physical entities, operating systems, and protocols. Attack means include system infiltration, computer virus attacks, deception attacks, denial of service attacks, attacks on physical entities, and network attacks. Of particular interest are information-deception attacks. Ma states that these are "the combined use of hacker attacks and computer virus attacks on the enemy's computer networks based on the use of such technology as computer images, electronic displays, voice recognition and synthesis, sensory transmission, and virtual reality in order to distribute and transmit false messages and false commands..."[578] Defensive measures include access control, network isolation, network surveillance, encryption, and physical protection.[579]

Ma notes that gaining information superiority is critical to determining victory in future war. Network superiority is comprised of ensuring sound network operations, network security, ensuring military information is not harmed, weakening or disrupting an enemy's ability to use its networks, and ensuring the control of one's networks. This also further develops one's sovereignty. Control of one's networks allows for gaining the initiative and preventing an adversary force from infiltrating Chinese networks.[580]

Countermeasure Experts Feng Yi and Zhang Jie: China must work hard, the authors note, to develop countermeasures to US equipment since China doesn't have the ability at the present time to follow the same path as the

---

[577] Ibid.
[578] Ibid.
[579] Ibid.
[580] Ibid.

US military-industrial complex and develop high-tech equipment. For example, the Chinese ability to counter GPS technology is now a key to countering satellite guided weapons. The weapons can't work properly without a good GPS system. The Chinese note that the GPS receiver on an opponent's missile cannot work normally or may not even work at all if an interfering signal with a noise level intensity equal to or greater than 80 decibels is used. This greatly reduces the missile's hit accuracy.[581]

Chinese scientists also report that a GPS interference device with a transmission power of five watts can prevent a GPS receiver on cruise missiles from working within a radius of 50 kilometers; and that an omni-directional radio interference device with a transmission power of 100 watts can disrupt GPS receivers within a 1,000 kilometer radius.[582]

China's counter technology path is following the development of six concepts: anti-satellite equipment, counter warning systems/reconnaissance equipment, counter-GPS systems, electronic warfare technology, and concealment devices. Simultaneously, a knowledge military must be developed along with a sensor force, precision strike force, and intelligence and logistic forces[583] in order to implement new modes of thinking.

The struggle to control information is at the heart of IW. Countermeasures will be key to ensuring that the struggle comes out in China's favor. Fast-breaking developments in civilian technology will also play an important role here.[584]

Conclusions

The key thoughts of Shen and his co-authors reflect many of the same methods and points of emphasis as other writers in The Dragon's Quantum Leap. Control, knowledge, trump cards, psychological operations, and countermeasures were all highlighted and usually by multiple authors.

The struggle to control information is at the heart of IW. Controlling information was defined as "the volume of information acquired within a defined domain of time or space that is far greater than that of an opponent. One's flow of information must also be greater than that of an opponent." Li

---

[581] Feng Yi and Zhang Jie, "China's Military Countermeasures against the Development of Informatized Equipment," Information Warfare in China, Xinhua Publishing, 2005, New Military Affairs Reference (Special Edition), pp. 202-216.
[582] Ibid.
[583] Ibid.
[584] Ibid.

underscored that warfare is changing from destroying the enemy to "controlling the enemy and looking out for your own interests." Kong Lingtong wrote that network attacks are an entirely new combat force the goal of which is to control the enemy instead of annihilating him. To control an adversary, China must prepare asymmetric responses to counter foreign advantages and "design programs which coerce the enemy into playing according to our rules."

With regard to knowledge, Li envisioned that a melding of East-West military cultures is occurring. This is due to factors such as the East's craving for science and technology and the West's search for wisdom and knowledge. Each can help the other. China realizes that without innovation in its science and technology potential it will fall further behind the West. The PLA's battlefield reconnaissance capabilities must improve, more effort must be put into network warfare, and precision weapons must be developed. It must pay attention to all of the new technologies that are now emerging.

The revolution in military technology has produced a corresponding revolution in military thinking, operational methods, and structural organization. There is a new focus on the attainment and use of knowledge. Shen focused on the application of knowledge with his prediction that robot war, clone war, leader war, star wars, virtual war, ideological war, media wars, and cognitive wars all reflect the features of ideal wars of the future. Wang Baocun stated that the informatization buildup relies on the comprehensive integration of mechanized forces "materials and energy" with the informatized forces "information and knowledge" focus.

Mei Jun wrote that a knowledge military must be developed simultaneously with a sensor force, guiding mobile force, precision strike force, and an intelligence and logistics force. Electronic destruction capabilities will be one of the important "trump cards" that must receive priority development. The idea behind the development of trump cards is to achieve a new strategic advantage (or *shi*) over an adversary. Mei wrote that whoever achieves advantages in the fight for network space will possess the strategic initiative in the twenty-first century, implying that control over network space is also a trump card. This is because a paralyzed network can cause losses to the national economy, create social chaos, and reduce combat capability among other consequences.

Feng Yi notes that China's information space must be closely analyzed for the penetration of adversarial psychological operations specialists. Chinese specialists should look at the conditions present in information space, examine what detection methods are available to monitor information space, develop defensive deception capabilities for information space, and develop a survivable system structure for China's information space. The deception mechanism is designed to create success in the mind of an enemy force when in fact his actions have failed.

Feng Yi and Zhang Jie note that China's counter technology path must develop six concepts: anti-satellite equipment, counter warning systems/reconnaissance equipment, counter GPS systems, electronic warfare technology, and concealment devices. Countermeasures will be key to ensuring that the struggle comes out in China's favor.

Finally, Ma Yexi wrote that computer network war includes deterrence, reconnaissance, disruption, deception, and protection. CNW's ability to distract an adversary or enable superiority (and convince an opponent that capabilities and advantages lie with friendly forces) can cause CNW to become a "network deterrent" that forces opponents to respect the rules of the game. It fully represents the integration of knowledge with materials and energy.

CHAPTER NINE: TAIWAN EXAMINES CHINESE INFORMATION WARFARE

This chapter summarizes the views of several Taiwanese specialists who focus on Chinese information warfare (IW) tactics, organization, and policy.[585]

Currently Communist China is pushing a revolution in military affairs and information war is at its core. In this military thinking the "pre-emptive strike" strategy is a very important component.[586]

Introduction

Taiwanese military specialists have studied Chinese IW topics for over two decades. Due to their common language, culture, and close proximity with the mainland, the Taiwanese are capable of discerning nuances in the People's Liberation Army's (PLA's) approach to IW that might escape a Western analyst. Some of the interesting PLA IW concepts that Taiwanese military professionals have discussed, for example, include:

- Acupuncture war
- Highly-controlled war
- Strategic information war
- Political work Web sites
- Intangible war
- Net force
- Surgical war

Understanding the PLA's potential use of information technology and IW theory is key to the future security strategy of the Republic of Taiwan (ROC). It is mandatory for Taiwanese government and civilian professionals to study Chinese IW intensely and be able to predict and foresee the PLA's potential use of IW against Taiwan in both peacetime and wartime.

This chapter will examine Taiwan's analysis of several issues (asymmetric war, IW theory, political work and psychological war, media war, and PLA IW institutes) associated with PLA IW. Also covered in this chapter will be Taiwan's view of the PLA's focus on the revolution in military affairs and how that revolution has transformed the PLA from a mechanized to an

---

[585] This chapter first appeared as an article in <u>High Frontier</u>, Vol. 5, Number 3, 2009, pp. 26-35.
[586] Lin Tsung-ta, <u>Strategic Dominance Initiative of the PRC's Information War</u>, Crystal Books, May 2005, page unknown.

informatized force. These developments impact the PLA's policy, organization, education, structure, and theory of IW.

A Taiwanese View of the PLA's Revolution in Military Affairs

The Chinese military has studied the meaning and impact of the revolution in military affairs (RMA) for more than two decades. While it might be assumed that China's understanding of the RMA would be similar to that of the US or other nations, it is not. For example, in 2001 retired Chinese Major General Wang Baocun defined the term as a process of military informationalization where theory and practice are the focus. He added that Chinese progress toward an RMA is signaled by its command, control, communications, computers, and intelligence modernization, network-based war-gaming, IW personnel training and field exercises, and informationalized equipment.[587] Thus Wang's Chinese perspective indicates that the information revolution is the key component of the current RMA. US analyst Richard O. Hundley of RAND defined the RMA in 1999 as "a paradigm shift in the nature and conduct of military operations which either renders obsolete or irrelevant one or more core competencies of a dominant player; or creates one or more new core competencies, in some new dimension of warfare; or both."[588]

The US and Chinese differences most likely are a direct reflection not only of capabilities but also of culture. The US lead is in technology while the Chinese rely on theory and strategy to enable (in their opinion) their inferior force to overcome US superiority. Further, Wang is not the only Chinese military figure with an opinion on the RMA. One Chinese author noted that the RMA is really a cognition system revolution and a new phase in military strategy research. Another author added that the RMA involves a series of changes to military theory, methods of operations, weaponry, systems organization, command organization, and so on; an understanding closer to most US RMA concepts.

One thing is certain: the Chinese hope to develop an RMA concept with "Chinese characteristics." A Chinese general noted that "Only with superior thought processes and superior moves, and by seeking a developmental strategy of 'imbalance' will we truly be able to avoid traveling the 'path that the enemy expects.' In the realm of IW, trying to keep up with the

---

[587] Wang Baocun, "China and the Revolution in Military Affairs," China Military Science, No. 5 2001, pp. 149, 154.
[588] O. Hundley, Past Revolutions, Future Transformations, RAND, 1999, p. 9.

Jones' by developing whatever they possess will lead to falling into traps set by others…"[589]

Taiwan's understanding of the Chinese RMA does not necessarily coincide with these views completely. Major Li An-yao, who was serving in the Air Force Command of the Ministry of National Defense of Taiwan when he wrote about this topic, stated that the revolution in military affairs has changed China's strategic views on international security and on constructing fast response and projection capabilities. He listed five characteristics of the Chinese Communist's revolution in military affairs that concern Taiwan: the gap in military technologies has affected China's national security and forced the PLA to place priority on technological development; the transformation has forced adjustments in battle thought, theory, equipment, and training (this point coincides with Chinese theorists noted above); a "show of weakness" by the PLA can help thwart the China threat theories being developed; the study of asymmetrical and unrestricted warfare has developed deterrents and counters to Western developments (currently such thinking includes the use of a preemptive strike); and IW can help win a future war in the Taiwan Strait since it is marked by high technologies, a brief time period, and few casualties.[590]

Li was impressed with the contributions of former Chinese leader Deng Xiaoping to new thinking and its impact on current projections. Deng emphasized People's War (PW) under modern conditions and he recommended a shift in the center of gravity in Chinese decision-making to economic construction and the development of science and technology. Today top-level decision-makers in China understand fully the importance of economic modernization alongside military modernization. Modernization helps China change its way of conducting a war. Li writes that the Chinese link IW to a technical form of war defined by the widespread use of information technologies. People's War refers to a political form of war defined by the righteous nature of a war. China's RMA must be laced with such Chinese characteristics in accordance with the societal shift in the forms of technology and war from the mechanized to the information age.[591]

---

[589] Dai Qingmin, "Discourse on Armed Forces Informationization Building and Information Warfare Building," On the Chinese Revolution in Military Affairs, ed. Shen Weiguang, New China Press, 2004, pp. 39-47.
[590] Li An-yao, "PLA Thinking on War, 'Revolution in Military Affairs' with Chinese Characteristics," Taipei K'ung-chun Hsueh-shu Yueh-k'an, Internet Version, 25 April 2008 as translated and downloaded from the Open Source Center (OSC) website, document number CPP20080421312006.
[591] Ibid.

However, Li also pointed out China's RMA weaknesses. First among them is the age of the military leadership. Next are obstacles in the development of new weapons and equipment such as increased costs, the lag in domestically produced weapons, the technical integration of weapons purchased from foreign nations, and the reliability of precision guidance components. Finally, China lacks experience in offensive operations and in Navy and Air Force operations. Li concluded by noting that Taiwan "must pay close attention to the direction of China's army building, study the course and results of PLA military reform, and draw upon the experience of the rise of the Chinese Communists following the path of overcoming strength with knowledge as soon as possible."[592]

Major Hsu Hsieh-jung was another Taiwanese officer who wrote about China's RMA concept. While noting that the PLA must expedite its "military reform with Chinese characteristics," Hsu believes China must also take into account the recent successes of the US and its coalition partners in Iraq, Afghanistan, and elsewhere. In those locations, decapitation operations were utilized against the leadership of the regimes. These actions indicate one must innovate (the soul of the RMA to Hsu) and learn from other experiences such as those of the US if it wants to avoid perilous situations.[593]

One of those lessons, Hsu writes, is that China must be adept at "highly-controlled warfare" since it was a special characteristic of the war in Iraq. The PLA's Academy of Military Science noted that the 2003 US-Iraq war was characterized by "a high control level, high demand for control, and a high degree of control." War is evolving from general war to highly controlled war. This change is felt not only in military affairs but also in the emphasis on control over political, economic, and other sectors to include psychological control. Highly-controlled war is a new form of warfare in which "the direct purpose is to control a political regime and in which political, economic, diplomatic, and other resources are integrated effectively to control the scale, form, means, and results of the war, with the backing of absolute military superiority."[594] War is expanding from tangible to intangible war as a result.[595]

---

[592] Ibid.

[593] Hsu Hsieh-jung, "An Investigation of the Impact of the Second Gulf War on the PRC's New Revolution in Military Affairs," Hsien-ping Hsueh-shu Pan-nien-k'an, online 1 December 2007 as translated and downloaded from the Open Source Center website, document number CPP20080701312002.

[594] Ibid.

[595] Ibid.

Other ways in which China's RMA differs from Western countries include:

- Pursing a different strategic purpose than the West (which pursues world hegemony in China's opinion).
- Utilizing different motivations than the West to stay in line with the profound changes in modern warfare.
- Starting from a different technological point than the West, since China is still going through the late stages of mechanization.
- Utilizing different operational RMA forms, such as leapfrog developments instead of the West's gradual development.[596]

For these reasons, Hsu notes, the PLA cannot copy the model of advanced Western countries. It must be familiar with the laws of the RMA and apply their contextual situation to it in order to avoid being trapped in an arms race with the West as happened to the former Soviet Union. Study of the Iraq war and US successes in Kosovo convinced China that the idea of winning local wars under high-tech conditions had evolved to that of winning informatized war based on high-tech conditions.[597]

A Taiwanese View of the PLA's Asymmetric War Concept

In the information age, stratagems and psychological operations of all types can play havoc with an opponent especially when combined with the use or even potential use of exotic weapons. Chinese asymmetric warfare operations fit this description and they are not restricted by time and space. Stratagems used in the time of Sun Tzu are equally applicable in the virtual environment of today.

Asymmetric warfare is a method for China to deal effectively with its current potential superpower opponent, the US. Surgical war, paralyzing war, and unrestricted warfare operations are all examples of asymmetric warfare operational measures that the Taiwanese ascribe to the PLA. Taiwanese author Chen Wei-K'uan used the definition of a PLA military strategist, Kuo Yung-bing, to define asymmetric warfare as "operations in which any two opposing parties in a war can try their best in using their own advantages in strategy, weapons technology, and applications of their arms and services as much as

---

[596] Ibid.
[597] Ibid.

possible to locate and attack the vulnerabilities of the opponent fiercely and overwhelmingly."[598]

Chen states that stratagems are one of the most typical ways that China uses asymmetric warfare. He notes that a stratagem is used "to force an enemy to make mistakes which can then be taken advantage of." He quoted from a few Chinese military classics to demonstrate this point:

- In the art of warfare, a psychological offense is better than capturing a city, and a psychological war is preferable to an armed war.–Zhu Ge Liang
- A whole army may be robbed of its spirit; a commander-in-chief may be robbed of his presence of mind.—Chapter VII: Maneuvering, Sun Tzu's Art of War
- All warfare is based on deception.—Chapter I: Laying Plans, Sun Tzu's Art of War
- In war, the way is to avoid what is strong and to strike at what is weak—Chapter VI: Weak Points and Strong, Sun Tzu's Art of War
- In all fighting, the direct method may be used for joining battle, but indirect methods will be needed in order to secure victory—Chapter V: Energy, Sun Tzu's Art of War
- Attack him where he is unprepared, appear where you are not expected—Chapter I: Laying Plans, Sun Tzu's Art of War
- In war practice dissimulation and you will succeed.—Chapter VII: Maneuvering, Sun Tzu's Art of War
- Thus the highest form of generalship is to frustrate the enemy's plans.—Chapter III: Attack by Stratagem, Sun Tzu's Art of War
- The key to overcome an enemy relies more on the use of strategy to deceive the enemy than the use of force. Thus, people who are good at commanding the troops are those who can deceive and who also can avoid being deceived.—Chapter on Deception, Jie Xuan's 100 Stratagems of War.

Chen focused on technological aspects of asymmetric warfare operations that aim to paralyze an opponent before their destruction, if the latter scenario was even needed. First are soft-kill weapon systems, which include electronic jamming equipment, computer viruses, directed-energy weapons,

---

[598] Chen Wei-k'uan, "A Study of Our Due Perception of the PLA's Asymmetric Warfare," Taipei K'ung-chun Hsueh-shu Yueh-k'an, 25 July 2007 as translated and downloaded from the Open Source Center website, document number CPP20080507312001.

laser beam weapons, and non-directed-energy weapons. Second are precision and remote tactical missile attacks, not only aimed at troop assembly points or hardware construction targets but also aimed to paralyze command, control, communications, computers, intelligence, surveillance, and reconnaissance (C4ISR), radar reconnaissance systems, and command center targets. Third is the development of an electronic warfare (EW) capability, electromagnetic pulse weapons, and the ability to construct a comprehensive surgical warfare infrastructure (based on importing weapons from Russia at an increased tempo). Surgical warfare aims to attack the vulnerability of high-tech weapons systems to achieve final victory, namely, attacking one point to cripple the whole system. Finally, the development of a space warfare capability puts the crowning touch on China's asymmetric warfare capability: the ability to sabotage or destroy an enemy's space systems.

Chen's conclusion was that China is headed quickly in the direction of winning a regional war under high-tech conditions via asymmetric warfare operations. It is unfortunate that he did not go into more detail as to how the two areas he covered (stratagems and technology) might be integrated.

Another author, Chung Chien, wrote that a symmetric war involving the PLA and other nations may last for a long time and is not an option sought by China. An asymmetric warfare operation, on the other hand, has the opportunity to last but a matter of hours or weeks and would be a preferred operation, one "without bloodshed." Two types of operations that Chung mentioned the PLA might enact were: a PLA long range blockade of Taiwan's sea lines of communication, cutting Taiwan's logistic life-line through the Spratlys; and an electromagnetic pulse attack that would shut down all services in Taiwan and make command and control impossible.[599]

A Taiwanese View of the PLA's Information Warfare Concept

Taiwanese professor P'an Chin-chang wrote in 2007 that the PLA views informatized warfare (another way of saying IW) as "a war pattern which refers to that included under nuclear deterrence in the information age, where two sides in a war use information as the lead, comprehensively use information to integrate platforms and informatized weapons, and conduct joint combat efforts by multiple services and branches in all-dimensional space,

---

[599] Chung Chien, "High-Tech War Preparation of the PLA, Taking Taiwan without Bloodshed," Taiwan Defense Affairs, 1 September 2000, as translated and downloaded from the Open Source Center website, document number CPP20050411000204.

including land, sea, air, space, and electronics." [600] Informatized warfare includes precision combat, network combat, special operations, and space combat. Such combat includes direct attacks that "jump over time and space" and aim to take multi-dimensional control of battlefields and to destroy and paralyze the opponent's combat system. [601] Informatized warfare will require the comprehensive integration of four capabilities: sensing the battlefield, information transmission, rapid mobility, and accurate strikes. [602] The PLA's IW focus is on the control of information. The ability to manipulate information and seize information supremacy is the preeminent quality in future war, according to P'an. [603]

This was not always the view that Taiwan took of PLA IW theory and practice. In fact, Taiwan's views of the PLA's IW capability have evolved over time. In the late 1990s, Lin Chin-ching, director of the Telecommunications Bureau of the Ministry of National Defense (MND) in Taiwan, served as a prominent spokesman for IW issues and continued to do so for several years. He listed three ways that China might strike at Taiwan's digital infrastructure. First, he stated that China's goal was to paralyze Taiwan "by destroying its command and control system using an electromagnetic device the size of a briefcase."[604] Second, citing EW theory, he said China would use "acupuncture-point-prodding," the ancient Chinese martial art theory of taking out an enemy with a strike on a pressure point. Finally, he noted that China would try to steal Taiwan's military secrets via the Internet or the use of computer viruses. [605]

In response to the Chinese IW threat, Lin says Taiwan set up a Strategy Planning Committee for IW. He noted that Taiwan had also established Computer Emergency Response Teams (CERT); established a telecommunication and information security committee; stipulated laws and relations concerning telecommunications and information security; improved procedures to access computers; and installed warning devices on all networks

---

[600] Pan Chin-chang, "On the Role of Psychological Warfare as a Part of the PLA's Informatized Warfare Operations," Lu-chun Hsueh-shu Shuang-yueh-k'an, 4 June 2007 as translated and downloaded from the Open Source Center website, document number CPP20071119312002.
[601] Ibid.
[602] Ibid.
[603] Ibid.
[604] Maubo Chang, Taiwan Central news Agency, 1350 GMT 21 May 1999, as translated and downloaded from the Open Source Center website, document number FTS19990521000902.
[605] Ibid.

to strengthen the awareness of computer personnel about potential threats.[606] Taiwan is also trying to make people aware of the Chinese potential to spread false news about the stock market through the mass media and cause confusion or panic in society.[607]

In 2000 Lin predicted that the next five years would be crucial for the development of IW capabilities on both sides of the Strait. He noted that China had established an IW simulation center, developed viruses to be used in attacks against networks, and imported foreign information technology and equipment. By 2005 he believed the PLA could establish a neural network center to execute joint simulations; develop battlefield command systems to provide better troop mobility; develop a tactical data link system; digitize and mobilize command and control systems; strengthen satellite communications research and development; and establish an optical fiber communications network. As a "communist totalitarian nation," China will also use the entire nation's effort to mobilize IW's development.[608]

Also in 2000, Taiwan Defense Minister Wu Shih-wen stated that a military unit in charge of cyber warfare would be established. The unit would be responsible for protecting Taiwan's computer systems from hackers and for denying access to unauthorized individuals. Lin Chin-ching added that all officers under the rank of lieutenant general would be tested on their knowledge of IW and computer information, and that their test results would be taken into consideration when their files are reviewed for promotion.[609] The initial military cyber unit would be a battalion sized unit of specialized troops with a focus on the development of IW and EW capabilities, especially C4ISR. These areas will account for 23 percent of the defense budget according to Lin.[610]

---

[606] Lin Jui-yang, "The ROC Armed Forces Strengthen Security over Information," Chung-Yang Jih-Pao, 17 August 1999, p. 3 as translated and downloaded from the Open Source Center website, document number FTS19990818000447.

[607] Seiji Yajima, Interview in Japanese Journal with Lin Chin-ching, Sankei Shimbun, 5 November 1999, as translated and downloaded from the Open Source Center (OSC) Web site, document number FTS1999110500047.

[608] Lin Chin-ching, "Comparison of PRC-ROC Information Warfare Capabilities, Ch'uan-Ch'iu Fang-Wei Tsa-Chih, 1 March 2000, pp. 68-73, as translated and downloaded from the Open Source Center website, document number CPP20000725000181.

[609] Maubo Chang, Central News Agency, 1456 GMT, 22 November 2000, as translated and downloaded from the Open Source Center website, document number CPP20001122000162.

[610] Brian Hsu, (no title provided) Taipei Times, 23 November 2000, as translated and downloaded from the Open Source Center website, document number CPP20001124000107.

In 2005 another Taiwanese author with the last name of Lin, Lin Tsung-ta, who by reputation is one of Taiwan's most outstanding scholars on Chinese IW, wrote a book titled All Out War on the PRC's Information Warfare. He focused on Chinese IW's asymmetric character, its use of civilian entities and applicability to People's War theory, and its preemptive and deterring qualities. Chinese IW requires "attacking vital points," words that are conceptually similar to Lin's focus on acupuncture war.[611]

Lin noted that China's National Defense Science and Technology Information Center divides IW into three parts. The first is EW/command and control warfare equipment. The second is offensive information weaponry, described as: computer virus weapons, nano-machines, chip microbes; hackers; high energy radio frequency guns; and power damaging munitions. The third type of weaponry is defensive weapons, to include: network sentries; information defense encryption systems; firewalls; and multi-layer Internet defense networks. Further, Lin added that combat power in the opinion of many Chinese scholars lies in the control and counter-control of information since those who control information control the initiative on the battlefield in future wars.[612]

There are new types of People's War, Lin stated, such as hacker force and propaganda force People's War. Like military forces they can obtain military intelligence, bolster morale, and interfere with an enemy information system. Combat goals can be reached simply by damaging another side's economy. People's IW is an asymmetric and non-violent type of national war. China is deepening the study of "Network People's War" mobilization education to make every Netizen (Internet citizen) a "network combatant." Mobilizing IW talent in the military and in society will be the key to future successes. As of 2005, the PLA had carried out deliberations on organizational institutions for People's War, civilian mobilization plans, strategies and tactics, and training for Network People's War. Strategies provide an intangible combat power asset that compensates for insufficiencies in material conditions according to Lin. Legal systems, secrecy, market competition, and intellectual property rights are other ways to add intangible power to the PLA's arsenal.[613]

---

[611] Lin Tsung-ta, All Out War on the PRC's Information Warfare, Crystal Books, May 2005 as translated and downloaded from the Open Source Center website, document number CPP20071102320002.
[612] Ibid.
[613] Ibid.

People's IW uses asymmetric operational methods to enable opening up a second battlefield for the PLA far from the combat zone and in the enemy's rear area. Moreover the goal of Chinese People's War

> is to proactively protect international information infrastructures while attacking enemy rear political, economic, and military information systems, damaging the enemy's economic order in the rear, weakening the enemy's combat potential, and further influencing the progression of war. During this process, enterprises and individuals nationwide use their computers, communications equipment, and other information systems' signals and resources to provide sustained support to the nation's information infrastructure in the strategic rear.[614]

Finally, People's War strategy relies heavily on military modernization. Economic growth is crucial and a high-tech national defense industry must be developed. Lin notes that China intends to pursue international exchanges to increase its national defense economic potential.[615]

In September 2007 Major General Tschai Hui-chen, the director of Information Assurance for Taiwan's Ministry of National Defense and deputy chief of the General Staff for Communications, Electronics, and Information (J6), spoke at a conference at Fort Leavenworth, Kansas. MG Tschai noted in a section of her report to conference attendees that with regard to threats and challenges before Taiwan, China remains the greatest concern in both areas. She discussed general information security threats, strategic information warfare threats, and general security threats posed by China's emphasis on IW. Of interest is that in her report, she covered many of the topics listed in Taiwan's view of Chinese IW from the mid-1990s: deterrence, paralysis, network force, asymmetric war, strategic information war, long-range precision war, and network psychological war.[616] Thus it appears that Taiwan's concerns with regard to Chinese IW have not changed much over the years other than to stress that the Chinese are more advanced in both their budgetary spending on and development of information technology.

Naturally, even though the general categories Major General Tschai listed have remained basically the same, each is much more sophisticated and advanced than it was in the 1990s.

---

[614] Ibid.
[615] Ibid.
[616] Tschai Hui-chen, "A Discussion of Information Warfare from a Taiwanese Perspective," IO Sphere, Special Edition 2008, pp. 15-21.

A Taiwanese View on the PLA's Political Work and Psychological War

The PLA has always been expert at the use of psychological warfare techniques, particularly the application of psychological pressure. The firing of missiles near Taiwan into the Taiwan Strait in 1996 and the development of an Anti-Secession Law in 2005 exerted psychological pressure on Taiwan to "toe the line" and to abandon any thoughts of independence from the mainland. A recent episode of psychological pressure involved the former Russian Kuznetsov class aircraft carrier Varyag. Chinese sailors and civilians refurbishing the carrier state that it will soon be renamed the Shi Lang (after the Chinese general who took possession of Taiwan in 1681, which was the first time China paid attention to the island).[617]

Mr. P'an Chin-chang, a teacher at Taiwan's National Defense University in 2007, wrote a few excellent articles on the PLA's "informatized" political work and use of psychological warfare techniques. P'an described the PLA's political work database and political work Web site that enhances the combat functions of informatized political work. The PLA believes, he writes, that informatized warfare is not just competition in weapons and equipment but also in ideology, will power, political strength, spiritual factors, and psychological capacity. Information "includes not only military information transmitted by digitized weapons and equipment but also political and ideological information to be used to launch psychological offensives against the enemy. Informatized warfare involves not only the competition of military force but also non-military competition of political and psychological power."[618]

P'an stated that on 20 October 2005 the PLA inaugurated its political work Web site. No longer would paper be the only way to convey teaching materials. The Web site's operations center is located at the General Political Department in Beijing. The six major functions of the Web site are operational guidance, news and information dissemination, propaganda and education, study and training, culture and entertainment, and communication and interaction. The site offers online lectures, distance learning, and even psychological counseling.[619]

---

[617] See http://www.strategypage.com/htmw/htnavai/articles/20080109/aspx.
[618] P'an Chin-chang, "A Study of the PLA's Informatized Operations for Political Work," <u>Kung-chun Hsueh-shu Yueh-kan</u>, online, 25 July 2007 as translated and downloaded from the Open Source Center website, document number CPP20080616312009.
[619] Ibid.

The site is carrying "some 3,000 items per day, the Web site is updated every minute, there are 44 channels, including nine interactive and online-posting channels, which carry 382 second-level columns, 2,530 third-level columns, 53 large-sized databases, numerous books, videos, and games, more than 1,000 kinds of newspapers and journals, and every article document can be opened and refreshed instantly."[620] National Defense University has developed six types of software for political work command platforms for the site and is researching over thirty projects concerning the informatization of political work.[621]

The PLA is studying other aspects of political work as well. A symposium held at Nanjing's Academy of Political Science in December 2004, for example, highlighted eight aspects of the informatization of political work. P'an described the findings as: developing the theory of informatization of political work; training professionals; applying information technology to political work; developing and enriching information resources; allocating information equipment and facilities to political work; constructing political work for an information network; formulating policies, laws, ordinances, and standards for the informatization of political work; and enhancing information-related capabilities of political work cadres. The Nanjing Academy stressed the importance of political competition in future wars, citing competition in political stratagem, media propaganda, and psychological manipulation as well as legal competition.[622]

Psychological warfare, a major aspect of informatized warfare and political work, is now a part of the PLA's state strategy, P'an added. This has resulted in the development of the following categories: political psychological warfare, economic psychological warfare, military psychological warfare, diplomatic psychological warfare, religious psychological warfare, cultural psychological warfare, propaganda psychological warfare, and deterrent psychological warfare. All of these types of psychological warfare can be used to enhance "beheading" an enemy force instead of attacking it with conventional forces.[623]

---

[620] Ibid.

[621] Ibid.

[622] Ibid.

[623] P'an Chin-chang, "On the Role of Psychological Warfare as a Part of the PLA's Informatized Warfare Operations," Lu-chun Hsueh-shu Shuang-yueh-k'an, 4 June 2007 as translated and downloaded from the Open Source Center website, document number CPP20071119312002.

Regarding the future development of psychological warfare, the PLA proposes:

- Establishing psychological warfare command institutes
- Creating psychological warfare specialty troops
- Setting up psychological warfare research institutes
- Cultivating a team of psychological key members
- Developing psychological warfare technologies and devices
- Establishing special psychological warfare training venues
- And establishing psychological warfare platforms with computer networks.[624]

The use of these facilities will enable the PLA to stealthily substitute one thing for another, to replace and edit people and landscapes in a virtual world, and to produce some false and shocking scenes to deceive and incite discontent. Network confrontation training is required to improve the conduct of network psychological warfare and help develop countermeasures against its use by enemy forces. Troops are developing and conducting simulated training using sound, light, electronics, and information technologies.[625]

When fighting an enemy force, the deputy director of the Political Work Research Institute of the PLA's Academy of Military Science, Gong Fangbin, wrote that:

A study by the PLA General Staff Department also concluded that the actual cases of the several high-tech wars in recent years have shown that information technology, when applied to the psychological warfare battlefield, has promoted the development of instant psychological warfare propaganda operations, the invention of intellectual equipment for psychological warfare, the diversification of the means of psychological warfare, and the integration of psychological warfare and armed warfare.[626]

Political cadres must be capable of buttressing local opinion and demoralizing enemy attitudes. With regard to local opinion, cadres must be able to manipulate information and launch the "three types of warfare" (legal, public opinion, and psychological) before a military operation begins. This will ensure that the people are on the side of the armed forces and that they will trust that

---

[624] Ibid.
[625] Ibid.
[626] Ibid.

the war being fought is a just war, according to P'an's interpretation of the PLA's work. With regard to demoralizing the enemy, P'an cites PLA Professor Zhang Zhaozhong, who noted that it is necessary to "distort the enemy's cognition system through IW and psychological warfare, and thus win a war without really fighting a battle, or by fighting fewer battles, or by fighting only small-scale battles."[627]

Zhong also stressed the importance of strategic IW as a new form of war that can take on an independent posture and even be launched several months or years before an armed invasion takes place. Targets of strategic IW include national political, monetary, communications, and other crucial sectors down to single weapon systems such as aircraft carriers. Developments can lead to the use of strategic deception, strategic psychological warfare, strategic deterrence, or strategic information attacks.[628]

Not all is well with political work in the PLA, however, according to P'an. He notes that duplicate organizations still exist, coordination is difficult, lateral communication is not as prevalent as top-down communications, and communication equipment is still susceptible to damage. These constraints continue to limit the effectiveness of the PLA's political work Web site. However, the PLA will continue to use military force alone in the absence of other psychological factors to continue to intimidate Taiwan. [629]

A Taiwanese View on the PLA's Media Warfare

Closely related to political work and psychological operations is the concept of "media warfare." A relatively new field of research in terms of terminology, media warfare appears to be an updated version of "propaganda work" whose importance, the PLA ascertains, has not diminished. As Mao noted, "the Red Army's priority in conducting its propaganda work is to expand its political influence and win the trust of the majority of our people…the Red Army's propaganda work is the first and most important work for the Red Army."[630] In a high-tech environment, the PLA is concerned that its officers and soldiers will have to overcome a psychology of fear, panic, isolation, and

---

[627] P'an Chin-chang, "A Study of the PLA's Informatized Operations for Political Work."

[628] Ibid.

[629] Ibid.

[630] Liu Wan-lin, "An Investigation into the Impact of the PRC's Military Media Warfare on the ROC Military," Taipei Hai-chun Hsueh-shu Yueh-k'an, 22 April 2008, as translated and downloaded from the Open Source Center website, document number CPP20080602312005.

pessimism. Solid media warfare prepared ahead of time can help alleviate some of these concerns.[631]

Taiwan researcher Liu Wan-lin discussed how China had closely followed the two Gulf Wars and drawn several important conclusions. The PLA believes that the media must be managed and controlled to establish an effective propaganda system that puts pressure on an opponent. The true nature of a war must be publicized, as well as world opinion about the war and the PLA's policy. World opinion should be prepared ahead of time since modern war is a political and diplomatic process as well as a military process, according to Liu's analysis of Chinese media. Media warfare can create opportunities and conditions that help win a war by influencing national strategy and military strategy simultaneously.[632]

Media warfare is an aspect of former Chinese President Jiang Zemin's three warfare concept for political work that includes media war, legal war, and psychological war. Due to media wars strategic significance, the General Political Department of the PLA issued a new "PLA Political Work Regulation" and directed military educational organizations to increase their focus on this topic. More than 50 software suites on political work, battlefield propaganda methods, and so on have been created. The Academy of Military Science created a "Research Center for Cross-Strait Issues" and a "Research Institute for Political Work."[633]

At the regional level, the Nanjing Military Region's officers and soldiers were provided a booklet titled "Concise Handbook of Law-Abiding Combat Operations" and the Nanjing Political Academy opened a new course called "Media Warfare." The PLA's Xi'an Political Academy handed out materials on "100 Questions and Answers on Media Warfare, Psychological Warfare, and Legal Warfare." They prepared a course on "Political Warfare Operational Command Automation" and established more than 10 new research and teaching divisions to include a psychological warfare department, a military security protection department, a wartime political warfare work division, and an information technology and political warfare work division.[634]

Media warfare measures can help China win the consent and support of the international community. The PLA hopes to offset the use of deceptive propaganda by a potential opponent and thereby assure that the direction of the

---

[631] Ibid.
[632] Ibid.
[633] Ibid.
[634] Ibid.

media and public opinion is on the side of the PLA. The PLA will also continue to contain Taiwan, in Liu's opinion, via the use of the US while promoting its "One China" policy.[635]

A Taiwanese View of the PLA's Electronic Warfare Assets

Taiwanese officers and professors frequently write on the PLA's electronic warfare capabilities. They cover topics such as the PLA's capabilities, troops, EW attack potential, and Taiwanese responses. Navy Commander Hsu Keng-wei wrote on the PLA's EW attack options in 2008 and his article will be highlighted here.[636]

Hsu stated that the PLA has built a dense network of electronic monitoring stations and radar early warning installations opposite Taiwan. The function of these assets is to surveil, detect, and jam Taiwanese anti-air, early warning, and control facilities. Recently, the PLA has succeeded in reverse engineering the EW equipment of several countries which has greatly improved their capabilities. They have also learned how to attach EW equipment to unmanned aerial vehicles. Hsu added that the "East China Electronic Warfare Network" has learned how to integrate all EW troops stationed in Zhejiang and Fujian and focus them on Taiwan.[637]

Taiwan scholars believe that by 2012 the PLA will have electromagnetic pulse weapons capable of paralyzing Taiwan's electronic business, aviation controls, banks, the stock market, and the Internet if war erupts. A computer network attack could also take the form of a preemptive move by the PLA to jam and paralyze US support before a war begins.

Hsu named the HD 5, HD 6, and TU-154 aircraft as EW reconnaissance and jamming platforms designed for use against Taiwan's air and sea fleets. In addition to the multitude of EW platforms available to the PLA, recent Chinese successes in space have added to Taiwan's concerns.

---

[635] Ibid.

[636] Hsu Keng-wei, "How to Effectively Counter the PRC Military's Electronic Warfare Attacks," Taipei Hai-chun Hsueh-shu Yueh-k'an, 22 April 2008, as translated and downloaded from the Open Source Center website, document number CPP20080602312007. For a more detailed examination of the PLA's EW capabilities (too extensive for this brief survey), see Liu Yi-Chung, "How to Enhance the EW Capabilities of the ROC Military to Satisfy War Requirements across the Taiwan Strait," Taipei Hai-chun Hsueh-shu Yueh-k'an, 1 June 2006, as translated and downloaded from the Open Source Center website, document number CPP20061004312001.

[637] Ibid.

These successes, from Hsu's perspective, indicate that China can collect a huge amount of information on Taiwan and "establish an electronic order of battle to weaken our military's EW capability…and further destroy our EW facilities for command, control, communication, and intelligence."[638] The PLA regularly practices working in an intense EW environment in their military exercises which has increased their practical experience in this area. In acupuncture war, Hsu concludes, using EW can enable "the first battle being the final battle."[639]

A Taiwanese View of China's Military Information Warfare Institutes

Taiwanese reporter Liao Wenzhong, in a set of two articles on China's military net force, listed a series of institutes and programs in China associated with the IW effort. He set the stage for his first article by citing the January 2002 PLA release of its Seventh Generation Training and Evaluation Outlines in which it disclosed that the PLA had formed a science and technology experimental force in order to respond to twenty-first century warfare challenges.[640] The force included a space, net, EW, and psychological warfare force that serves as the basic force for IW. The PLA would be responsible for offensive network warfare and EW while other aspects (network security, psychological warfare, and intelligence warfare) would be the responsibility of other government departments.

This was far from the beginning of the Chinese effort, as the following timeline for IW developments demonstrates. Much of the work began in the early 1990s. All of these references were included in Liao's two articles.

1992 Chinese authorities develop the "China Internet Plan" controlled by the mainland.[641]

1997 The Communist Party of China (CPC) creates the National Informatization Leadership Group.[642]

1997 The General Office of the State Council upgraded and renewed the project for the main computers of the general office. For the top secret portion of the project, multi-field encryption, transmission encryption, mandatory

---

[638] Ibid.

[639] Ibid.

[640] Liao Wenzhong, "China Military Net Force: National Security, Public Security, and the People's Liberation Army," Taipei Ch'uan-Ch'iu Fang-Wei Tsa-Chih, 1-31 March 2007, pp. 58-65 as translated and downloaded from the Open Source Center website, document number CPP20071023318001.

[641] Ibid.

[642] Liao Wenzhong, "China Military Net Force: National Security…"

identification cards, mandatory access control, and the use of equipment with low electromagnetic leaks were instituted.[643]

1998 The State Council created the Ministry of Information Industry;[644] and the Third Research Institute of the Ministry of Public Security created the State Research Center of Anti-Computer Invasion and the Prevention of Viruses. The Third Research Institute trains information security agents to be responsible for the prevention and handling of computer viruses and basic testing. It takes on projects from the State 863 Plan and the Design Plan of the Gold Shield Project Security Support System.[645]

1999 The CPC started to create "information warriors."[646]

1999 The Central Military Commission of the PLA established the first psychological warfare research and teaching section at the Xi'an PLA Political College. Courses taught included military and social psychology, psychology under high-tech conditions, network warfare and psychological warfare, and psychological warfare theories and practices.[647]

2001-2003 The PLA created research centers within related IW forces or research institutes in five large cities, Zhengzhou (IW simulation research center), Jinan (IW confidentiality research center), Beijing (IW operations research center), Nanjing (IW intelligence research center), and Xian (IW operations research center). The IW operation research center in Beijing has worked with the "special information research center," formerly known as the psychic function research center.[648]

2002 The IW division of the national strategic level of the CPC determined that the PLA would be responsible for EW and IW, also known as integrated network and electronic warfare; the 4th Department of the General Staff is to form a net force composed of the PLA and information militia from the

---

[643] Liao Wen-chung, "China Military   net Force: Network Decapitation Strike and Public Security Net Force," Taipei Ch'uan-Ch'iu Fang-Wei Tsa-Chih, 1-30 April 2007, pp. 58-65, as downloaded and translated from the Open Source Center website, document number CPP20071016318001.
[644] Liao Wenzhong, "China Military Net Force: National Security…"
[645] Liao Wen-chung, "China Military Net Force: Network Decapitation…"
[646] Liao Wenzhong, "China Military Net Force: National Security…"
[647] Ibid.
[648] Ibid.

National Defense Mobilization Commission and civil information technology industry, officials, and academia.[649]

2002 It is predicted that there are 46 million Internet users in China.[650]

2002 The Ministry of Defense set up scholarships and accepted more than 200 students from different universities to study and then work for the military after graduation.[651]

2002 The PLA presented the concept of a "local war under informatized conditions" to replace the term "local war under high-tech conditions."[652]

2002 The formation of an information militia for all of China was finished. Organizationally, it has four components: an EW unit, a network warfare unit, a hacker unit, and an information rescue unit. Wartime tasks include extensive reconnaissance, information defense, and information attacks.[653]

2003-2004 Large information technology companies in developed in cities on the east coast of mainland China create national defense information militia units.[654]

2003 The CPC and State Council approved the Ministry of Public Security's effort to build the "Gold Shield Project," which would transform the entire information management sector of the public security system into an electronic version.[655]

2003 The State Development and Reform Commission of the State Council approved the 1203 Project of the Ministry of Public Security, the public key infrastructure, and authorization management systems.[656]

2004 The Ministry of Public Security and departments of public security in six provinces and municipalities were connected to security application systems with the PKI/PMI platform.[657]

---

[649] Ibid.
[650] Liao Wen-chung, "China Military Net Force: Network Decapitation…"
[651] Liao Wenzhong, "China Military Net Force: National Security…"
[652] Ibid.
[653] Ibid.
[654] Ibid.
[655] Liao Wen-chung, "China Military Net Force: Network Decapitation…"
[656] Ibid.
[657] Ibid.

2004 The number of Internet crime cases rose from 2,700 in 2000 to 13,600 in 2004; the number of network police and "network security guards" in China rises to 230,000. China recognizes the need for an independent Chinese Internet.[658]

2005 News networks in the US focusing on propaganda against China were modified, meaning that a guerilla war at the enemy's rear had been formed.[659]

2005 A Network Security Information Agency was organized, a social mechanism more like informants for intelligence agencies. They monitor social situations, perform social control, and conduct special case investigations of network use. Among network friends they are referred to as "net spies."[660]

2005 The Information Office of the State Council and the Ministry of Information Industry jointly issued the Provisions on the Administration of Internet News and Information Services. Anti-government speeches are not allowed under this provision.[661]

2005 There were close to 130 million Internet users in China.[662]

2006 The CPC declares that a wireless local area network (WLAN) Authentication and Privacy Infrastructure (WAPI) Association has been created in Beijing. It is the Chinese National Standard for WLAN to which China has independent intellectual property rights.[663]

2006 The People's Liberation Army Daily reports that the Second Artillery Force has created an "informatized blue army" formed by professional electronics information officers. The army's task is to simulate electronic and network attacks against the red army.[664]

2006 China cracks down on Internet crime and requires network users to go online with their actual names, identification, and registration.[665]

---

[658] Ibid.
[659] Liao Wenzhong, "China Military Net Force: National Security..."
[660] Liao Wen-chung, "China Military Net Force: Network Decapitation..."
[661] Ibid.
[662] Ibid.
[663] Liao Wenzhong, "China Military Net Force: National Security..."
[664] Liao Wen-chung, "China Military Net Force: Network Decapitation..."
[665] Ibid.

Other organizations and programs do exist but no dates were provided for their founding. In his article on network decapitation, Liao listed state (party) and PLA organizations. At the state level there is the Network and Information Security Team of the Informatization Work Office of the State Council. It is responsible for coordinating all institutes responsible for information security, such as the Ministries of Public Security, State Security, Information Industry, and the State Certification and Accreditation Administration, among others. The Public Information Network Security Supervision Bureau and the Net Supervision Division are in charge of the national network for information security. Some responsibility is also shared with the Division of Network and Information Security under the Information Communication Bureau for network secrets protection and security.[666]

With regard to the PLA, Liao noted that it is the 4th Department of the General Staff that is responsible for compiling IW textbooks in China. The PLA has conducted many red versus blue IW exercises. It was noted that the formation of the "blue army" by the PLA is meant to copy the combat methodology of the Red Team in the US's "IW development center." Military exercises with IW subthemes, such as "Vanguard 206B,"showed how different sub-phases, characteristics, armed services, branches, and transportation equipment could be integrated through the information power of an electronic warfare troops' "net force."[667]

The PLA believes there will be a battle for virtual territory and for the material battlefield. The true "net force" lies in the information militia of the Information Mobilization Office under the State Mobilization Commission. It will continue to try to become independent of the world of networks by developing a China Internet as well. Liao concluded the article by noting the following

> The 'net force' is a brand new type of 'Grand War' scheme that combines high-tech knowledge with politics, economy, psychology, and information networks and that is 'all people being soldiers, the integration of peace and warfare, and dual usage for the military and civilians.' The combat types of the 'net force' include both offense and defense. It must cooperate with strictly designed psychological warfare, and must possess the capability of acquiring 24-hour accurate intelligence. Furthermore, it requires a set of rapid and dense 'network

---

[666] Ibid.
[667] Liao Wen-chung, "China Military Net Force: Network Decapitation…"

platforms' for intelligent attacks on enemies at any time, covering the whole field and from all directions.[668]

China's independent and dedicated "net force" will be able to hide while Taiwan's Microsoft system will be exposed. Taiwan will have to figure out how to deal with this as soon as possible.

In the article on network security, Liao also discussed organizations and the PLA. The CPC formed an Information Mobilization Office under the National Defense Mobilization Commission that is parallel to the Defense Ministry. The office is mainly responsible for the overall mobilization of Chinese manpower and resources during wartime. Thus the military can "incorporate the local information forces through the information mobilization offices to generate combat power, and achieve the goal of utilizing the civil forces for military purposes and integrating peacetime and wartime." Civil forces include the information industry, communications management posts, communications science and technology, information education, broadcasting and TV, and satellite communications.[669]

The CPC's Department of Information Industry has a secret office that "recruits and absorbs computer geniuses" in computer science. These individuals are termed "network warriors" and have the freedom to test computer programs. They are taught to monitor Internet surfers or become hackers, software designers, or decoders. Others are sent abroad to settle in a foreign country and become a station for China's IW efforts in that country.[670]

The Psychological Warfare Institute concluded that psychological warfare must be integrated from the beginning of a conflict. It must be combined with precision strikes and utilize the media to influence public opinion and enhance the strength of deterrence; must utilize network warfare throughout while preventing the enemy from breaking into friendly units; and must have a design aligned with national policies, strategies, and stratagem. The strategic office of the CMC plans and conducts the CPC's military strategy and psychological warfare effort. The latter is the base for strategic warfare and uses the Internet and networks as representative operational techniques.[671]

China's State Council has proposed that it will use McWILL (Multi-carrier Wireless Internet Local Loop) as its broadband wireless Internet system,

---

[668] Ibid.
[669] Liao Wenzhong, "China Military Net Force: National Security…"
[670] Ibid.
[671] Ibid.

to which it has independent intellectual property rights. It can cover a radius of 19 kilometers and its urban single station coverage can be one to three kilometers. It can maintain good communication while moving at 72 miles per hour.[672]

An organization that the PLA created is the Institute of Technology. It was created from the Communications Engineering College, the College of Engineering Force, the Meteorological College of the Air Force, and 63 other related research institutes with General Staff affiliations. The director of the Institute of Technology was the director of the 4th Department of the General Staff (it is unknown if this affiliation has remained). The Institute founded a Research Center for Internet Technology for the entire army and allocated more than 400 experts and professors to the center. The institute plans to accept 60 students with doctorate degrees each year to enrich its faculty. Research projects are focused on the organizational structure of the military, weapons and equipment, campaign and tactics, education, training, and logistical support.[673]

Conclusion

There are areas of agreement between Taiwanese and Western analysts as to the direction of Chinese IW. One obvious area of agreement is both groups focus on the Chinese interest in gaining "control" of cyber operations. Information supremacy is another area of common agreement. Another common point regarding terminology is the use of both groups of the term "strategic information warfare." Taiwanese IW experts do, however, extract a different terminological understanding in some instances than do Western analysts and these differences lead to different degrees of emphasis.

Some of the interesting PLA IW concepts that Taiwanese military professionals highlight in the discussion above included:

- Acupuncture war, which establishes the examination of critical points in a network that, much like the pressure points in martial arts, when taken out, can shut down an entire system.
- Highly-controlled war, which is a new form of warfare that attempts to control the scale, form, means, and results of a war with information.
- Strategic information war, which is understood to be the integration of political, economic, military, diplomatic, and other areas to

---

[672] Ibid.
[673] Ibid.

produce an overall or comprehensive information victory. The targets of strategic IW include national political, monetary, communications, and other crucial sectors down to single weapon systems such as aircraft carriers.

- Political work Web sites, which have established distant learning capabilities and data-bases for quick access to information not readily available in the past.
- Intangible war, which focuses on strategies, market competition, legal systems, and intellectual property rights. These are areas of importance that the West must not overlook.
- Network warriors are computer geniuses in computer science who have the freedom to test computer programs. They are taught to monitor Internet surfers or become hackers, software designers, or decoders. Others are sent abroad to settle in a foreign country and become a station for China's IW efforts in that country.

Further, it is important to remember that China obtained Microsoft's code. We do not have the code that the Chinese will use internally and probably never will. This allows them to "interact" with our systems and code to a degree unimaginable in the past and in a way that we cannot replicate with their system.

Other Taiwanese observations of PLA capabilities in 2008 were also of interest. For example, when reviewing China's military strategies after the 17th National Party Congress, several points were made by Taiwanese officials, especially in regard to the PLA's military strategy, for which Taiwan must be prepared. First, military strategy toward Taiwan revealed the requirement "to win a partial war under informatization conditions" by 2050.[674] The three step strategy to do so involves creating a solid information base by 2010, achieving a quantum leap in technology around 2020, and achieving the goal of winning an informatization war by the middle of the twenty-first century.

Further, Taiwan must consider not just "how" the PLA has turned from a semi-mechanized force to an informatized force but more importantly what this implies for their mode of operations and application of military strength against Taiwan. Increased reconnaissance, monitoring, and long-range capabilities will increase the PLA's overall capacity and impact on Taiwan's

---

[674] Liu Wen-hsiang and Wu Chien-te, "Investigation into the PRC's Taiwan Military Strategy after the 17th National Congress of the Communist Party of China (CPC)," Taipei K'ung-chun Chun-kuan Shuang-yueh-k'an, as translated and downloaded from the Open Source Center website, document number CPP20080819312002.

current assumptions about CPC invasion options. Decisive battle may be replaced by "hide-and-seek" operations under informatization conditions that use deterrence, blockades, paralysis, and other information measures. Harassing attacks may be supplemented with a "threat put forward to take massive military action to force us into political peace talks."[675]

Taiwan is rightly concerned with the aggressive direction that the Chinese have taken with their informatized force. A close eye must be kept on the scientific and technological advances that the PLA is making and how it will integrate them with their military forces' operations and strategy.

---

[675] Ibid.

PART FOUR:
Conclusions

CHAPTER TEN: CONCLUSIONS

Introduction

The purpose of The Dragon's Quantum Leap was to describe the PLA's new mode of thinking. This was accomplished through examining specific articles dedicated to the topic and through examining selected applications of new, digital-oriented thought in the fields of deception, reconnaissance, stratagems, military culture, and other areas. The PLA continues to make progress toward an informatized mode of thought. This is evident in PLA military field exercises and in their professional discussions in military journals where practice and theory are furthered.

The apparent goal of the PLA's newly-developed digital prowess/quantum leap is to allow it to be fully prepared to achieve electronic *shi* (electronic strategic advantage)[676] early in the twenty-first century. An electronic advantage could be attained by uncovering vulnerabilities in a potential enemy's digital systems through electronic reconnaissance activities or by disseminating viruses to vulnerable systems. Both activities would likely occur in peacetime to allow the PLA an initial advantage if war broke out. With electronic *shi* the PLA can utilize the Sun Tzu concept of "win victory before the first battle." Victory is won by having identified the vulnerabilities capable of crashing or destroying a potential adversary's information systems before the first shot is fired. Has the attainment of this advantage already happened? An adversary of China may not know until their systems crash or are destroyed.

Perhaps the most important document indicative of China's transformation and quantum leap in thought was the PLA's 2009 Chinese Defense White Paper. In this document, the term mechanization, which usually was the centerpiece of prior White Papers, was used only seven or eight times while the terms informatized and informatization were mentioned nearly 50 times. The emphasis on the latter terms clearly indicates that these concepts now serve as the theoretical and developmental path for the armed forces.

Of course, this has not been an entirely smooth journey for the PLA. The transformation and application of informatized thought has had its

---

[676] For a more detailed examination of the concept of electronic *shi*, see Timothy L. Thomas, "China's Cyber Tool: Striving to Attain Electronic *Shi*?", forthcoming in Law, Policy and Technology: Cyberterrorism, Information Warfare, and Digital Immobilization, Pauline C. Reich and Eduardo Gelbstein, Editors, IGI Global publishers, 2010.

problems. However, the PLA fully recognizes the current shortcomings of its force in relation to the technically-advanced forces of the West. The PLA has worked to overcome these shortcomings, highlighting the need for officers to think strategically and operationally and to be creative and innovative in all areas of military affairs. Innovation and creativity are key to the thoughtful development of new technological ways to affect strategic, operational, and tactical issues. This includes, for example, how information technologies can enhance deception, campaign stratagems, and crisis management techniques.

By 2009 most of the problems from earlier years were solved. In May the PLA announced that it would hold a massive information warfare exercise in the second half of 2009. For the first time the exercise would involve troops from four military regions. The exercise was

> aimed at assessing and improving the PLA's overall combat capacity in the context of information warfare. It will put to the test the PLA's capacity in command and decision-making, joint operations of land and air troops, operations in complicated electro-magnetic conditions, assault operations, simulated battles, and comprehensive exercises by specialist units.[677]

The conclusions that follow summarize the general changes uncovered in the preparation of this book that are reflective of the PLA's new mode of thinking. These changes appear to have the required digital legs to take China to new levels of achievement and advancement. However, readers should remember that while this new mode of thought may represent a quantum leap for China in the opinion of this author, it may or may not for other analysts or for other nations. Context matters as does a willingness to move outside one's own "template and paradigm" comfort zone.

Indicators of New Modes of Thought

The PLA's focus on cognitive issues (especially strategic issues) over its long military history undoubtedly has buttressed its search for new modes of thought in the information age. Thinking is a way that the PLA can defeat western technology, a way for the inferior to defeat the superior. The authors of Unrestricted Warfare noted, for example, that "…proposing a new concept of weapons does not require relying on the springboard of new technology, it just demands lucid and incisive thinking. However, this is not a strong point of the

---

[677] Yang Yang, "China to Hold Massive Military Drill in Second Half of 2009," downloaded from http://english,cri.cn/6909/2009/05/05/1361s481984.htm

237

Americans, who are slaves to technology in their thinking."[678] It is unnerving to imagine some of the new strategic methods the Chinese government or PLA may be developing to influence world affairs through digits (manipulating the Stock Market, engaging in currency exploitation or real estate deals, using blackmail to control the price of rare earth elements, etc.). The work of Marx and Engels inadvertently (or presciently!) support the view of adapting to the information age. It was Engels who noted that "The theoretical thinking of each era, including the theoretical thinking of our times, is a historical product. It has completely different forms in different times and has completely different content."[679] China is working to uncover both the forms and the content of IW.

One Chinese author cited earlier in this book noted that "In confrontations on the future battlefield, what is scarier than inferior technology is inferior thinking." This reminder shines light on the PLA and the fact that new modes of thought are not limited to geopolitical issues, although the latter certainly does influence the former.

The US focus on technology at the expense of thought is well-documented and recognized, even by Americans. It is also represented in the legislation America passes and in hearings on Capitol Hill. Technology is often the key or only focus. The fiscal 2008 National Defense Authorization Act, for example, passed by the House, contains a provision requiring the US's annual Military Power of the People's Republic of China report to include a new section on Beijing's "efforts to acquire, develop, and deploy cyber warfare capabilities" in its assessments of China's "asymmetric" warfare capabilities.[680] A study of new modes of thought is not a part of this or most organizational agendas in Washington. This is understandable from the vantage point of the US's reliance on its military-industrial complex to solve most problems. No one pays attention to the military-thinking complex until it is late in the game, as the US counterinsurgency effort in both Iraq and Afghanistan proved. The surge played as large a role in success in Iraq as did technology.

In abbreviated form, some of the major changes uncovered or captured in the transformation discussion in The Dragon's Quantum Leap include:

- The PLA's new mode of thinking is placing more emphasis on the offense (which contradicts China's stated goal of defense).

---

[678] Qiao Liang and Wang Xiangsui, Unrestricted Warfare, Pan American Publishing Company, Panama City, Panama, 1999, p. 15.
[679] Selected Works of Marx and Engels, Beijing, The People's Press, 1995, Second Chinese Edition, Vol. 4, p. 248.
[680] Early Bird, 14 December 2007.

- The PLA's new mode of thinking focuses more on the strategic environment, as they have done historically, than US analysts who focus on the operational environment. China doesn't do PMESII-PT.[681]
- The PLA's new mode of thinking is emphasizing increased military and civilian technological integration.
- The PLA's new mode of thinking is developing CULTURAL battle simulations to accumulate the necessary information and experience to improve offensive and defensive abilities in the conduct of media warfare.
- The PLA's new mode of thinking is emphasizing informatized non-war military operations and military operations other than war (MOOTW) as the US did years ago. However, they are doing so, as they note, under informatized conditions.
- The PLA's new mode of thinking is emphasizing what the Chinese term "advanced (informatized)" military culture.
- The PLA's new mode of thinking is stressing combinations of means, "cocktail mixtures" that range beyond the traditional battlefield. This is a worrisome point and ties in with MOOTW strategies.
- The PLA's new mode of thinking is applying Sun Tzu's concepts, especially ways for the inferior to defeat the superior with information age developments. Packets of electrons now can "win victory before the first battle." (see Appendix Two for a section on "The *Shi* of Virtual Reality" that covers this topic in more detail)
- The PLA's new mode of thinking is being discussed openly in the Chinese press. This is not a covert undertaking yet it is one we do not comprehend or understand even when it is in black and white. Perhaps this is because some western analysts are stuck in their own templates and paradigms.
- The PLA's new mode of thinking is exploiting the integration of cognitive and technological topics.
- The PLA's new mode of thinking is taking into account lessons learned from watching other militaries, especially the US and its coalition partners. From these observations the Chinese have developed a huge opposing force (OPFOR) known as the "blue Force" that engages the PLA with informatized warfare theory and equipment.

---

[681] PMESII-PT is an analysis of the operational environment in terms of political, military, economic, social, infrastructure, and information with the addition of physical environment and time variables.

- The PLA's new mode of thinking is switching from a branch source, level by level (tactical to operational to strategic) thought process to a joint, integrated process.

These changes in China's mode of thinking have been quietly developing over the past ten years. For the PLA, informatized warfare concepts have opened more new avenues for innovative thinking and creative conceptualization than at any time in the past. Retired General Wang Pufeng stressed the idea of thinking a few years ago in a military journal. Wang, a former head of the Academy of Military Science's War Theory and Strategy Research Department, states that thinking and ideas are not the same thing. Thinking is the process of using a method to arrive at a reasonable understanding of something. An idea is the result of the thinking process. Strategic informatized thinking is a comprehensive process (providing new ideas for plans and operations) that stresses informatized characteristics and methods.[682]

Wang listed three factors that cannot be lacking when measuring the quality of strategy: accurately knowing the situation, possessing abundant knowledge, and possessing outstanding ability and keenness in perception (that is, a discerning or sagacious person). New modes of thought motivated by information age developments ensure these factors will be dramatically improved.[683]

To know the situation, information must be understood, the amount and flow of information must be controlled, information must be quickly processed and utilized, the good differentiated from the bad, and one must be able to see what is coming from a small clue. Knowledge must be gained from both direct experience and history. Ability refers to wisdom and knowledge while sagacity involves both strategic planning and management. The latter two (ability and sagacity) are the most essential for strategic thought in Wang's opinion.[684]

The Integration of Military and Civilian Technologies and Thought

No chapter in this book covered this topic. However, during the research for this work, the topic appeared on several occasions and clearly became worthy of mention. Informatized thought has found new ground for expansion due to the growing integration of military and civilian thought over

---

[682] Wang Pufeng, "On Strategic Thinking," China Military Science, 2004, No. 3, pp. 86-91.
[683] Ibid.
[684] Ibid.

cyber issues, an integration occurring at an ever-quickening pace. The forecast by the authors of <u>Unrestricted Warfare</u> that there would be closer integration of military and civilian assets and personnel (civilian hackers, computer industries, etc.) in the future has come true. <u>Time</u> magazine, for example, published an article demonstrating this integration. Reporter Simon Elegant wrote that "a picture is emerging of a coordinated effort by Chinese-military authorities to recruit hackers…" As proof of his accusation, Elegant refers to an interview with a Chinese hacker, Withered Rose, in a Sichuan University campus newspaper. The story not only relates information about Rose but details links between hackers and the military. Rose later won a military-sponsored hacker contest and the PLA subsequently hired him to represent the Sichuan Military command in competitions that bring military and civilian practitioners closer together.[685]

An examination of statistics and other reporting measures indicate that Chinese society is also on the cusp of some revolutionary, quantum-leap type changes in information technolgies. China now has some 298 million Internet users[686] and over 600 million mobile phone subscribers.[687] Both figures exceed such numbers in the US by a wide margin. Access has offered Chinese students a wider variety of data and expanded their reach to things and thoughts once not available. People, in this sense, take quantum leaps in their capability to access and share information in a society where information access was once very tightly controlled.

Statistics back up claims that China's social network and computer use are increasing at a quickening pace. The Chinese search engine Baidu is now the fourth most visited site in the world according to one report. It has 60% of the Chinese market compared with Google's 20%. Rebecca MacKinnon, a professor at the University of Hong Kong, notes that the Chinese will drive how the Internet evolves in the coming years since they soon will have the largest number of users. Tudou and 6rooms are more popular than YouTube in China; Xiaonei is a Facebook near equivalent; and web portals such as Qihoo are there for comparison against Yahoo. Users are younger than in the US. Their social,

---

[685] Simon Elegant, "Enemies at the Firewall," <u>Time</u>, 6 December 2007, downloaded in May 2009 at http://www.time.com/time/printout/0,8816,1692063,00.html
[686] Robin Wauters, "Meanwhile Internet Usage in China Still Booming," 14 January 2009, located at http://www.techcrunch.com/2009/01/14/meanwhile-internet-usage-in-china-still-booming/
[687]"China Mobile Phone Subscribers Pass 600 Million Mark," Textually.org, 24 July 2008, located at http://www.textually.org/textually/archives/2008/07/020854.htm

cultural, and political clout are still to be judged.[688] Most important is that these developments are changing society's mode of thinking much like the military. The common man now realizes he can participate to an extent never imagined in assisting the government with state matters (collecting data and other information across the globe) and in accessing new opportunities.

Finally, with regard to computing expertise, China reports that its quantum computing capability is now beginning to show improvement. For example, author Gregory Huang described the dreams and aspirations of the Chinese to quickly develop a quantum computing device in the journal New Scientist. In an interview with Pan Jian-Wei of the University of Science and Technology (UST) of China, Huang described how Pan is trying to combine "quantum memory with a new architecture known as cluster states."[689] Quantum computing inspires researchers to use quantum mechanics to perform tasks that current computers cannot. As Huang explains

> The power of a quantum computer comes from the fact that a quantum particle can exist in more than one state at a time. So unlike a data bit in an ordinary computer, which can have the value of either 0 or 1, a quantum bit (or qubit) can simultaneously have the value 0,1 or any "superposition" of the two. So perform a calculation using qubits and you get a huge number of calculations for the price of one.[690]

When the quantum theory known as entanglement is added to the quantum phenomenon, Huang notes, it can link the properties of several qubits. Then, in principle, it is possible to represent more numbers than there are atoms in the universe.[691] Problems do exist, however. In this case the problem is the stability of an "entanglement." It turns out they are very fragile. "Cluster states," where each step has its own calculation, is Pan's attempt to overcome this problem and maintain stability with the use of photons for quantum communication. No entanglement manipulations are necessary, as they are prepared and left alone. This does, however, require preparing more entanglements before the calculations start.[692] This progress indicates that Chinese scientists are moving quickly forward and making progress in many technical areas to which new thinking (or the application of old stratagems) can be applied.

---

[688] Gregory Huang, "Boys from the Wang Ba (Internet Bar)," New Scientist, 10 November 2007, pp. 66-67.
[689] Gregory Huang, "Master of Qubits," New Scientist, 10 November 2007, p. 69.
[690] Ibid.
[691] Ibid.
[692] Ibid., p. 70.

Future War

The most prominent US author on the topic of Chinese future war is Michael Pillsbury. In his 1997 book <u>Chinese Views of Future Warfare</u>, only one chapter dealt specifically with future military trends while his 2000 book on <u>China Debates the Future Security Environment </u>was more specific. Here Pillsbury covered the broad category of forecasting future wars from a Chinese perspective and discussed topics such as force structure, the revolution in military affairs, power projections, and future People's War theories. Nothing approaching Pillsbury's work has subsequently appeared.

Bits and pieces of the future war puzzle do appear from time to time in Chinese journals and, when assembled, they make an intriguing mosaic. For example, in regard to futuristic systems, there is Chinese interest in quantum and optical computer developments; micro-nano technologies; gene technologies; supersonic technologies; ion invisibility technology; unmanned platform technology; and developments in directed energy technology among many other high-technology projects. These developments indicate steady progress. The Chinese also discussed the development of a laboratory of future war and, from 2005 to 2007, the development of a command post of the future, network war, and virtual space. Bio technologies and other issues (twenty-first century inertial technologies, electromagnetic pulse bombs, thermobaric weapons, laser units, merciful (non-lethal?) weapons, and space weapons) were also topics of discussion between 2000 and 2008.

Shen Weiguang mentioned future war weapons in his work on <u>Information Warfare in China</u>. He predicted that robot war, clone war, leader war, star wars, virtual war, ideological war, media wars, and cognitive wars will all reflect the features of what he termed ideal wars of the future. Other authors in Shen's book stated that countermeasures will be key to ensuring that a future struggle comes out in China's favor. Feng Yi and Zhang Jie wrote that China's counter technology path must develop five concepts:

- Anti-satellite equipment
- Counter warning systems/reconnaissance equipment
- Counter GPS systems
- Electronic warfare technology
- Concealment devices.

Concluding Thoughts

The examination of these selected aspects of China's new mode of thinking offers various portraits that could be painted. For example, is China aggressive or helpful in its new mode of thinking? The former picture could be

243

painted by China's network reconnaissance and development of digital stratagems and deception. The latter picture could be painted by China's apparent desire to work hard at developing its crisis management techniques and interest in working closer with the west. Books like Unrestricted War also help, in a strange way, to move discussion forward due to the PLA authors open critique of future conflict.

On the whole, however, China's new mode of thinking is worrisome. It has produced many new issues to which the west must pay attention. Network psychological warfare, Chinese-specific adaptations to new information technologies, and the concepts of system attack warfare and pre-emptive strikes with electrons will require our constant attention. The Chinese recognize that information technologies can be used in politics, on the battlefield, or in combinations of political and military means.

The revolution in military and information technology, of course, has produced a corresponding revolution in military thinking, operational methods, and structural organization. Retired Chinese Major General Wang Baocun wrote that the informatization buildup relies on the comprehensive integration of a mechanized force's "materials and energy" and an informatized force's "information and knowledge." First priority must be placed on the development of C4I systems, the integration of early warning and interdiction, command and control, and precision strikes.

Ma Yexi wrote that computer network war (CNW) of the future must include deterrence, reconnaissance, disruption, deception, and protection methods. CNW's ability to enable superiority (and convince an opponent that capabilities and advantages lie with friendly forces) can cause CNW to become a "network deterrent" that forces opponents to respect and play by China's rules of the game. Finally, Mei Jun wrote that "trump cards" must receive priority development. They must focus on electronic destruction capabilities. Intensive microwave interference equipment, electromagnetic pulse weapons, and laser anti-satellite equipment represent three types of trump card weapons. Mei wrote that whoever achieves advantages in the fight for network space will possess the strategic initiative in the twenty-first century, implying that control over network space is a critical trump card. A paralyzed network can cause losses to the national economy, create social chaos, and reduce combat capability among other consequences.

With regard to the US focus on technology, authors Qiao and Wang write that war will not follow a fixed race course based on technology and weaponry as the US believes. Focused and lucid thought can still allow the inferior to defeat the superior in their opinion.

Technology use in politics or economics, in consort with economics, can be a deadly pairing for use against other nations. Perhaps most important for national security personnel studying the PLA is that stratagems can be applied to political, economic, and other fields of study. One can hypothesize that Chinese civilian institutes in existence now are involved in the study of stratagems to manipulate US financial flows or to create situations against which the diplomatic community must react. Therefore, the US and its allies must think about such contingencies and eventualities in peacetime. Stratagems can be silent manipulators that cause decision-makers to do as the Chinese desire.

China's interest in culture must also be monitored. In the words of one author, China must construct socialist culture with Chinese characteristics; must create cultural diffusion hardware and software over which China has autonomous intellectual property rights; and, most important for Western audiences, China must take action to "propel China's culture industry and media industry beyond China's borders in an effort to take over the international culture market."[693] China is already engaged in spreading its culture beyond its borders. For example, is the spread of the Confucius Institutes an aggressive or helpful project? Based on the thought of "taking over the international culture market" the project would be deemed aggressive. There are now 282 Confucius Institutes in 272 classrooms in 88 countries according to a Chinese source. There are 87 such institutes in 205 classrooms in 12 countries in the Americas alone.[694] If the purpose of the institutes is to broaden cooperation and understanding, then they certainly would be viewed as helpful.

The battlefield has become a testing ground for many technological advances. Today's battlefield is characterized by continually changing direction and many irregular factors due to the existence of so many technological advances that can be purchased "off the shelf" by nation-states or insurgents. Outcomes on the battlefield will depend as much on creative thought in the application of technological advances as on the technology itself. Chinese authors recognize that the PLA must create power for itself on the battlefield by creating situations and developing them as they intend. Thinking matters in

---

[693] Wang Shudao, "Modern Cultural Diffusion and National Security," China Military Science, 2005, No. 3, pp. 64-69.
[694] Information downloaded from http://college.chinese.cn/node_1941.htm. The author would like to thank Mr. Scott Henderson of FMSO for pointing out this website.

such cases. For example, the PLA is working to find technological ways to obscure the outlines of military equipment in the field to prevent their acquisition by enemy targeteers and thus attain deception. These new technological advances are combined with stratagems or perception management techniques to provide new and innovative ways to fool potential enemy decision-makers. Stratagems are designed to induce cognitive confusion into an opponent's decision-making process and cause enemy commanders to make decisions based on false information. Using advanced surveillance equipment to obtain a top-down image of an area provides a "vision" for stratagem (perception management) developers to work from and with. Stratagem designers then provide input to computers to produce more technologically based strategic deception options. However, this requires sophisticated commanders who understand how to exploit the most recent scientific and technological breakthroughs and combine them with stratagem and deception techniques to enable the optimum level of combat efficiency.

The Chinese government and PLA's use of potential combinations of technical, political, and battlefield elements buttressed by new modes of thought must continue to be a top priority area of study for western analysts and their consideration of Chinese strategy. The Chinese most likely have continued to work with the thoughts of selected officers like Qiao and Wang. Perhaps they have developed new elements and new combinations of unrestricted warfare techniques. For example, in order to "win victory before the first battle" China may be considering a combination of the following means: cyber preemption + control of financial resources + network reconnaissance + new concepts of weapons (ways to crash the stock market, for example) + high-tech campaign stratagems + high-tech deception. Qiao and Wang added other stimulating and at times scary messages for Western audiences (not the least of which is that war with the US is "inevitable"). Western analysts need to think and be aware of these proclivities if they hope to counter them.

In conclusion, the West's technological advantage is still applicable and far superior to that of the PLA. However, the PLA's transformation leap and reliance on new modes of thought has the nation postured to conduct informatized war in both peacetime and wartime. It is the peacetime use of informatized concepts that should worry the West most since this is where the West is the most vulnerable.

While there are many reasons to fear China's peacetime use of informatized warfare, two stick out. They are China's interest in using a combination of methods to manipulate the information and financial security of another nation in China's favor; and the ability of China to conduct reconnaissance and offensive activities anonymously and, if detected, to declare plausible deniability. Such activities make China a wily and confident adversary who is willing to take enormous risks to "design programs which coerce the enemy into playing according to our [China's] rules." Chinese analysts also have written that in some cases Chinese systems will be defended by attacking adversary systems. Such thoughts imply that deception and offensive actions are at the heart of many Chinese IW moves.

The West must ensure to its utmost ability that China's risk-taking is forecasted and monitored properly. If not, Western leaders may fall prey to some ancient stratagem that has been technologically developed and hidden; or an unintended conflict may emerge over issues that can be settled outside of the battlefield. The PLA's ideas expressed in this work indicate that western nations must prepare now some realistic methods for better uncovering and exposing Chinese designs. Otherwise, the Chinese will have no obstructions on their path to attaining electronic *shi* and the strategic electronic advantage the term implies.

Hopefully, analysts will continue their interest and study of the PLA and its new thinking deep into the twenty-first century. Western analysts must become as adept at studying the Chinese as the Chinese are at studying us. Only in this way will the west truly comprehend if someone is trying to impose a stratagem on them in an act of aggression; or if someone is just trying to help alleviate a crisis or confrontation. If the world truly is on the cusp of witnessing the emergence of China the world's most influential power, then Chinese specialists should be able to find employment for many years to come.

APPENDIX ONE: IW ARTICLES IN CHINA MILITARY SCIENCE: 2007-2009

The titles listed in English below are from the journal China Military Science and are representative of the IW content of this PLA journal. Dragon Bytes listed the IW articles in this journal from 1999-2003. Decoding the Virtual Dragon listed IW articles from 2004-2006. This section thus updates that list. The titles in this section are listed as they appeared in China Military Science, starting with the most current issue available and working backward to No. 1, 2007. As noted earlier, all PLA journals and newspapers continue to write extensively on the subject of informatization in China.

To continue a procedure initiated in Dragon Bytes, only those titles with "high-tech," "digitalization," "precision," "network," "system of systems" "information," or some other clear IW related term in the title are listed. Any Chinese discussion of US IO is also listed as are articles about psychological operations since they are an ingredient of Chinese IW.

Number 6, 2009 (not available at time of printing)

Number 5, 2009
"On Relations between Military Soft Power and Comprehensive National Power and State's Soft Power," Long Fangcheng and Li Decai, pp. 120-129
"Study of Network Warfare in Terms of International Law," Zheng Guoliang and Zheng Ming, pp. 130-135.

Number 4, 2009
"Air Superiority in Local Wars under Informatized Conditions," Wu Wenjun and Tan Fuzhi, pp. 77-83.
"On Fire Warfare under Informatized Conditions," Li Yun, pp. 84-89, 97.

Number 3, 2009
"Analysis of New Changes in Principles of Information Warfare," Wang Hui and Geng Haijun, pp. 18-23.
"On the Nature and Categories and Forms of Information Operations," Dong Xuezhen and Tian Yuping, pp. 24-35.
"Considerations on Innovative Development of Military Armament Science under Informatized Conditions," Guo Shizhen, pp. 79-90.
"Fundamentals in Theories of PLA Informatization," Li Jing, pp. 100-105.

Number 2, 2009

"Transformation of Military Science Research Patterns under Informatized Conditions," Geng Weidong and Jiang Shaosan, pp. unknown at time of printing.
"Recent Development in the Study of the Idea of People's War under Informatized Conditions," Wang Wei and Yang Zhen, pp. unknown at time of printing.

Number 1, 2009
None

Number 6, 2008
None

Number 5, 2008
"Study of the Law of Army Informatization Building," Li Yanbin, et al, pp. unknown.

Number 4, 2008
"On the Content and Method System of Military Training under Information Conditions," Chai Yuqiu and Zhou Daolei, pp. 21-26.
Research into Fundamental Issues of Operations under Information Conditions (special section in this issue of China Military Science that included the following four articles)
"On the Changes of Relations between Strategy and Campaign-Combat in Modern War," Cui Yafeng, pp. 27-37.
"A Study of the Complex Systems Theory of Information War," Zhu Xiaoning and Xia Liang, pp. 38-48.
"A Systematic Analysis of the Factors that Affect the Generation of Combat Capability," Yang Xin and Zhang Zhiyu, pp. 49-61.
"On the Fundamental Issues of Complex Electromagnetic Environments," Wang Ruqun, pp. 62-70.

Number 3, 2008
"On Creative Development of National Defense Science and Technology Theory under Informatized Conditions," Li Decai and Ou Lishou, pp. 42-51.
"Outline of Strategic Theory of Army Informatization Building," Niu Li and Zhang Sanhu, pp. 52-59.
"On the Trend of Transformation of Operations Theory under Informatized Conditions," Li Zhilin, pp. 60-68.

Number 2, 2008

"Military Soft Power in the Field of Vision to Win Informationalized Wars," Wang Lianshui and Ni Heliang, pp. 63-67.
"Science and Technology: the First Combat Power of the Information Age," Song Li, pp. 115-126.

Number 1, 2008
"Promote a Better and Faster Scientific Development of Informationalization in Political Work," Shen Guoquan, pp. 98-105.
"On the Weak Defeating the Strong under Information Conditions," Peng Hongqi, pp. 142-148.

Number 6, 2007
"Revolution in Military Thinking in the Information Age," Deng Yifei, pages unknown.

Number 5, 2007
"Get Hold of the Essence of the New Revolution in Military Affairs and Advance the Integration of Information Technology and Military Science," Ren Haiquan, pp. 77-85.
"Understand the Characteristics and Laws of Military Training under Information Conditions and Promote Further Development in the Transformation of Military Training," Cui Yafeng, pp. 109-115.

Number 4, 2007
"Implement the Scientific Development Concept and Advance the Training of Talents under Information Conditions," Cadres Department of the PLA General Political Department, pp. 78-82.
"A Study of Issues in Military Training under Information Conditions," Wang Xibin, pp. 88-95.
"A Study of the Basic Characteristics of Modes of Thinking in Information Warfare," Li Deyi, pp. 101-105.

Number 3, 2007
None

Number 2, 2007
None

Number 1, 2007
"Ensure Historical Orientation and Promote All-Round Innovation of Army Informationalization," Dai Qingmin, pp. 77-83.

"On Building Soft Military Power," Wang Xingsheng and Wu Zhizhong, pp. 92-98.

"On Logistics Information Warfare—Offense and Defense of Military Losistic Supply Chain," Li Li, Chen Hong, and Wang Jinfa, pp. 99-108.

APPENDIX TWO: ON DEVELOPING VIRTUAL *SHI* AND A VIRTUAL THIRTY-SIX STRATAGEMS

This appendix examines the term "shi" and the thirty-six stratagems of war. Both concepts form a part of the foundation of classic Chinese thought. The appendix focuses on the concepts applicability in the information or cyber age.[695]

Introduction

China's history and culture is rich in military wisdom and philosophy. An examination of the thought processes that support this wisdom offers templates, insights, and models from which to do three things: better evaluate the Chinese military's potential intentions and methods; work with the PLA based on this understanding; and develop new Western military concepts.

This appendix examines two Chinese concepts of importance that may assist in these endeavors. The term *shi* (pronounced like the English word "sure") is one such concept. The word *shi* appears eighty or more times in Chinese dictionaries and each time it is expressed by a different Chinese character with a different meaning (but is still pronounced *shi*).[696] *Shi* (as is the case with many Chinese pinyin expressions) can be expressed linguistically via four tones, which are: neutral, ascending, descending, or descending-ascending. For each tone there are twenty or so different Chinese characters. For example, the words ten, teacher, non-commissioned officer, time of day, to begin, to be, to test, to make, to see, to know, room, and thing are all pronounced via one of the four tones of *shi*. Each one is expressed/written with a different Chinese character. Therefore it is important to know just which Chinese character of *shi* one is speaking about and defining.

In the case of this chapter, different Chinese and English speaking authors have translated the *shi* character under examination in several different ways adding to the confusion. *Shi* is defined as energy, power, momentum, and strategic advantage, among other translations. An examination of this *shi* character is discussed below.

---

[695] This author reviewed the articles herein and credits the content, concepts, and ideas to the primary authors noted. Translation credit belongs to a private company used by FMSO for the article by Ren Li and to the Open Source Center for the remaining articles.

[696] Discussion with Chinese language instructors Marn-Ling Wang and David Dai at the US Defense Language Institute, July 2009.

Why should this concept be of any concern? Noted Western Sinologist Roger Ames has called the concept of *shi* "the key and defining idea in Sun-Tzu: The Art of Warfare." Ames translates the term as "strategic advantage." He also notes that *shi* "is a level of discourse through which one actively determines and cultivates the leverage and influence of one's particular place."[697] The popular Western Sinologist Ralph Sawyer defines this type of *shi* as the "strategic configuration of power."[698] Other Western and Chinese specialists' definitions of the same character are offered as well, with some specialists agreeing and some disagreeing with the concepts of strategic advantage and strategic configuration of power.

The other concept under consideration is that of a stratagem, most often discussed in conjunction with the thirty-six stratagems of war. A stratagem is designed to mislead enemy processes of perception, thinking, emotion, and will. It is used to deceive an opponent and result in a favorable tactical advantage. *Shi* and stratagem are important military concepts adaptable to the age of electrons as reviews of recent Chinese articles indicate.

The examination of *shi* that follows is based on different linguists' translations of the concept in The Art of War, on the views of experts on the topic, and on definitions from dictionaries or philosophical compendiums. Such an examination allows one to consider all the linguistic variants of the term. The concept is also examined from the contemporary context of what might be expected from the "strategic configuration of electrons" or from one of the other definitions of *shi*.

The section on the thirty-six stratagems examines the views of a strategic thinker at the Chinese Academy of Military Science. His discussion compares the Art of War and the Thirty-Six Stratagems. The comparison enlightens a Western reader's understanding of Chinese "informationized" military thought and culture and how stratagems are also being applied in the age of electrons.

In essence, this appendix explains how concepts developed thousands of years ago are still applicable today and worthy of further consideration.

The Difficulty in Understanding the Concept of *Shi*

A Chinese term that has eluded a precise Western definition is "*shi*" (also spelled "*shih*"; the spelling of *shi* or *shih* used in the following pages is

---

[697] The Book of War, The Modern Library, New York, 2000, p. 50.
[698] Ralph D. Sawyer, The Art of War, Fall River Press, 1994, pp. 143-147.

dependent on the spelling used by individual authors who are quoted). It is a concept familiar to the Chinese and foreign students of Chinese philosophy, such as US sinologists. But it is a concept hardly ever encountered by others not in these categories.

William H. Mott IV and Jae Chang Kim, authors of The Philosophy of Chinese Military Culture: Shih vs. Li, write that *shih* was the defining theme in The Art of War and that "the essence of *shih* was the dynamic power that emerged in the combination of men's hearts, military weapons, and natural conditions."[699] Thus, while the significance of *shi* is clear to major writers and translators, what is exactly meant by *shi* is not! Further, if these scholars consider *shi* to be the key and defining theme of the Art of War, then analysts should pay attention to the term and investigate why it is of such significance to these scholars and linguists.

Ralph Sawyer writes in his edited version of The Seven Military Classics of Ancient China that *shih's* definition varies with its use in the Art of War; is interrelated with developments in Legalist thought; can represent tactical power where strategic power appears inappropriate in scope; and is defined differently by most expert US translators.[700]

Roger Ames believes *shih* can be traced back to Legalist, Confucian, and even Taoist philosophical sources.[701] In his 1993 Sun Tzu: The Art of War volume, Ames explains the difficulty in correctly translating *shih* in ancient texts in the following way:

> These texts, emerging as they do out of concrete historical experience, tend to communicate through the medium of image, historical allusion, and analogy. What constitutes evidence and makes things clear in the text is often an effectively focused image, not a theory; an inexpressible and inimitable experience, not an argument; an evocative metaphor, not a logically demonstrated truth. The style, then, respects the priority of the unique particular–a defining characteristic of emergent harmony.[702]

Dr. Michael Pillsbury, one of America's foremost authorities on the PLA and author of several comprehensive works on Chinese military thought,

---

[699] William H. Mott IV and Jae Chang Kim, The Philosophy of Chinese Military Culture: Shih vs. Li, Palgrave MacMillan, 2006, p. 11.
[700] Ralph D. Sawyer, The Seven Military Classics of China, Westview Press, 1993, pp. 429-432.
[701] Roger Ames, Sun Tzu: The Art of Warfare, 1993, Ballantine Books, p. 281.
[702] Ibid., p. 73.

used his study of PLA materials to explain several components of *shi* that appear key to understanding the concept:

- *Shi* assesses your side's potential, the enemy side's potential, weather, and geography to identify the moment in a campaign when an advantage can be gained over an opponent. *Shi* is a certain moment in the campaign when you could take the advantage from the enemy (He Diqing, <u>Campaign Course Materials</u>, AMS 2001);
- *Shi* is created in five ways, through maneuver, posture, position, psychology, and calculations. The timing and speed of creating *shi* in war has changed under conditions of high-tech warfare (Yue Lan, "High Tech Warfare and Contemporary Military Philosophy," <u>Liberation Army Daily Press</u>, 2000)
- *Shi* is the moment when it becomes apparent one side can win the war (Guo Shengwei, <u>Deng Xiaoping's Military Stratagems</u>, Central Party School, 2000)
- *Shi* according to the Tang founder used psycho-shi, geo-shi, and shaping-shi (Zhang Wenru, <u>China's Strategic Culture</u>, Beijing University Press, 1997);
- and *shi* can be created with stratagems (Li Bingyan, <u>Stratagem and Transformation</u>, 2004).[703]

Definitions of *shi* by a host of US sinology and Chinese experts are quite varied as Sawyer and Ames suggest. Thirteen Western and ten Chinese definitions of *shi* follow. Each represents a different way of explaining the concept:

Western:

- Roger Ames, a leading interpreter of Chinese philosophy and culture, from <u>The Art of War</u>: *shih* is strategic or battle advantage.[704]
- Ralph D. Sawyer, translator and commentator on Sun Tzu's <u>The Art of War</u>: *shi* is the strategic configuration of power, a strategic concept; advantage from superior position and power (an army's overall capacity [endurance, spirit, equipment, command, etc.] instead of just numbers) of the force involved.[705]

---

[703] This information was taken from a slide presentation that Dr. Pillsbury sent to this author.
[704] Ames.
[705] Sawyer.

- Samuel B. Griffith, translator and commentator on The Art of War: *shih* means force, influence, authority, energy. Griffith used "energy" as the translation for Chapter Five of the Art of War. He stated in a footnote that *shih* could mean energy or potential in some cases and situation in others.[706]
- Lionel Giles, The Art of War: Giles also translated the term *shih* as energy.
- Mark McNeilly, author of Sun Tzu and the Art of Modern Warfare: *shih* is translated as energy. His footnote is identical to Griffith's and he clearly used Griffith's entire translation in his work.[707]
- Denma Translation Group's The Art of War: *shih* is the power inherent in a configuration.[708]
- Francois Jullien, author of The Propensity of Things: *shi* is the potential that originates not in human initiative but instead results from the very disposition of things.[709]
- William H. Mott IV and Jae Chang Kim, authors of The Philosophy of Chinese Military Culture: *shi* is the dynamic power that emerged in the combination of men's hearts, military weapons, and natural conditions.[710] Also used to mean the following: threaten, manipulate, deter, power, force, influence, situation's natural features, tendency, trend, gestures, and a person's circumstances.[711]
- Dr. Gary Bjorge of the US Army's Combat Studies Institute: S*hi* is "like the force of rushing water that lifts stones from a stream bed, like a drawn crossbow, and like round rocks rolling down a steep mountain slope;" it offers a sense of potential energy in a situation and the existence of momentum and force.[712]

---

[706] Samuel B. Griffith, The Art of War, Oxford University Press, 1958, p. 90.

[707] Mark McNeilly, Sun Tzu and the Art of Modern Warfare, Oxford University Press, 2001. McNeilly provided commentary on Griffith's translation.

[708] The Denma Translation, The Art of War, Shambhala, 2003, explanation of *shih* on a card sold with the book.

[709] Francois Jullien, The Propensity of Things, Zone Books, New York, 1999, p. 13.

[710] William H. Mott IV and Jae Chang Kim, The Philosophy of Chinese Military Culture, Palgrave MacMillan, 2006, p. 11.

[711] Ibid., p. 15.

[712] Gary J. Bjorge, Moving the Enemy: Operational Art in the Chinese PLA's Huai Hai Campaign, Leavenworth Paper Number 22, [no date given], p. 53.

- Alastair Iain Johnston, author of <u>Cultural Realism</u>: *shi* is actualized military power.[713]
- T. W. Kuo, <u>Sun Tzu: Manual for War</u>: Kuo used the term "force" for his definition of *shih*.[714]
- <u>Military Power of the People's Republic of China</u>, 2007: *shi* is the strategic configuration of power, also understood as the alignment of forces. There is no direct Western equivalent of the term, according to the report.[715]
- Dr. Michael Pillsbury, 2009: see two pages prior for his citations from PLA materials.

Chinese:

- <u>Chinese-English Dictionary</u>: *shi* is power, force, influence; momentum, tendency; outward appearance of a natural object; situation, state of affairs, circumstances; sign, gesture; male genitals.[716]
- Lin Wusun, translator of <u>Sun Zi: The Art of War, Sun Bin: The Art of War</u> (advertised as "two great Chinese military classics in one volume"): *shi* is momentum and the term *xing* is disposition.[717]
- <u>Chinese Encyclopedia of Philosophical Terms</u>: *shi* is "an inevitable trend in historical development."[718] S*hi* and reason are inseparable, the "divine reasoning in the intention." S*hi* is "availing oneself of advantage to gain control, a natural interest" while law is the basis for governing with *shi*. S*hi* "changes with each passing day and cannot return to its former self."[719]
- Tao Hanzhang, Chinese General: *shi* is "the strategically advantageous posture before a battle that enables it to have a flexible, mobile, and changeable position during a

---

[713] Alastair Iain Johnston, <u>Cultural Realism</u>, Princeton University Press, 1995, p. 97.
[714] T. W. Kuo, <u>Sun Tzu: Manual for War</u>, 1989, ATLI CORP, p. 47.
[715] <u>Annual Report to Congress: Military Power of the People's Republic of China</u>, 2007, US Government Printing Office, p. 7.
[716] Wang Zuomin and David Crook, chief editors, <u>Chinese-English Dictionary</u>, Beijing Foreign Language Institute of English, 1992, p. 625.
[717] Wu Rusong and Wu Xianlin, chief editors, <u>Sun Zi: The Art of War, Sun Bin: The Art of War</u>, People's China Publishing House, 1995, pp. 32-34.
[718] Feng Qi, <u>Chinese Encyclopedia of Philosophical Terms</u>, Revised Edition, Shanghai Lexicographical Publishing House, 2001, p. 1355.
[719] Ibid.

campaign."[720] Chapter Five (*Shi*) in Tao's translation of The Art of War was translated as "posture of the army."[721]

- Sui Yun, translator for the ASIAPAC book The Art of War: *shi* is defined as "momentum."[722]
- Tienzen Gong, in the online article "Satellite Killer, Unbreakable Codes, and More:" literally, the word *shi* means "holding forces with hands." Those with *shi* can control a boulder rolling down a mountain. A general must control and articulate *shi*, creating *shi* for friendly forces and controlling the *shi* of enemy forces and reducing it to nothing.[723]
- Chinese Golden Treasure Book on The Art of War: *shi* is defined as momentum in the Chinese book published by the China Society of the Art of War.[724]
- Li Rulong at the 6th International Symposium on Sun Tzu's Art of War: *Shi* (energy/power) strategy has always been a significant proposition. "Acting according to the situation," "planning and concocting the power," and "selecting men and employing strategic power" have always been important subjects for study by strategists throughout the ages… "power" is actually a kind of potential energy; once the external condition is provided, this energy will demonstrate a mighty power and become a force. Such an understanding can be allied to all fields of social practice including military affairs.[725]
- Xinhua Zidian (New China Dictionary): Power, authority, might (abuse one's power to take advantage of others); a condition that is manifested, appearance (pertaining to the natural world [physical features of a place, terrain, precipitous mountains], pertaining to movement [posture, gesture, sign, signal], pertaining to politics, military affairs, or other areas [current situation, trend of the times, the way things are going,

---

[720] Tao Hanzhang, Sun Tzu's Art of War: The Modern Chinese Interpretation, Sterling Innovation, 2007, p. 124.
[721] Ibid., p. 44.
[722] The Art of War, ASIAPAC BOOKS PTE LTD, 2003, p. 123.
[723] Tienzen Gong, "Satellite Killer, Unbreakable Codes, and More," www.chinese-word-roots.org, accessed on 15 January 2009.
[724] Golden Treasure Book, The Art of War By Sun Zi, Xiyuan Publishing House, 2004.
[725] Li Rulong, "A Brief Discussion of the 'Shi' Strategy," The 6th International Symposium on Sun Zi's Art of War, selected paper abstracts, pp. 71-72.

general trend, take advantage of circumstances to attack a fleeting enemy); male genitalia (castrate)[726]

- Chinese book <u>Campaign Stratagems</u>: *Shi* is situation, status, and state of affairs; the combination of the friendly situation, enemy situation, and the environment; trend in affairs; the integrated situation that has an impact on the effective performance of military strength; sum of all factors impacting the performance of the operational efficiency of both sides; general confrontational situation; hub of increase and decrease in operational efficiencies of two sides; the key factor determining the rise and fall of operational efficiency.[727]

Thus, the complexity of the term is clearly identifiable from the definitions. Posture of the army, strategic advantage, strategic configuration of power, the alignment of forces, availing oneself of advantage to gain control, potential from the disposition of things, momentum, energy, force, power, influence, and "holding forces with hands" were all used to define *shi*.

Ames writes that the translator, informed by context, must select the most appropriate definition.[728] In his view, the term *shih* is so difficult to translate since it can "combine in one idea the following cluster of meanings:"[729]

1. aspect, situation, circumstances, conditions
2. disposition, configuration, outward shape
3. force, influence, momentum, authority
4. strategic advantage, purchase[730]

Shih begins from the recognition that war unfolds within a broad field of unique natural, social, and political conditions, according to Ames, which are always changing. It includes intangibles such as morale, opportunity, timing, psychology, and logistics. Thus, with so many explanations, after awhile the analyst begins to question what is NOT *shi*.

---

[726] <u>New China Dictionary</u>, 1971, p. 395. Translation of the definition provided by Mr. Bart Zobel.
[727] Zhang Xing Ye and Zhang Zhan Li, <u>Campaign Stratagems</u>, National Defense University, 2002.
[728] <u>The Book of War</u>, p. 50.
[729] Ibid., p. 51.
[730] Ibid.

Dr. Bjorge, mentioned above, wrote that Su Yu's shaping of the 1948 Huai Hai campaign involved the fact that Su "believed that given the existing *shi*, simultaneously applying these Sunzian precepts would produce a major victory rapidly and set the stage for subsequent operations." If the energy of a good fighting man is like the momentum acquired by a round stone rolled down a mountain, then for Su and the situation before him (the capabilities and locations of the forces involved, the terrain features, and the Nationalists desire to relieve the Seventh Army) was like the mountain slope. Su's force had momentum and conditions presented the opportunity for even more. Physical and psychological energy flowed for him.[731]

Ralph Sawyer adds to this explanation, noting that *shih* is "a measure of the relative power an army derives from positional advantage combined with its overall combat strength." Positional advantage can include terrain, firepower, morale, superior provisions, and other force multipliers. The release of strategic power can vary based on these many factors.[732]

Shi has uses for other than military purposes since it has some eighty definitions as noted above. In March 2008 Qi Zhu, a Chinese national residing in California, published her doctoral dissertation on "*Shi* in Architecture: The Efficacy of Traditional Chinese Doors."[733] Qi used the <u>Chinese Encyclopedia of Philosophical Terms</u> which she states categorizes the ideogram *shi* in two ways. *Shi* is considered to be either a philosophical concept construed as power or authority derived from a dictatorial position (*shi* born out of political hierarchical systems); or as an aesthetic concept described as an elusive and marvelous force animating an artifact.[734] She adds that Jullien understands *shi* as "a potential or force spontaneously born out of a disposition" and his understanding, to her, recaptures a solid understanding and meaning of *shi*.[735]

In the Introduction to his translation of <u>The Art of War</u>, Samuel Griffith mentions that "only the *shih*—the chariot-riding nobility—and their immediate retainers carried primitive shields of lacquered leather or varnished rhinoceros hide. The footmen wore padded jackets…"[736] Only the shih were allowed to ride in chariots. Perhaps this is how "power" became associated with *shih* in that the nobility were referred to in this way. Qi's comment that *shi* is a

---

[731] Bjorge, p. 144.
[732] Ralph Sawyer, <u>Sun Pin Military Methods</u>, Westview Press, 1995, p. 64.
[733] Qi Zhu, "*Shi* in Architecture: The Efficacy of Traditional Chinese Doors," doctoral dissertation at Virginia Polytechnic Institute and State University, 25 March 2008.
[734] Qi Zhu, p. 1 of the Introduction to her doctoral dissertation.
[735] Ibid., p. 2-3.
[736] Griffith, p. 10.

"philosophical concept construed as power or authority derived from a dictatorial position" is then more understandable.

Shi as a situation or disposition may be a reflection of a historical thought process and conceptualization. These expressions and perceptions, when studied today, imply that the Chinese expressions and perceptions are more comprehensive and holistic than their Western counterparts. The Chinese mind, it appears, has been taught by its philosophical and cultural base to first locate the disposition or setting of reality before focusing on a solution to an actual problem at hand.

As an example of this conceptualization, The Geography of Thought describes a simple experiment where people of Western and Oriental races look at fish in an aquarium and describe what they see. The first sentence from an Oriental's viewpoint was a description of the environment ("It looked like a pond") whereas the Western mind was three times as likely to first mention the type of fish they saw.[737] This indicates that the Oriental mind is taking in the big picture, the disposition of things. Likewise, this propensity to examine a broader disposition appears to be reflected in Chinese theorists' descriptions and definitions of strategy, which are broader than US descriptions of the concept. Whereas US strategists focus on ideas or ways, ends, and means, Chinese strategists tend to first look at objective factors existing in the world today with reference to a particular country (level of science and technology, amount spent on defense, location of forces, geo-political setting, etc.) and how to subjectively manipulate these circumstances. An examination of the Chinese military's concept of strategy in the book The Science of Military Strategy offers frequent references to comprehensive overviews (the configuration of a setting) of subject areas, to include:

- Comprehensive national power (CNP)
- Comprehensive sea power (CSP)
- Comprehensive strategic interest (CSI)
- Comprehensive strategic targets (CST)
- Comprehensive strategic benefits (CSB)
- Comprehensive cyberized war (CCW)
- Comprehensive confrontation capacity (CCC)
- Comprehensive national defense construction (CNDC)
- Comprehensive support efficiency (CSuE)
- And comprehensive national strategy (CNS).

---

[737] Richard E. Nisbett, The Geography of Thought, Free Press, 2003, p. 90.

Mott and Kim did not focus as much on *shih's* comprehensive qualities as they did on a number of other qualities associated with *shih*. They write that

> *Shih*, an intangible power, encourages people who enjoy it and discourages those who lack it...*Shih* carries many meanings distinguishable within Chinese culture largely from the context. The most familiar meanings are power, force, or influence. Another common usage refers to a situation's natural features or a person's circumstances. Some Chinese use the term to suggest a tendency, trend, or series, or even people's gestures. The Chinese use *shih* in political theory, military strategy, the Wei-Chi game, and daily life to express a special form of power or influence.[738]

Shi is described in the next section as a way to visualize, explain, and comprehend one's current reality. It is the extension of *shih* from the age of mechanization to the age of informatization.

The *Shi* of Virtual Reality

It is informationized *shi* that should concern analysts today. The PLA is learning how to use the potential of electrons as they move from a mechanized to an informationized military force. Such a transformation involves an assessment of the electronic potential of other armed forces. Ames noted years ago that security, in the Chinese view, can only be found by continually redefining one's own strength, adjusting to an enemy force's new developments, and reevaluating where one's strategic advantage lies. Understanding these conditions allows a commander to once again control a situation, according to Ames.[739] The PLA's focus on "highly controllable war" indicates his analysis is on the right path.

With so many words to choose from, it is easy to make a *shi* definition fit an information or cyber age concept. The Chinese and other nations have written about the disposition and potential of electrons for years. For example, Western explanations of *shi* using the image of a boulder sitting on a mountain top or a crossbow pulled taut with the arrow waiting to be let go are examples of "potential." It is potential energy waiting to be let go. The Sun Pin notes that the bow and crossbow, able to kill a soldier over a hundred paces away, exemplify strategic advantage.[740] Then what must be the strategic advantage of electrons that can be used to guide a precision weapon to its target that is over

---

[738] Mott and Kim, p. 15.
[739] The Book of War, p. 56.
[740] Ibid., p. 52.

continents away! Digital age warfare also fits with the observation of Sun Tzu that "war is such that the supreme consideration is speed."[741]

In terms of the information age, a Trojan Horse virus in a computer could represent "potential." A Trojan Horse is a virus that "is a form of malware that appears to perform a desirable function but in fact performs undisclosed malicious functions that allow unauthorized access to the host machine."[742] If a hacker can gain access to a server through a backdoor and insert a Trojan Horse, and execute it at a time of his or her choosing, then the virus contains the characteristics of the drawn bow, sitting there and awaiting release.

Disposition and strategic advantage may be situations exploited by civilian hackers whose activities cannot be directly traced to the PLA or to government authorities and whose actions, so long as not internal oriented, are tolerated. This is the *shi* of the hacker. Further, the hacker uses packets of electrons as stratagems to develop strategic advantage into a force or power as Li implies.

There are also some very specific applications of *shi* to the PLA's experience. One such reference was an article on the strategic use of electrons in Jiefangjun Bao. The article noted that if form is the foundation and prerequisite for *shi* (translated as force), then *shi* also holds and directs form. The author added "not only should network warfare power be flexibly combined at a specific time and space, its use must be delayed for the best moment to attack or defend."[743]

The use of force (*shi*) depends on the potential of a state's ability to conduct strategic network warfare. Network warfare cannot exclude strategies and even has a higher requirement for them, according to the authors. Force involves the strength or weakness to control the direction and flow of information; the amount of data possessed by combatants; the degree of network architecture redundancy and the speed of recovery after being attacked; the different combat objectives of forces with different powers; and adopting a corresponding military strategy to attack, defend, hide, or move. All of these elements relate back to the ability to master a large number of attack

---

[741] Ibid., p. xxiii.

[742] Trojan Horse, Wikipedia, accessed 16 January 2009.

[743] Liu Wanxin, Dang Wanlong, and Zhang Dan, "Network Attack and Protection Also Need Strategies," Jiefangjun Bao, 2 January 2008, p. 6, as translated and downloaded from the Open Source Center website, document number CPP20080102436002.

computers or botnets. This ability can manifest itself as one's strategic advantage.

Mott and Kim discussed *shih* strategy and future war near the end of their book. They noted that the PLA has adapted its doctrine, organization, and strategy to the high-tech environment they witnessed in the Gulf War and that there are several trends the PLA is following. They are: improving a joint warfare capability; restructuring the ground forces; transforming the education system; establishing a modern logistic system to support joint warfighting; adopting a standard organization for effective management; and adopting simulations and modern training systems.[744]

Both Ames and Tao Hanzhang addressed the intangibles of *shi*. Ames noted that several factors implied by *shih* go beyond the physical. They are morale advantage, terrain advantage, and opportunity advantage.[745] Tao wrote that a commander must make use of advantageous terrain, seize upon favorable opportunities for fighting, and have superiority in the quality of troops.[746] Put in terms of the information age, this would indicate that troops must understand the terrain of the computer, seize opportunities where they exist such as in reconnaissance of networks (thereby setting the stage to win the fight before the first battle), and maintaining the morale advantage, which the Chinese feel they have accomplished through the renovation of their political system to now include media, legal, and psychological warfare types. A morale advantage can also be created or exploited when one works in the absence of any defining international cyber laws.

But it is Ames who appears to understand the concept of *shi* best and what it means for the PLA today. He noted that:

> All determinate situations can be turned to advantage. The able commander is able to create differentials and thus opportunities by manipulating his position and the position of the enemy. By developing a full understanding of those factors that define one's relationship with the enemy, and by actively controlling and shaping the situation so that the weaknesses of the enemy are exposed to one's acquired strength, one is able to ride the force of circumstances to victory.[747]

---

[744] Mott and Kim, p. 229.
[745] The Book of War, pp. 57-58.
[746] Tao, p. 130.
[747] The Book of War, p. 55.

The transformation of the PLA from a mechanized to an informationized force fits the criteria of trying to turn a situation to its advantage. Of concern to Western societies should be the question of whether "shaping the situation" now involves attempting to control market societies and manipulate the electronic flows of free societies? Tao notes that in China there is the saying: "With only one man guarding the mountain pass, ten thousand men are not able to pass."[748] Can one well-placed and educated computer specialist serve this purpose today, and stop the flow of ten thousand (and more) decisions in the market place?

A Comparison of Two Books: the Art of War and Thirty-Six Stratagems

Ren Li, a senior colonel in 2003 and director of the Fourth Research Department for War Theory and Strategic Research at the Academy of Military Science in Beijing, compared and contrasted two books: Sun Tzu's Art of War versus the Thirty-Six Stratagems (precise author unknown).[749] His analysis is one of the most interesting recent commentaries on these two classics.

Ren notes that the origins of the Art of War are quite clear, having been written during a time of social reform during the Spring and Autumn Period (722-481 B.C.) and Warring States Period (approximately 475 B.C. to 221 B.C.). The Art of War focuses on the importance of a fighting spirit, one in which "taking the initiative in launching attacks, probing deep within enemy territory, rapid combat, quick victories, and conquering a foe to augment one's own strength" were representative of the times.[750] The book was written more for generals and sovereigns than for the simple soldier.

The Art of War discusses basic theoretical problems related to war. It consists of thirteen chapters that are comprehensive, precise, and systematic, discussing the patterns in military affairs extensively and forming a system for viewing classical Chinese military science. A cornerstone of modern thought adopted from the Art of War is caution in going to war, as demonstrated by the very few instances over the past 50 years in which China decided to conduct combat operations. Other cornerstones of the book are strategic thought, power, and strategic initiative, preparations, and measures.

---

[748] Tao, p. 128.

[749] Ren Li, "Contrast and Analyze Sun Zi's Art of War and Thirty-Six Stratagems, China Military Science, 2003, No. 3, pp. 126-132. All references herein are to this article.

[750] Ibid.

Sun Tzu's ten guiding principles for war include rapid victory; achieving victory by unusual means (energy, indirect method); grasping the initiative (weak points and strong); military deception; flexible mobility; concentration of power (weak points and strong); suddenness or surprise; hiding one's intentions; striking against weak points; and seizing the initiative (maneuver).

The origins of the other book Ren reviewed, the Thirty-Six Stratagems, are somewhat murky. Ren writes that the earliest publication of the Thirty-Six Stratagems "appears to be a letterpress edition released by Rui Qinlou of Chengdu and printed by Xinghua Printers in 1941."[751] He feels the Thirty-Six Stratagems were written over a long period of time since the stratagems were used in the drama of the Yuan (1271-1368) and Ming (1368-1644) periods and in the novels of the Ming and Qing (1644-1912) periods. The period of time in which the Thirty-Six Stratagems was published was less innovative, more utilitarian, and less aristocratic than the time the Art of War was published. Thirty-Six Stratagems favored the deterministic nature of stratagems and practicality over theory. Stratagem titles are taken from theatrical songs, common sayings, and slang typical of novels of the period.[752]

Today, the Thirty-Six Stratagems has a broad range of readers in mind. The variety of publications based on the book is staggering in Ren's opinion (to include a popular variant similar to the US explosion in the "such and such for dummies" series of books). Current fascination with the Thirty-Six Stratagems is on its applied aspects rather than its theoretical research. It has expanded into every aspect of Chinese life. A few Chinese titles based on the thirty-six stratagems include the following:

- The Thirty-Six Stratagems for Business
- The Thirty-Six Stratagems for Diplomacy
- The Thirty-Six Stratagems for Making Money in the Stock Market
- The Thirty-Six Stratagems for Enterprises
- The Thirty-Six Stratagems in Commerce
- The Thirty-Six Stratagems for Love
- The Thirty-Six Stratagems for Networks
- The Thirty-Six Stratagems for QQ (an instant messaging program)
- The Thirty-Six Stratagems for Conversation
- The Thirty-Six Stratagems for Graduate School Examinations
- The Thirty-Six Stratagems for Getting an MBA

---

[751] Ibid.
[752] Ibid.

266

- The Thirty-Six Stratagems for Bargaining Down Prices
- The Thirty-Six Stratagems for the Art of War between a Husband and Wife[753]

Perhaps for its overall popularity the Thirty-Six Stratagems has been labeled the "Art of War of the People." Some worry that since the book focuses on deception and trickery, that the work may harm the trust that exists between people and businesses. Paradoxically, according to Ren, the military has shown little interest in The Thirty-Six Stratagems as a military work and thus its influence has been minimal on military science. Most Western audiences would not think that to be the case.[754]

The Thirty-Six Stratagems is devoted to maneuvers and strategies against an enemy on the battlefield. It is composed of a title of the stratagem, an explanation of the stratagem, and commentary. To Ren, the titles and explanations were not written at the same time as the commentary nor were they written by the same person. In some instances the commentaries do not correspond to the stratagems in question.[755]

The point of the Thirty-Six Stratagems is to offer answers to military problems when there are no hard and fast rules for doing so. The epilogue to the book states that "the stratagem with myriad fluctuations and which is the most cunning, bizarre, and unfathomable, is certainly the 36th Stratagem. This is the one which determines the greatness of a general." This stratagem discusses when retreat is the best option. The discussion indicates that surrender is total failure, peace is partial failure, and retreat can mean "turning defeat into victory."[756]

The six categories (under which there are six stratagems each) are: when in a superior position; stratagems for confrontation; stratagems for attack; stratagems for confused situations; stratagems for gaining ground; and stratagems for desperate situations. The first three categories refer to favorable circumstances and the latter three categories refer to unfavorable circumstances. The Thirty-Six Stratagems uses the philosophy of the book I Ching as the basis for many of its ideas. Twenty-nine of the thirty-six stratagems quote sections from the I Ching and the remaining seven stratagems touch upon I Ching logic, according to Ren.[757]

---

[753] Ibid.
[754] Ibid.
[755] Ibid.
[756] Ibid.
[757] Ibid.

Ren concludes his 2003 article with the following passage:

> The Art of War and the Thirty-Six Stratagems are two military treatises created at the beginning and end of China's feudal period, respectively, and in this they are branded with the characteristics of these two different eras. The Art of War comprehensively reveals the basic patterns of war, and provides the foundation for military science in ancient China together with a series of concepts and standards for it. It is the bedrock of Chinese military history. Thirty-Six Stratagems focuses upon forging and expounding upon military strategies, with reference to the ideas of the I Ching. Actual examples are provided, and it is concise and practical, making it worthy of being listed among the top-ranked treatises in Chinese military history.[758]

Stratagems and Virtual Reality

It seems apparent that an understanding of the disposition or configuration of forces also leads Chinese theorists, based on this understanding, to develop stratagems that exploit such dispositions. The stratagem could be visualized as the potential that forms in the mind of a commander after considering the disposition of forces and terrain at his disposal.

In a year 2000 article in the Chinese journal China Military Science, for example, authors Major General Niu Li, Colonel Li Jiangzou, and Major Xu Dehui (all from the Communications and Command Institute) defined IW stratagems as "schemes and methods devised and used by commanders and commanding bodies to seize and maintain information supremacy on the basis of using clever methods to prevail at a relatively small cost in IW."[759] They offered ten specific stratagems that can be applied to IW. These stratagems take into account disposition (muddy the flow, go with the flow, control time, etc.) and strategic advantage (to intimidate, demonstrate, use decisive technical equipment, all-round strength, deception, etc.):

(1) **Thought-Directing**—Direct others' thinking in the wrong decision by attacking cognitive and belief systems and force commanders to make errors.

---

[758] Ibid.

[759] Niu Li, Li Jiangzhou, and Xu Dehui, "Planning and Application of Strategies of Information Operations in High-Tech Local War," Zhongguo Junshi Kexue (China Military Science), Number 4 2000, pp. 115-122, as translated and downloaded from the FBIS website on 9 November 2000

(2) **Intimidation through Momentum-Building**—Generate heavy psychological pressure via intimidation by signaling inevitable victory, concentrating forces, and coordinating information networks. This is to be achieved by creating a situation favorable to China and unfavorable to the enemy. Intimidation is to be achieved via momentum building, achieved by enhancing one's own position, situation, and posture while blocking the flow of information to the enemy.

(3) **Information-based Capability Demonstrations**—Intimidate by demonstrating capabilities, an action that should not appear to be intentional. The right time, occasion, and modality must be chosen to make information believable to the enemy.

(4) **Prevailing over the Enemy with Extraordinary Means**—Adopt active and effective measures to generate surprise, and use decisive technical equipment and means of information warfare.

(5) **Using Fictitious Objects to Hide the True Picture**—Hide true reality by creating a fictitious reality. Simulate combat forces using high-tech means.

(6) **All-Encompassing Deception**—Apply deceptive schemes simultaneously or consecutively according to strategic or operational intentions.

(7) **Prevailing over the Enemy with All-round Strength**—Use all means of information warfare to maintain supremacy. Electronic soft attacks (reconnaissance satellite systems, etc.), hard attacks (informationized precision-guidance weapons, strategic bombings), and C3I battlefield control and management must all be present.

(8) **Going with the Flow**—Mislead the enemy by pretending to follow his wishes.

(9) **Releasing "Viruses" to Muddy the Flows**—Release viruses to contaminate information flows. A virus attack is "a technical act, which will have to be based on the use of stratagems in order to play an important role in IW." Stratagems should create a favorable time for releasing viruses.

(10) **Controlling the Time Element**—Control of the time element is crucial. Conducting information "inducement," "deception," concealment," and "containment" operations will help achieve the desired amount of control. [760]

Conclusions

This brief discussion of two concepts, *shi* and stratagem, is anything but definitive. It is included to remind analysts that there are undergirding pillars of Chinese thought such as these two examples that have survived through the ages and continue to influence contemporary thought and thus operations. The discussion attempts to put under one roof a number of ideas associated with the concepts and, most importantly, demonstrate their applicability in the age of informatization.

What strikes one immediately in the case of *shi* is the overwhelming number of definitions associated with the term. Ames broke his categorization of *shi* into four clusters. It is possible to arrange the definitions offered here in three different ways.

First there is the category of what will be termed "strategic posturing." Several definitions are included here from the discussion, to include posture of the army, strategic advantage, strategic configuration of power, availing oneself of advantage to gain control, "potential from the disposition of things," and "holding forces with hands."

A second category, represented by power and influence, is more closely associated with the concept of a ruler's abilities and the definition found in the Chinese Encyclopedia of Philosophical Terms. The third group includes momentum, energy, and force and is more aptly summarized simply as the release of energy.

Li Rulong provided an interesting Chinese summary and combination of all of these concepts when he noted that "'power'" is actually a kind of potential energy; once the external condition is provided, this energy will demonstrate a mighty power and become a force. Such an understanding can be allied to all fields of social practice including military affairs."

Ames's concept of strategic advantage evolves from potential energy aligned with the correct external condition. He wrote

---

[760] Ibid.

When looked at spatially from outside one's own 'skin,' *shih* is that set of conditions that is defining of one's situation. It is one's context in relationship to oneself. When looked at from an internal perspective, *shih* is one's own place and posture relative to one's context. When looked at temporally, taking into account the full calculus of dispositions, *shih* is the tension of forces and the momentum that brings one position in immediate contact with another.[761]

Stratagems are included, as they have been in other works by this author, to once again stress their importance in understanding the essence of Chinese thought. Stratagems imply deception and lie at the heart of Chinese strategic thought. If one ignores the influence of stratagems then one ignores perhaps THE basic pillar of Chinese thought.

---

[761] Ibid., p. 81.

APPENDIX THREE: MORE DECEPTION-RELATED TERMS IN THE <u>CHINESE MILITARY ENCYCLOPEDIA</u>

This appendix examines four terms on deception: decoy, infrared decoy, deceptive electronic jamming, and radio communication deception. These are truncated versions of the definitions that originally appeared in the 1997 <u>Chinese Military Encyclopedia</u>.

The <u>Chinese Military Encyclopedia</u> has definitions of other terms associated with deception. These include deceptive electronic jamming; camouflage inspection; radar camouflage and radar countermeasures; radio communication deception and radio communication disguise; strategic camouflage, strategic surprise, and strategic surprise attack; tactical camouflage and thermal camouflage; radar decoy; decoy; camouflage operations vehicle, light camouflage, and camouflage units; and computer security among others.

Four terms were selected from the <u>Chinese Military Encyclopedia</u> for inclusion in this appendix. They are "decoy," "infrared decoy," "deceptive electronic jamming," and "radio communication deception." As with the definitions of camouflage, these are abbreviated versions of the definitions taken directly from the encyclopedia.[762]

Decoy: A decoy is a mockup showing characteristics of a target, built and emplaced so as to deceive and confuse the enemy. Decoys are categorized as two types, standard or expedient. The use of decoys to simulate targets and set up false battle positions can divert the enemy's attention, lure the enemy's reconnaissance and assaults, and cover and conceal real targets. It can disperse the enemy's firepower and reduce losses to real targets. The degree of realism of a decoy is a major factor in the deception of enemy reconnaissance and assaults. To make an effective decoy normally requires the following: a decoy must be set up in a place which meets the same tactical and technical requirements as a real target, and the decoy must be sited a safe distance from real targets; the timing of decoy construction and the length of time the construction takes must be about the same as for a real target; a decoy must have the same surface dimensions and shape as a real target, as well as similar thermal radiation characteristics, electric wave reflection characteristics, optical and acoustic characteristics, and tracks evidencing movement; and a decoy needs imperfect camouflage. A decoy must normally be small, lightweight, with a solid and simple structure, and must be easy to carry, set up, and

---

[762] The Foreign Military Studies Office has a copy of the <u>Chinese Military Encyclopedia</u> in its office holdings.

recover. Decoys are mainly mockups of technical equipment and personnel, false constructions, false landmarks, and apparatus which simulate the optical, acoustic, thermal, and radar wave characteristics of real targets.

Mockups of artillery pieces, tanks, motor vehicles, aircraft, rocket launchers, and personnel are categorized according to the materials and methods of construction as inflatable, prefabricated for assembly, foam expansion type, and expedient material mockups. Inflatable decoys are made of plastic or rubber film or fabric and rubber composites. Their external appearance is realistic, and this facilitates the simulation of curved and pipe-shaped components. Inflatable decoys are lightweight and small. They can simulate technical equipment, tents, and other small and medium-sized targets. Inflatable decoys are the most widely used decoy. Decoys prefabricated for assembly are made with wood, metal, fiberglass, plastic, and some fabric skin. Their external appearance is very realistic. When part of it is destroyed, it can easily be repaired or replaced. Prefabricated decoys are suitable for simulating buildings, aircraft bunkers, weapons and equipment, and other large or medium-sized targets. Foam expansion decoys are constructed with polyurethane plastic foam. They may be either flexible or rigid. A flexible expansion decoy packed into a case is only one-tenth the size of the real target it imitates. When the case is opened, the decoy re-assumes a size close to that of a real target. A rigid expansion decoy can assume its shape after being soaked on site at normal outside temperature. Normally this takes only a few minutes. The decoy can withstand a certain amount of wind, rain, and snow. A rigid expansion decoy has a realistic external appearance. This type of decoy has attracted attention since the 1970s. Mockups of technical equipment can be made on site with wood, bamboo, metal, PVC panels, straw, woven mats, or concrete. Use of such decoys made with expedient materials is extensive because of the broad source of materials and the cheapness of construction.

Decoy constructions include false fortifications, bridges, command posts, and airfields. Normally such decoy constructions are fabricated on site using expedient materials and as part of a unified plan from a higher echelon. The simplest and most reliable way to set up a decoy construction is to install partially camouflaged decoy weapons, decoy vehicles, decoy boats, and decoy access roads at a site from which a unit has just withdrawn. The main types of decoy constructions are false trenches, false communication trenches, and false bunkers and covered works of various kinds. The three main types of decoy bridges are expedient bridges, false subsurface bridges, and false lightweight bridges. A decoy expedient bridge consists of a simple framework with cloth, reed mats, or mats of tree branches, stretching from bank to bank. A decoy submerged bridge has a false access road, an exposed portion on shore, and marker panels on the surface of the water. A decoy lightweight bridge can withstand a light load, and personnel and mockups of technical weapons can pass over it. Decoy airfields are categorized as either daylight or night airfields. A daylight decoy airfield consists of a fake runway, taxiways, aircraft parking aprons, hangars, a fuel depot, a tower, and so on built on a scale approximately the same as that of a real airfield. A night decoy airfield mainly uses lights to present the image of a real target airfield and its relative position. A decoy airfield is normally set up on the flight route to a real airfield, so that enemy aviators will discover it before they arrive at the real airfield. To make the decoy airfield realistic, normal operating status can be simulated by having small aircraft take off and land on a simple runway and by simulating an access road, airfield roads, etc.

Decoy landmarks are normally false objects constructed and emplaced to be quite obvious, such as a solitary tree, a bridge, a road intersection, a prominent building, or a fake river bend, lake, or farm field. To enhance the realism of a decoy landmark, the real landmarks must be camouflaged carefully at the same time a real target is camouflaged.

Simulation apparatus is equipment that simulates sound and light, heat, and radar return signals. Sound and light simulation apparatus is mainly used to simulate the sound and flash of artillery fire. Normally this is done with a gunpowder charge producing a sound equivalent to that of an artillery shot. Mixed into the charge is a suitable amount of a pyrotechnic agent to simulate the flash of a nighttime shot. Heat simulation apparatus is used to simulate the heat emissions of a target which would generate heat and a target's surface temperature. Radar return signal simulation is the simulation of the radar effective scattering cross-section aimed at a target and of the background. Besides using angle reflectors to simulate bridges, airfields, levees, water landmarks, and industrial targets, other angle reflectors can be set up in or near decoy targets to constitute full-size decoy targets.[763]

Infrared Decoy: An infrared decoy is a one-time use opto-electronic jamming device which can be dropped into the air or onto the sea surface and which can produce strong infrared radiation similar to that produced by the target which is being protected, so as to deceive point source detecting infrared seeking missiles and enable the target to evade attack. Infrared decoys are widely used for self-defense by aircraft and ships.

---

[763] Chinese Military Encyclopedia, Academy of Military Science Press, Volume 5, July 1997, p. 495. Entry by Tao Xiaodi.

Infrared decoys are categorized according to their radiation generating mechanism as pyrotechnic compound decoys, solid fuel decoys, hot air balloon decoys, and infrared compound chaff. Pyrotechnic compound decoys produce a large amount of smoke and infrared radiation by way of a chemical reaction in the mixing and combustion of substances such as incendiary and oxydizing agents. Solid fuel decoys use the combustion of solid fuel to produce infrared radiation. These decoys burn some combustible substance to produce infrared radiation which is very close on the spectrum to the infrared energy produced by the target being protected. Hot air balloon decoys are specially made balloons filled with a gas at high temperature and released into the air to act as a decoy. Infrared compound chaff is metallic strips used for radar jamming. One side is coated with smokeless rocket propellant, which is a combustible material that burns when the chaff is released in the air producing a "hot cloud." This type of decoy can deceive infrared seeking missiles and it can jam radar.

Infrared decoys are also called infrared jammers or infrared tracers. They are a type of smoke and flame decoy where the smoke and flame agent is usually a compound of powdered magnesium, nitrocellulose, and polytetrafluoroethylene. The external appearance of an infrared decoy is usually the same as that of a chaff jammer. Because most infrared seeking missiles use a point source detection, center of mass tracking mechanism, when such a missile discovers several infrared targets within the field of vision of its seeker, it will track the equivalent center of radiation of the targets.

An infrared decoy is used in the following manner. When a missile inbound on the attack is detected, an infrared decoy is released into the air by the carrier (aircraft or military ship) being targeted. The decoy's combustible agent ignites and burns quickly creating a false target emitting infrared radiation. As the distance between the decoy and the target gradually increases, the target moves further towards the edge of the field of vision of the missile's seeker, and ultimately it leaves the field of vision altogether. The missile loses the target and shifts its tracking to the decoy. In actual warfare, an aircraft or military ship will normally release a large number of infrared decoys to ensure its safety.

Ideally, an infrared decoy's infrared emission should be in the operating band of infrared guided missile seekers (1 to 5 microns or 8 to 14 microns) and have a spectral distribution similar to that of the target being protected. It should also radiate at an intensity five to seven times or more greater than that of the target being protected. Its ignition time is normally 0.5 seconds or less. Burn duration refers to the length of time the decoy maintains the specified intensity of infrared radiation. Burn duration must be greater than the length of time it takes for the protected target aircraft or ship to flee the missile seeker's field of vision to a safe distance from where the missile will strike the decoy. Infrared decoys for use by aircraft have a shorter burn time, often 8 to 12 seconds. Infrared decoys for use by ships have a longer burn time, about 40 seconds to one minute.[764]

Deceptive Electronic Jamming: This type of jamming causes enemy electronic equipment to receive false information, leading to misjudgment and wrong decisions/actions on the part of the enemy. Deceptive electronic jamming is categorized by how the interference is produced, either as active deceptive jamming or passive deceptive jamming. Deceptive electronic jamming can be categorized by its deception pattern as either camouflaged deception or deception by "pretending to be what it is not." Camouflaged deception is achieved by changing or simulating one's own electromagnetic signals, concealing the truth, and displaying something false. Deception by "pretending" is achieved by presenting electromagnetic signals which the enemy takes to be its own, tapping into the enemy's communication channels and transmitting false information to the enemy. For example, deceptive jamming aimed at radar mainly uses false target interference, angle deception interference, range deception interference, and speed deception interference, with the goal being to disrupt radar's ability to detect and track targets. Deceptive jamming of radio communication is also called communication jamming. This involves posing as a station on the enemy's communication net and establishing contact with the enemy's main station or other stations; sending the enemy false orders, false messages, and false images; and thereby duping the enemy. Deceptive jamming of the enemy's opto-electronic equipment mainly involves: emitting range deception and encoding deception laser signals; setting up false targets to diffuse strong laser signals; deceiving the enemy's laser sensing equipment and laser guidance equipment; and emitting infrared-coded pulse jamming, dropping infrared lures, and disrupting the enemy's ability to lock onto and track targets with infrared tracking and guidance equipment. Compared with suppressive jamming, deceptive jamming has the advantages of easier concealment and being difficult for the enemy to sense. But deceptive jamming is very focused, and before it is used, ample intelligence about the enemy's electronic equipment is essential.[765]

---

[764] Chinese Military Encyclopedia, Academy of Military Science Press, Volume 5, July 1997, p. 412. Entry by Yang Wenxuan.
[765] Chinese Military Encyclopedia, Academy of Military Science Press, Volume 6, July 1997, p. 738. Entry by Zhang Baolin.

Radio Communication Deception: This type of deception involves measures taken to confuse the enemy in the process of radio communication. Normally radio communication deception is organized centrally by a headquarters. The goals are to induce misjudgment and wrong actions on the part of the enemy and to conceal one's own intent and the location and disposition of one's own forces.

Radio communication deception requires content and action which is as close as possible to reality, with measures for adaptation which ensure that one's own communication systems operate normally. It requires tight security measures. Radio communication deception measures include radio feints, radio communication disguise [spoofing], and radio camouflage.

The usual method of carrying out a radio feint is to set up a radio net in an area where there are no combat operations, make frequent contact on the net, demonstrate one's presence to the enemy, create a false impression, and achieve, as the expression goes, "a feint to the east but an attack to the west." As one's own units redeploy and move, radio stations remain in place and continue operating as normal to confuse the enemy. On axes of secondary importance, send fake radio traffic to attract the enemy's attention and cover the operations of radio stations on the main axis of operations. Within radio nets, set up false linkages and change their locations at appropriate times to cause misperception on the part of the enemy, and thus conceal the composition and disposition of one's own forces.

Radio communication disguise is based on knowledge of the enemy's radio links, patterns of operation, and characteristics. Radio communication spoofing imitates enemy radio stations, infiltrates enemy radio nets, sends false intelligence reports, or intercepts enemy radio messages.

Radio camouflage is the use of measures to make it impossible for enemy radio reconnaissance to obtain any real intelligence. The main methods of radio camouflage are: change radio call signs and frequencies to make the enemy misjudge where the various stations in a net are located; use remote radio transmitters to make it difficult for the enemy to determine where stations are located and what the command relationships are; send fake messages within the net during peacetime, and in wartime when real message traffic increases, reduce the number of fake messages so as to conceal one's operational deployment. [766]

---

[766] Chinese Military Encyclopedia, Academy of Military Science Press, Volume 3, July 1997, p. 623. Entry by Yuan Chuangquan.

APPENDIX FOUR: TABLE OF CONTENTS OF FIVE CHINESE TEXTS OF POTENTIAL INTEREST

This appendix lists the table of contents from several texts not used in this book but perhaps of interest to readers who focus on Chinese military affairs and are interested in future study.

(1) <u>INTERNET WAR</u>
(A Brief History of How the Internet Changed the World)

Jiuzhou Press, 2009

TABLE OF CONTENTS

282

(2) A REVIEW OF WORKS ON US MILITARY INTELLIGENCE THEORY

Zhang Xiaojun, Chief Editor

Shi Shi Publishing House, 2005

TABLE OF CONTENTS

Introduction

Part I History, Strategy, and Military Intelligence

Part II Military Intelligence, War, and National Security

288

(3) A STUDY OF MILITARY INTELLIGENCE

Li Naiguo

Military Science Press, 2001

TABLE OF CONTENTS

(4) THE THEORY OF MILITARY STRATEGY

Fan Zheng Jiang and Ma Bao An

Beijing National Defense University Publishing House, 2007/11

TABLE OF CONTENTS

Main References/Bibliography 370

(5) MILITARY INFORMATION SUPERIORITY THEORY

Zhao Xiao Song and Wei Yu Du

Beijing National Defense University Publishing House, 2008/11, 2000 copies

TABLE OF CONTENTS

ABOUT THE AUTHOR

Mr. Timothy L. Thomas (BS, Engineering Science, USMA; MA, International Relations, University of Southern California) is a senior analyst at the Foreign Military Studies Office at Fort Leavenworth, Kansas. Mr. Thomas conducts extensive research and publishing in the areas of peacekeeping, information war, psychological operations, low intensity conflict, and political-military affairs. Mr. Thomas was a US Army foreign area officer who specialized in Soviet/Russian studies. His military assignments included serving as the Director of Soviet Studies at the United States Army Russian Institute in Garmisch, Germany; as an inspector of Soviet tactical operations under the Commission on Security and Cooperation in Europe; and as a brigade S-2 and company commander in the 82nd Airborne Division. He has written three books on information warfare topics, focusing on recent developments in China and Russia. Mr. Thomas is an adjunct professor at the US Army's Eurasian Institute; an adjunct lecturer at the USAF Special Operations School; and a member of two Russian organizations, the Academy of International Information and the Academy of Natural Sciences.